Thomas

Manchester University Press

Contemporary American and Canadian Writers

Series editors
Nahem Yousaf and Sharon Monteith

Thomas Pynchon

Simon Malpas and Andrew Taylor

Manchester University Press

Published by Manchester University Press
Altrincham Street, Manchester M1 7JA, UK
www.manchesteruniversitypress.co.uk

British Library Cataloguing-in-Publication Data is available

Library of Congress Cataloging-in-Publication Data is available

ISBN 978 0 7190 9934 2 *paperback*

First published by Manchester University Press in hardback 2013

This paperback edition first published 2015

The publisher has no responsibility for the persistence or accuracy of URLs for any external or third-party internet websites referred to in this book, and does not guarantee that any content on such websites is, or will remain, accurate or appropriate.

Printed by Lightning Source

Contents

Series editors' foreword

This innovative series reflects the breadth and diversity of writing over the last thirty years, and provides critical evaluations of established, emerging and critically neglected writers – mixing the canonical with the unexpected. It explores notions of the contemporary and analyses current and developing modes of representation with a focus on individual writers and their work. The series seeks to reflect both the growing body of academic research in the field, and the increasing prevalence of contemporary American and Canadian fiction on programmes of study in institutions of higher education around the world. Central to the series is a concern that each book should argue a stimulating thesis, rather than provide an introductory survey, and that each contemporary writer will be examined across the trajectory of their literary production. A variety of critical tools and literary and interdisciplinary approaches are encouraged to illuminate the ways in which a particular writer contributes to, and helps readers rethink, the North American literary and cultural landscape in a global context.

Central to debates about the field of contemporary fiction is its role in interrogating ideas of national exceptionalism and transnationalism. This series matches the multivocality of contemporary writing with wide-ranging and detailed analysis. Contributors examine the drama of the nation from the perspectives of writers who are members of established and new immigrant groups, writers who consider themselves on the nation's margins as well as those who chronicle middle America. National labels are the subject of vociferous debate and including American and Canadian writers in the same series is not to flatten the differences between them but to acknowledge that literary traditions and tensions are cross-cultural and that North American writers often explore and expose precisely these tensions. The series recognises that situating a writer in a cultural context involves a multiplicity of influences, social and geo-political, artistic and theoretical, and that contemporary fiction defies easy categorisation. For example, it examines writers who invigorate the genres in which they have made their mark alongside writers whose aesthetic goal is to subvert the idea of genre altogether. The challenge of defining the roles of writers and assessing their reception by reading communities is central to the aims of the series.

Overall, *Contemporary American and Canadian Writers* aims to begin to represent something of the diversity of contemporary writing and seeks to engage students and scholars in stimulating debates about the contemporary and about fiction.

Nahem Yousaf
Sharon Monteith

Abbreviations

Introduction: 'the fork in the road'

Fifty years after the publication of his first novel, *V.*, in 1963, Thomas Pynchon remains the most elusive and important writer of American postmodernity. For an author whose novels return again and again to the processes by which identity is structured by, and limited to, the shapes that society fashions for it, Pynchon's own biographical self has remained tantalisingly out of focus, as if always one step ahead, or to the side of, attempts to locate and define him. It is one of the contentions of this book that such a stance of invisibility is more than a desire for privacy on Pynchon's part (although it certainly is that); rather, his deliberate refusal to participate in the customary round of interviews and readings – the expected forms and functions of authorship – performs the kind of struggling resistance to social interpellation that we see at work in his texts. The tension between containment and freedom, in which the creation of precarious sites of dissent is inevitably threatened by the systematic force of mainstream culture, represents one of the structuring paradigms of Pynchon's work. From the early short story 'Entropy' (1960) to the encyclopaedic reach of the recent *Against the Day*, Pynchon has been concerned to map the fault-lines of privacy and publicity, of interiority and exposure. His career has been feted by the literary establishment, with the award of the William Faulkner Foundation Award in 1963 for his first novel *V.*, the Rosenthal Foundation Award of the National Institute of Arts and Letters in 1967 for *The Crying of Lot 49*, and the National Book Award for *Gravity's Rainbow* in 1974. Yet Pynchon has also refused such accolades, famously turning down the prestigious William Dean Howells Medal of the American Academy of Arts and Letters in 1975 (imploring Richard Wilbur, President of the Academy, not to 'impose on me something I don't want. It makes the Academy look arbitrary and me look rude').[1]

By refusing fully to play the part of celebrity author but yet doing enough within the culture to retain our interest in his mysterious status (twice appearing on *The Simpsons*, albeit masked by a paper bag over his head, for instance; and contributing the voice-over narration for the promotional video of his 2009 book, *Inherent Vice*), Pynchon enacts the oscillation between cherished autonomy and compromised engagement that is at the heart of his writing.[2]

Pynchon's desire for privacy has ensured that the story of his life remains sketchy, and the quest to uncover details of his biography has generated much academic interest.[3] One aspect of it, though, is worth noting at this point. His earliest American ancestor, William Pynchon (1590–1662), was one of the founders of the Massachusetts Bay Colony and established the colonial settlement at both Roxbury and Springfield. William's place within the colony was undermined by the publication in 1650 of *The Meritorious Price of Our Redemption*, a book whose nuanced revision of Puritan doctrine was perceived as theologically and politically subversive by the governing elite. It bears the dubious honour of being the first book to be banned in the New World.[4] As we discuss in subsequent chapters, in the writing of William Pynchon's descendant, Thomas, struggles over the legacy of Puritan structures of thought continue to reverberate. This is most explicitly found in *Gravity's Rainbow*, in which William Slothrop, a mess cook who arrives in America in 1630 on the *Arbella*, soon finds himself 'sick and tired of the Winthrop machine' (*GR* 554–5). Heading west to farm pigs, he enjoys their 'nobility and personal freedom, their gift for finding comfort in the mud on a hot day – pigs out on the road, in company together, were everything Boston wasn't'. This somewhat bizarre but sincerely felt incarnation of the outsider prompts Slothrop to write *On Preterition*, 'among the first books to've been not only banned but also ceremoniously burned'. By focusing on the preterite, defined as 'the many God passes over when he chooses a few for salvation', attention is shifted from 'the Elect in Boston [who] were pissed off about that' (*GR* 555) to those constituencies ostracised by, yet offering attractive alternatives to, religious and social orthodoxies. Slothrop, like William Pynchon, is forced to return to England, and the novel encourages us to consider this instance of fictionalised intellectual history as a defining moment in America's prospects. The narrator muses on the counterfactual significance of what might have been, before the reader is granted access to the thoughts of Slothrop's mid-twentieth-century descendant, Tyrone, who wonders if there is a 'route back' to 'the fork in the road America never took', to encounter 'inside the waste of it' a terrain 'without even nationality to fuck it up' (*GR* 556). As we discuss in Chapter Four, this passage signals Pynchon's interest in the subjunctive potentiality of space (also an important element, as we shall see, of *Mason & Dixon*) that opens up the possibility, even if only an imagined one, for William's early America and Tyrone's Zone to be freed from those markings of division and control, including ones of national identity, that structure the social and political environments of both Slothrops. The 'waste' of such emancipated spaces resonates with the potential, paradoxically, to generate meaning, those 'coordinates from which to proceed' unencumbered by the coercions of hierarchy and difference. But the precisely conditional phrasing of Tyrone's thoughts, as mediated by the narrator, should give us pause: 'there might be' and 'maybe for a little while' articulate the tentativeness of Pynchon's conviction in an emancipated future, for the 'single set' of apparently enlightening directions that Tyrone hopes for might just as easily cohere into rigid discriminations. America's 'fork in the road' inscribes the failure of the nation's promise and the potential for its progressive reconstitution. However, such a vision of the future, as subsequent chapters discuss, is always prone to incursion by the solidifying forces of reaction.

As Deborah Madsen, amongst other critics, has noted, Pynchon's fiction is frequently structured around, or at least plays with the conventions of, the American quest narrative. Madsen writes that such a form, indebted to the romance tradition, 'seeks meaning in a sequence of hermeneutic encounters ... [T]he American emphasis on interpretation introduces complexities until the narrative proves incapable of making present any hermeneutic absolute'.[5] Indeed, the tension between the drive to interpret and an inability to make interpretation cohere into secure knowledge might be regarded as the central dilemma for Pynchon's protagonists, and the key challenge for his readers. The desire to imaginatively reach a site of inhabitation untouched by the corrosive effects of entropy (of which more in Chapter One) holds out the possibility of an alternative politics, a moment of genuine transgression that signifies our resistance to the enforcing structures of any given culture. Madsen's definition is instructive because it points to the provisional, precarious nature of the epistemology that Pynchon's work both performs and provokes. The transcendent flights of emancipation offered by the Beat generation of writers, who at the time Pynchon admired, are not sustainable in the postmodern landscape of his narratives, saturated as it is with the markers of technology, popular culture and political coercion. In the introduction to his collection of early short stories, *Slow Learner*, he notes the importance of Jack Kerouac and William Burroughs to apprentice authors like him who were trying to write against the perceived conformity of 1950s American culture: *On the Road* he cites as 'one of the great American novels', and he retrospectively describes one of his own stories published at the start of the following decade, 'Entropy', as 'as close to a Beat story as anything I was writing then' (*SL* 7, 14). In addition, the year before *Slow Learner* appeared, Pynchon had provided the introduction to a reprint of Richard Fariña's 1966 novel *Been Down So Long It Looks Like Up to Me*, a book that reads now as both a late addition to the Beat generation canon and, in its playful surrealism, an example of the kind of postmodern sensibility that Pynchon himself was developing at the time. It is that very sensibility, however, that ensures that Pynchon's narratives cannot accede wholeheartedly to a state of dissenting transgression. The countercultural impulses which the United States generates continue to fascinate (and Pynchon traces their genealogy across decades of literary and political history), yet these eruptions of resistance exist – and can only exist – in a dialectical tension with those powerful forces of containment which both oppose and create them.

Within this dialectic of freedom and constraint, Pynchon's characters find themselves in networks of signification they struggle to understand but which urge them to make connections and establish forms of relationship. The alternative – that 'nothing is connected to anything, a condition not many of us can bear for long' (*GR* 434) – becomes unthinkable. The period of Pynchon's development and emergence as a writer saw the cultural and political consequences of threatened coherence, with the paranoia of McCarthyism supplanted by moments of mass-mediated conspiracy (the Zapruder film of the Kennedy assassination; the subsequent assassination of Lee Harvey Oswald broadcast on television; the photographic images of the immediate aftermath of the Martin Luther King and Robert Kennedy killings) which in turn fed cinema's embrace in the early 1970s of paranoid narratives.[6] The literary consequences of paranoia, defined as the need to uncover or assume webs of interdependency, produce what Emily Apter has called 'a delirious aesthetics of systematicity' in which the absence of secure knowledge provokes instances of forced kinship, the imagination of systems that have the potential to be either liberating or persecutory.[7] In *The Crying of Lot 49* Oedipa Maas, the novel's central character, describes the hermeneutic possibilities such thinking allows as a series of epistemological options that, as Chapter Two describes, are incompatible with each other and thoroughly undermining of interpretative certitude but are nevertheless representative of what John Johnston describes as 'four possibilities, each with its own implicit probability'.[8] The paranoid sensibility is at one moment convinced of the reality of connection, at another thrown into doubt and confusion. The 'cybernetic on-off, us-them circuit board' that Apter identifies as the structuring principle behind such imagined systems of relationship produces what she calls 'discrete limits of an autonomous self, abolishing mechanisms of agency'.[9] This is indeed one of the effects that paranoia generates in Pynchon's texts, not only evident in Oedipa Maas's fraught engagement with her Californian reality but also foundational to the way in which Herbert Stencil, in *V.*, attempts to read and interpret proliferating references to the novel's mysterious central figure, V. The presence of omnipresent global corporations, extensive structures of government surveillance and rapidly changing forms of information technology all encourage the kinds of anxiety that paranoia fosters. Moreover, as *The Crying of Lot 49*, *Gravity's Rainbow* and *Vineland* all make explicit, technologies come to structure both the epistemological and ontological contours of Pynchon's world such that, as Leo Bersani points out, these aspects of social reality work to legitimate the paranoid narrative: 'at least in the traditional sense of the word', Pynchon's paranoids are 'really not paranoid at all'.[10]

Emily Apter's vision of a paranoiac 'oneworldedness' that stands opposed to the more pluralising, cosmopolitan impulses of transnationalism embodies the dark, persecutory side of the kinds of interrelationship that underwrite our contemporary world. But, as the lines from *The Crying of Lot 49* quoted above suggest, other iterations of connection might carry more progressive resonances. Networks of association (such as trade unions, countercultural collectives, religious observances, family ties) can also establish bonds of resistance to that nexus of government–technology–capitalism which so frequently in Pynchon's writing signifies as the source of oppression. His 1984 novel *Vineland*, for instance, traces a genealogy of political dissent through trade union activity, eastern mysticism and, finally, family solidarity. Certainly the book is sober about the prospects of such spaces of resistance being able to defeat once and for all the overwhelmingly powerful forces of reaction ranged against them, but in its delineation of affiliations of progressive thought Pynchon posits the possibility of a precarious but precious 'real life alternative to the exitlessness' of contemporary political culture. Amy Elias has usefully characterised this double sense of paranoia, the idea of connection working in two ways:

> The 'connectedness' that is desired by the Elect and which must be resisted by the Preterite is the monovocal, universalist connectiveness of totalitarian control. The 'connectedness' that Pynchon's characters pursue as an act of resistance, however, is a polyvocal connectedness of association and community that resists standardization. For Pynchon's characters, paranoia is thus *creative* in two ways, as a hermeneutic that unmasks totalitarian control that wishes to remain invisible and box life into rigid, limiting, and controllable categories, and conversely as an open, polyvocal approach to the world that allows one to see connections, associations and creative difference.[11]

What Elias identifies here is the degree to which Pynchon's characters are invested in the process of exerting control over their narratives, in which the paranoid sensibility, in both its progressive and reactionary incarnations, attempts to read order into the unstructured chaos of life. The inscription, in *Mason & Dixon* (1997), of a cartographic line across swathes of continental America is just one explicit – and historically resonant – instance of this impulse to structure the proliferating realities of Pynchon's fictional worlds, in which the presence of 'orders behind the visible' (*GR* 188) is detected, imagined or embraced. In *Gravity's Rainbow* we read of one such space, 'The Zone', an occupied central Europe in the summer of 1945 in which 'frontiers' and 'subdivision' have been abolished – one character tells Slothrop, 'It's all been suspended ... [A]n "interregnum." You only have to flow along with it' (*GR* 294). Pynchon introduces this section of the novel by quoting Dorothy from *The Wizard of Oz* ('Toto, I have a feeling we're not in Kansas any more ...' [*GR* 279]), thereby preparing the reader for a location in which the conventional spatial categories have been erased, 'a geographical slate momentarily wiped clean', as Steven Weisenburger has characterised it.[12] Such spaces of precarious possibility, in which the declarative mode of assertion and control gives way, for a time, to a more subjunctive mood, are a recurring figuration in Pynchon's work. These are ambiguous terrains, often populated by the disenfranchised and marginal who yet also embody the potential for a future regenerative state.[13]

The encyclopaedic range of reference and allusion in Pynchon's writing inaugurates the drive for hermeneutic capture that readers share with many of his characters. That this impulse is inevitably undermined by the narrative's textual openness and discursive fecundity is both its frustration and its delight. Even the perfectly wrought form of a text like *The Crying of Lot 49* or 'Entropy' (Pynchon's own subsequent dismissal of this tale notwithstanding) resists the shallow satisfactions of interpretative closure; this sensation of poised uncertainty can build into something like bewilderment in more expansive works such as *Gravity's Rainbow* and *Against the Day*. Henry James famously noted that 'relations stop nowhere', and it is both the duty and the burden of the novelist (his 'perpetual predicament'), to 'draw, by a geometry of his own, the circle within which they shall happily *appear* to do so', to circumscribe experience so as to render it narratively comprehensible.[14] Pynchon's writing is acutely attuned to the competing demands of these impulses, in which the freedoms of expansion are confronted by the (maybe necessary) coercions of borders, in which the proliferation of fictional possibility and its assembled knowledge is (maybe necessarily) shaped by narrative structure. David Cowart helpfully points us in the direction of 'Menippean' satire (which he characterises by its 'voluminous, encyclopedic ambitions, its scatology, its digressiveness, and its descent into the fantastic') as a literary historical context in which we might place Pynchon's aesthetic.[15] Indeed works like Swift's *Gulliver's Travels*, Voltaire's *Candide* and Sterne's *Tristram Shandy* can usefully be read as progenitors of the kind of playful, baroque postmodernism that, typically, comes to stand for the Pynchonesque. Prior to Cowart, Edward Mendelson's 1976 article 'Encyclopedic Narrative: From Dante to Pynchon', had described a model of fiction that includes Dante's *Comedy* and Melville's *Moby-Dick* and argued, somewhat tendentiously, that each national literature produces a single text that can be described as encyclopaedic. Mendelson writes that such works 'attempt to render the full range of knowledge and beliefs of a national culture, while identifying the ideological perspectives from which that culture shapes and interprets that knowledge'.[16] The degree to which the

encyclopaedic text is able to generate what Daniel Punday sceptically describes as 'a whole image of human knowledge' is, of course, a
recurring concern for and in Pynchon's writing.[17] As our subsequent
chapters hope to demonstrate, the formal (and often elliptical) diffusion of encyclopaedic narrative does not obscure from his pages
our sense of Pynchon's political and ethical concern; moreover, *pace*
Mendelson, that concern is often most acutely articulated when the
authorised national narrative is traversed by disruptive incursions
and migrations. Pynchon's writing is born out of the social tensions
of the 1960s, a decade which it frequently inhabits or ponders
from a historical distance, either past or future: from 'The Secret
Integration' (1964), and its analysis of the period's racial prejudice
through the prism of childhood imagination, to *Inherent Vice*, and
that novel's concern to map the frightening after-image of 1960s
psychedelia, he has reflected continually on the political idealisms
and declensions of the United States, as they are rendered explicit
in that decade of the nation's history. Towards the end of *Inherent
Vice*, the lawyer Sauncho Smilax comments ruefully on a ship that
reappears, under different names, in the novel: 'May we trust that
this blessed ship is bound for some better shore, some undrowned
Lemuria, risen and redeemed, where the American fate, mercifully,
failed to transpire' (*IV* 341). The ship, as ship of state, as a version of
the United States yet to find a harbour in which to flourish, always
has the subjunctive potential, within the parameters of Pynchon's
jeremiad, to arrive at its destination. Stanley Cavell's sense of
America as 'a territory of magic or exemption' is an apt definition for
the impulse that we find in Pynchon's work to retain an investment
in New World exceptionalism, but one which is invariably tempered
by the knowledge that all too frequently what is glimpsed is 'a realm
that [we] cannot preserve'.[18]

   The structure of this book recognises the ways in which Pynchon's
work tends to be encountered by its readers. While, from *Gravity's
Rainbow* onwards, we have organised our chapters in correct chronological sequence, according to date of publication, there is a (characteristically Pynchonesque) temporal looping at the beginning of
our discussion. *Slow Learner* is a mixed text: appearing in 1984 with
a lengthy introduction by the author, it contains stories that were
initially published between 1959 and 1964 – that is to say, prior to
the appearance of Pynchon's first novel *V.* as well as subsequent to it.
Our decision to begin with *Slow Learner* acknowledges its status as

early work, and allows us to consider Pynchon's playful reflections on his much younger self. The readings of *Slow Learner* also help to crystallise many of the aesthetic and political preoccupations that get more expansive, confident iteration in Pynchon's later writing. In 'Entropy', for instance, Pynchon's most anthologised piece, we have a highly poised exploration of the tensions between order and chaos, restraint and freedom, that work themselves out in increasingly fraught, compromised forms as his art develops. From the very beginning Pynchon's textual allusiveness has been a feature of his writing, and (his own rather dismissive, retrospective comments notwithstanding) it is instructive to chart the ways in which literary and scientific references (to T. S. Eliot, Henry Adams, Mark Twain, and Norbert Wiener, for example) swirl in and out of these early stories as Pynchon begins to experiment with the contours of cultural and psychological disaffection. Our second chapter, on *The Crying of Lot 49*, obviously disrupts the chronological sequence, but in the purity of its complex form, in its perfect marriage of narrative structure and thematic concern, this short novel enacts, to continuing resonant effect, the postmodern strategies for which Pynchon is justly celebrated, as well as providing a document of the United States on the cusp of profound social and political change. *Slow Learner* and *The Crying of Lot 49*, then, are taken as concentrated embodiments of the theoretical and contextual obsessions of a long writing career, but are in no way to be regarded as templates against which Pynchon's other work is to be measured. Luc Herman's observation that Oedipa Maas is an 'archaeologist of American society' applies equally as well to her creator, whose continued digging into America's domestic and global identities provides us with a series of ongoing interventions into the national psyche at moments of historical pressure.[19] The Second World War in *Gravity's Rainbow*; both world wars and a series of other European and colonial crises from the first half of the twentieth century in *V.*; the liberations and traumas of the 1960s in *Slow Learner*, *The Crying of Lot 49*, *Vineland* and *Inherent Vice*; the imminent First World War and future 9/11 attacks in *Against the Day*; the colonisation of continental America and the future United States Civil War in *Mason & Dixon*; and the Cold War Reaganomics of *Vineland*: Pynchon's art is truly transhistorical and transnational. This book explores the ways in which postmodernity, and its embrace of epistemological, ethical and ontological aporia, is put to work in the service of profound reflections on the political possibilities of narrative.

Notes

1 Thomas Pynchon, 'To Richard Wilbur', in 'Presentation to Thomas Pynchon of the Howells Medal for Fiction of the Academy', in *Proceedings of the American Academy of Arts and Letters and the National Institute of Arts and Letters* 26 (1976): 43–6 (45).

2 Pynchon appears in 'Diary of a Mad Housewife' (first aired 25 January 2004) and 'All's Fair in Oven War' (first aired 14 November 2004). Pynchon's elusiveness is the subject of a film by Fosco and Donatello Dubini, *Thomas Pynchon: A Journey into the Mind of <P>* (2001).

3 Mathew Winston's 'The Quest for Pynchon' represents one relatively early instance of this kind of biographical detective work, *Twentieth-Century Literature* 12.3 (1975): 278–87. A more recent summary of Pynchon's life is John M. Krafft's 'Biographical Note', in *The Cambridge Companion to Thomas Pynchon*, ed. Inger H. Dalsgaard, Luc Herman and Brian McHale, Cambridge: Cambridge University Press, 2011, 9–16.

4 For more on William Pynchon's book – and its subsequent banning – see Michael P. Winship, 'Contesting Control of Orthodoxy among the Godly: William Pynchon Reexamined', *William and Mary Quarterly* 54.4 (1997): 795–822.

5 Deborah L. Madsen, 'Pynchon's Quest Narratives and the Tradition of American Romance', in Thomas H. Schaub ed., *Approaches to Teaching Pynchon's 'The Crying of Lot 49' and Other Works*, New York: Modern Language Association, 2008, 29. See also Kathryn Hume, *Pynchon's Mythography: An Approach to 'Gravity's Rainbow'*, Carbondale: Southern Illinois University Press, 1987, especially Chapter Four.

6 For more on cinematic paranoia of the period, see Ray Pratt, *Projecting Paranoia: Conspiratorial Visions in American Film*, Lawrence: University of Kansas Press, 2001, 113–44.

7 Emily Apter, 'On Oneworldedness: Or Paranoia as a World System', *American Literary History* 18.2 (2006): 365–89 (366).

8 John Johnston, *Information Multiplicity: American Fiction in the Age of Media Saturation*, Baltimore: The Johns Hopkins University Press, 1998, 43.

9 Apter, 'On Oneworldedness', 367.

10 Leo Bersani, 'Pynchon, Paranoia, and Literature', *Representations* 25 (Winter, 1989): 99–118 (101).

11 Amy J. Elias, 'History', in *The Cambridge Companion to Thomas Pynchon*, ed. Dalsgaard, Hermand and McHale, 126.

12 Steven Weisenburger, *A 'Gravity's Rainbow' Companion: Sources and Contexts for Pynchon's Novel*, Athens and London: University of Georgia Press, 2006, 177–8.

13 Theophilus Savvlas draws a useful parallel here with Henri Lefebvre,

Introduction **11**

whose discussion of the *mundus*, an Italian town's rubbish tip, establishes the potential of waste to exert a counter-hegemonic pull. Lefebvre writes of this place as a 'passageway through which dead souls could return to the bosom of the earth and then re-merge and be reborn' (*The Production of Space*, trans. Donald Nicholson-Smith, Oxford: Wiley-Blackwell, 1991, 242). See Savvlas, 'Pynchon Plays Dice: *Mason & Dixon* and Quantum History', *Literature & History* 20.2 (2011): 51–67 (62–3). From one of his earliest stories, 'Low-lands', to the more recent *Against the Day* Pynchon has been preoccupied with the portals that exist between worlds and through which the living and the non-living are able to pass.

14 Henry James, 'Preface to *Roderick Hudson*' (1907), in Henry James, *The Critical Muse: Selected Literary Criticism*, ed. Roger Gard, London: Penguin Books, 1987, 452. In 1884, in 'The Art of Fiction', James had already pondered the tension between structure and diffusion, articulating a preference for the latter: 'In proportion as in what she [Fiction] offers us we see life *without* arrangement do we feel that we are touching the truth; in proportion as we see it *with* rearrangement do we feel that we are being put off with a substitute, a compromise and convention' (200).

15 David Cowart, *Thomas Pynchon & the Dark Passages of History*, Athens: University of Georgia Press, 2011, 200.

16 Edward Mendelson, 'Encyclopedic Narrative: From Dante to Pynchon,' *MLN* 91 (1976): 1267–75 (1269).

17 Daniel Punday, *Writing at the Limit: The Novel in the New Media Ecology*, Lincoln: University of Nebraska Press, 2012, 169. Punday links Pynchon's novel *Gravity's Rainbow* to the development of the electronic encyclopedia, specifically Wikipedia, to explore the text's pragmatic rather than totalising hermeneutic principles: 'Like *Gravity's Rainbow*, the [electronic] encyclopedia moves away from an idealized model of knowledge based on transcending the limits of specific media, and toward an emphasis on agency and use' (170).

18 Stanley Cavell, *Philosophy the Day After Tomorrow*, Cambridge, MA: Harvard University Press, 2005, 78, 79.

19 Luc Herman, 'Early Pynchon', in *The Cambridge Companion to Thomas Pynchon*, ed. Dalsgaard, Herman and McHale, 27.

1

Refuge and refuse in *Slow Learner*

With the publication in 1984 of *Slow Learner*, Thomas Pynchon made easily available some of his earliest writing. At least one of the stories, 'The Small Rain', had been published (in the *Cornell Writer* in March 1959) while Pynchon was studying for his undergraduate degree at Cornell University. The other pieces in the collection are: 'Low-lands' (published in *New World Writing* in March 1960); 'Entropy' (in the spring 1960 edition of the *Kenyon Review*); 'Under the Rose' (in *The Noble Savage* in May 1961); and 'The Secret Integration' (written after *V.* and appearing in the *Saturday Evening Post* of 19 December 1964). In addition to the interest that the appearance of these early works generated, Pynchon's decision to include an autobiographical introductory essay in which he described the genesis of his literary style and offered evaluations of the stories the reader was about to encounter set in train some feverish critical speculation about the author and his writing career. For a figure who had so successfully maintained a level of invisibility within the public sphere that had become part of our fascination with him, the confessional tone of the volume's introduction was startling. By placing the stories in a biographical frame, Pynchon proposes a reading of them as essentially juvenilia and of himself as a 'slow learner' who had failed to acquire the necessary skills and strategies of the successful writer of fiction:

> It is only fair to warn even the most kindly disposed of readers that there are some mighty tiresome passages here, juvenile and delinquent too. At the same time, my best hope is that, pretentious, goofy and ill-considered as they get now and then, these stories will still be of use with all their flaws intact, as illustrative of typical problems in entry-level fiction, and cautionary about some practices which younger writers might prefer to avoid. (*SL* 4)

Yet, as we will argue towards the end of this chapter, the apparently artless tone of the 'Introduction' conceals forms of narrative posturing that the unwary reader might miss. Pynchon offers a strong authorial judgement and watches as we are foolishly tempted to collude with it.

Of the stories reprinted in *Slow Learner*, this chapter discusses three in detail: 'Low-lands', 'The Secret Integration' and 'Entropy'. These have been selected because they best represent Pynchon's earliest articulations of some of the tropes and ideas that have preoccupied him throughout his writing career: spatial instability, the regulation of systems (bodily, social, political), the eruption of the fantastic into the quotidian, and the usefulness of waste. All three tales are also especially concerned with allusiveness, and show a writer aware of and, at times, struggling with his literary and cultural inheritance, whether that be the high modernism of T. S. Eliot in 'Low-lands', the entropic patterning of Henry Adams in 'Entropy', or the Mark Twain-like delight in children's imaginations in 'The Secret Integration'. While it would be foolish to claim that these stories are fully rendered, neither is it wise, as the chapter goes on to show, to accept the wholesale critique of them that Pynchon, in his guise as unhelpful introducer, offers. Although often uneven in execution, they nevertheless seek to excavate some of the submerged aspects of an American culture determined to present a face of contented conformity to itself. Pynchon's stories are fascinated by our reliance on structures of rational control – systems of containment through which we aim to organise ourselves – as well as those moments of disruption via fantasy or violence whereby we attempt to contest the inexorable narratives of convention. *Slow Learner*, then, allows readers to see more clearly how the canonical (if still mysterious) writer of *Gravity's Rainbow* and *Against the Day* emerges, for while the subjects and locales of each of the stories in the volume varies widely, their concern with, amongst other things, consumerism, social instability and the possibilities of imaginative rebellion marks them, in retrospect, as typical of their author.

Relentless rationality: 'Low-lands'

Of all the pieces republished in *Slow Learner*, 'Low-lands' concerns itself most explicitly with the pressures of American conformity as they exert themselves at mid-century, and the possible paths (real or

imagined) that might lead to liberation or transcendence. In its narrative of Dennis Flange's withdrawal from the illusory comforts of a
bourgeois marriage to an explicitly marginal, and increasingly fantastic, space of escape, the story participates in a contemporary cultural
anxiety around questions of autonomy and resistance. Underneath
the veneer of middle-class contentment, of the economic boon of
a post-war economy, cultural critique of the 1950s was frequently
preoccupied with the implications of conformity and containment
within the body politic. The success of American capitalism had led,
it was argued, to the occlusion of dissenting voices from debates
about national identity. The marginalising of such forms of social
grievance and division by the 'vital center' (a term coined in 1949 by
the historian Arthur M. Schlesinger whose book of the same name
advocated a centrist liberalism untainted by the extremes of left and
right) helped to foster repressive images of cultural homogeneity in
post-war American life. Such repression in turn met with criticism
in works such as David Riesman's *The Lonely Crowd* (1950) and
C. Wright Mills's *White Collar: The American Middle Classes* (1951).
Riesman declared that there had been a gradual transformation in
the conception of selfhood, so that American character had become
'other-directed' in ways that had brought about a generic identity
that was continually susceptible to 'signals from others', 'the mass
media: movies, radio, comics, and popular culture media generally'.[1]
Inner-directed persons, Riesman argued, had a complex interior life,
indicative of the conception of character imagined to be the norm
under a politics of liberal individualism. Moreover, he imagines the
transition from inner to outer in explicitly class terms:

> [W]e could say that inner-direction is the typical character of the 'old'
> middle class – the banker, the tradesman, the small entrepreneur, the
> technically oriented engineer, etc. – while other direction is becoming
> the typical character of the 'new' middle class – the bureaucrat, the
> salaried employee in business, etc.[2]

The notion of other direction articulated a crisis of agency, reified
as a conflict between Self and Society in which changes in economic
conditions are configured as threats to private property. In *White
Collar*, Mills had similarly diagnosed a post-war self suffering from
the loss of a privatised identity within the machinations of capitalist
bureaucracy: 'The decline of the free entrepreneur and the rise of
the dependent employee on the American scene has paralleled the

decline of the independent individual and the rise of the little man in the American mind'.[3] Riesman and Mills desire to recuperate Enlightenment conceptions of the individual, and, as Timothy Melley points out, both men ground their ideas in the assumption that 'persons are self-made and acquire their own attributes through the labour of self-creation'.[4] Our introductory chapter has already noted that Pynchon was appreciative of the countercultural impulses of Jack Kerouac and the Beats, and the structural antagonism between conformity and dissent, social incarceration and creative self-determination, is obviously key to the ethical debates played out in novels like *On the Road* (1957) and Richard Fariña's *Been Down So Long It Looks Like Up to Me* (1966, and for which Pynchon provided the introduction in a 1983 reprint). As we will show in 'Low-lands', the kinds of freedom possible in Pynchon's story are aligned with a movement down into interior space that is increasingly removed from the demands and expectations of the everyday. The rhetoric of interiority and exteriority that underwrites Cold War narratives of decline like those of Riesman and Mills is central to 'Low-lands', where spatiality – sometimes constricting, sometimes protective – provides the tale's organising trope. But the assurances of a renewed privatised space and a reconstituted individuality are ambiguously treated, for the story concludes on a note of escape that might also be a descent into madness.

'Low-lands' opens with Dennis Flange, a lawyer, who has decided not to go to work, but is instead drinking with his friend, Rocco Squarcione, the garbage man – much to the disapproval of Flange's wife, Cindy. Pynchon provides the reader with an efficiently detailed description of Flange's domestic arrangements, suggesting the degree to which his marriage has become stultified by routine and commercialism. Flange, Pynchon writes, 'sat with Rocco for the rest of the day drinking muscatel and listening to a $1,000 stereo outfit that Cindy had made him buy but which she had never used, to Flange's recollection, for anything but a place to put hors d'oeuvre dishes or cocktail trays' (*SL* 55). Cindy hangs paintings by Mondrian in a police booth in the front yard, to which Dennis is relegated whenever they argue. He begins to suspect an affinity between his wife and the painter, 'both austere and logical' (*SL* 61) in the way that they regard the world. The two-storey marital home on Long Island is carefully positioned above sea-level – the sea itself becomes a central trope in the story – and within its conventional mock English cottage exterior there are more oblique spaces, 'priest-holes and concealed passageways and oddly angled rooms', and a cellar containing 'innumerable tunnels, which writhed away radically like the tentacles of a spastic octopus into dead ends, storm drains, abandoned sewers and occasionally a secret wine cellar'. Underground, then, are to be found alternative spaces, some of which are redundant, others lead to potentially interesting rewards, but all suggestive of something that runs counter to the uniformity of Flange's surface domesticity. We learn that the original owner of the house himself embodied a multiplicity of aspect, being 'an Episcopal minister who ran bootleg stuff in from Canada on the side' (*SL* 56).

Cindy orders Dennis and his friend down to 'the rumpus room', an early indication that the figures of disruption and non-conformity will relocate to spaces below the ground-level of society. But when Pig Bodine also arrives at the house, Cindy tells them all ('the weird crew' [*SL* 56]) to leave, Bodine having been responsible for interrupting Flange's wedding night to take him on a two-week drinking session. Much of the information we learn about Bodine is repeated in *V.* (Pynchon was writing that novel as he worked on 'Low-lands'), where he is a friend of, and foil to, Benny Profane.[5] His importance to the tale lies in his embodiment of a homosocial world that represents a retreat from the responsibilities of marriage and a career; Bodine's is a chaotic and unpredictable lifestyle. In this, Pynchon's story explores the impulse to equate conformity with heterosexual relationships, suggesting that the (re)construction of male bonding is one strategy through which the containments of a mainstream culture might be resisted. This notion had been most influentially articulated by Leslie Fiedler in a 1948 essay on Mark Twain's novel *Huckleberry Finn* (and later expanded to provide the organising thesis of his book *Love and Death in the American Novel* [1960]). For Fiedler this movement away from what he regarded as the representation of complex sexual encounter into a realm of homosocial innocence was an indictment of the immaturity of American literary culture.[6] Pynchon's tale choreographs fantasies of escape as they present themselves to Dennis Flange, but it withholds from offering the kind of outright critique that Fiedler levels, choosing instead to be more circumspect about its judgements. Flange certainly regards his earlier, pre-domesticated self as an idealised ego, one formed by the experience of communal masculinity during his navy service in the Second World War. In his memory this figure – his 'peculiar double' (*SL* 59) – is 'Fortune's elf child and disinherited darling, young and randy and more a Jolly Jack Tar than anyone human could conceivably be; thews and chin taut against a sixty-knot gale with a well-broken-in briar clenched in the bright defiant teeth ... [T]here he had been, Dennis Flange, in his prime, without the current signs of incipient middle age' (*SL* 59–60). As David Seed astutely notes of this passage, Flange's depiction of his ideal self here is constructed with an awareness of its own artificiality: 'Although the story is narrated in the third person we rarely sense a sharply defined ironic gap between narrator and protagonist ... because Flange demonstrates a humorous self-consciousness about his own fantasies'.[7] What is clear, though, is that sexuality is allied with youthful vitality, 'disinherited' from the ageing protocols of marriage and freed from the constraints exerted by a wife back in the United States.

Flange's recollection of his time in the Pacific is just one of many references to water in the story. Geronimo Diaz, Dennis's crazed psychoanalyst (and the forerunner of Dr Hilarius in *The Crying of Lot 49*) encourages his impulse away from domesticity through his 'wonderful, random sort of madness' (*SL* 58), one which nevertheless offers a version of Freud's theory of the centrality of the sea ('the true mother image for us all') to life's development; and the story also references a connection between water and amniotic fluid ('the sea was a woman' [*SL* 59], 'the snorings of one's wife are as the drool and trickle of amniotic fluid somewhere outside the blankets' [*SL* 58]). The sea becomes, as Seed notes, an 'imagistic core' (*SL* 58) at the heart of the story,[8] and is the subject of a complex meditation as Flange remembers a 'Filipino steward' (*SL* 64) during the war who would sing sea shanties, one of which provides the title of the story:

A ship I have got in the North Country
And she goes by the name of the Golden Vanity,
O, I fear she will be taken by a Spanish Gal-la-lee,
As she sails by the Low-lands low.

Flange translates the term 'Low-lands', meaning the south of Scotland, into a spatial metaphor for the sea:

Anyone who has looked at the open sea under a special kind of illumination or in a mood conducive to metaphor will tell you of the curious illusion that the ocean, despite its movement, has a certain solidity; it becomes a gray or glaucous desert, a waste land which stretches away

to the horizon, and all you would have to do would be to step over the
lifelines to walk away over its surface ... (*SL* 65)

In a compressed form this passage articulates the story's consideration of the non-literal as the means by which convention in all its
forms might be avoided. The perspective here is refracted through
the distorting/illuminating lens of art ('illumination', 'metaphor' and
'illusion'), such that the water is transformed into an endless vista
that can be explored by the unfettered imagination by stepping 'over
the lifelines' of the quotidian. The 'waste land' described here is not
T. S. Eliot's vision of modernity's malaise, but instead an imaginary
expanse which for Flange 'almost demanded a single human figure
striding across it for completeness' (*SL* 65). The sea, then, becomes
reconstituted as a surface onto which Dennis can project his surrogate self, an explorer freed from the demands of marriage and
a career. As John Dugdale notes, 'The sea is identified throughout
the text with fantasy, waking and sleeping, and the "sea change"
is the main image for the sort of metamorphosis achieved by the
dreamwork'.[9]

This imaginary space exists alongside the ostensibly material
reality of the rubbish dump, the location where Dennis and his
friends find sanctuary after Cindy has thrown them out of the house.
Tony Tanner describes Pynchon as 'the real lyricist of rubbish',[10]
and indeed his fiction is full of waste dumps and those regarded by
society as outcasts, outsiders or the disinherited. Pynchon's writing
is preoccupied with the waste products, material and human, of
America's national body. As we have already noted, collectively
Pynchon calls such items the 'preterite', a term taken from Puritan
vocabulary to distinguish the fallen from the elect who organise and
police theological and social structures. As David Evans has recently
explained, Pynchon's rubbish 'represents all the waste material,
human and other, which is discarded to realise any design – the
unsaved remnant, the excluded middle, the Preterite, for whom
not even God's commodious plan has a place'.[11] In this Pynchon
participates in a reinvented American standard, the jeremiad, whose
insistent lament is aimed at the failure of the United States to realise
the utopian possibilities of its destiny. The journey to the dump
in 'Low-lands' is a descent towards an area 'sunk fifty feet below
the streets of the sprawling housing development that surrounded
it' (*SL* 64); presided over by a figure called Bolingbroke (alluding

to Shakespeare's *Henry IV*), it is 'an enclave in the dreary country around it' (*SL* 67), a country from which Flange is taking his leave. The dump has created its own aesthetic shapes and textures which are more tangible than the imagined realm of the sea that we noticed above. Here is an underworld of refuse, a 'discrete kingdom' with its own rationale of organisation. Bolingbroke leads them 'past half an acre of abandoned refrigerators, bicycles, baby carriages, washing machines, sinks, toilets, bedsprings, TV sets, pots and pans and stoves and air-conditioners and finally over a dune to where the mattresses were' (*SL* 66). The compositional qualities of this space are emphasised further when, at the mid-point of the story, we reach Bolingbroke's shack and his collage of magazine photographs. Here is an alternative realm, presided over by a ruler who wears a pork-pie hat for a crown, in a kingdom decorated with the visual debris of the surface world.

In Bolingbroke's shack the cast of characters begin to tell each other sea stories, except for Flange, who relates instead how he and a number of other fellow-students stole a corpse and put it on the bed of the fraternity president. Flange's refusal to tell a narrative of the sea is explained in a rather torturous sentence, but one to which it is worth paying some attention:

> [I]f you are Dennis Flange and if the sea's tides are the same that not only wash along your veins but also billow through your fantasies then it is all right to listen to but not to tell stories about that sea, because you and the truth of a true lie were thrown sometime way back into a curious contiguity and as long as you are passive you can remain aware of the truth's extent but the minute you become active you are somehow, if not violating a convention outright, at least screwing up the perspective of things, much as anyone observing subatomic particles changes the works, data and odds, by the act of observing. So he had told the other [story] instead, at random. (*SL* 69)

This is a difficult passage which refuses to come into pristine focus, yet it signals concerns that are important to the story as a whole. Poised between fantasy and reality, artifice and truth, Flange's decision is to maintain a stance of passivity. If, as we have argued, the sea is the location for both evolutionary development and the transformative imagination, Flange is unwilling to disrupt these possibilities by intervening with a story of his own. Alluding to Heisenberg's uncertainty principle (which states that accurate measurement of subatomic particles cannot be achieved without disturbing the network in which they move), Flange decides to listen rather than risk participation. What he hears is comforting, for the tall tales of Bolingbroke and Bodine, with their colourful episodes of mutiny and invasion, allow him to conflate the peculiar underworld of the dump with the creative potential of the sea:

> [I]t was right that there should be gypsies living in the dump, just as he had been able to believe in the rightness of Bolingbroke's sea, its ability to encompass and be the sustaining plasma or medium for horse-drawn taxis and Porcaccios [elements in both Bolingbroke's and Bodine's stories]. Not to mention that young, rogue male Flange, from whom he occasionally felt the Flange of today had suffered a sea change into something not so rare or strange. (*SL* 71–2)

The stories he hears, then, serve as therapeutic triggers for an imaginative reconstitution of the self. Gypsies and tall tales combine to suggest the value of the tangential and digressive, of a condition of heroic marginality from which, Dennis fears, he has declined. While, as Richard Patteson has suggested, Pynchon's insistent concern is to explore 'the conflict between the human need to create meaningful form and the unavoidable tendency towards formlessness in the universe',[12] this opposition, as one might expect, begins to collapse almost as soon as it is articulated. As we will attempt to demonstrate in the discussion of *Mason & Dixon*, the impulse to measure and codify is constantly being undermined by irrational and fantastic impulses that cause us to question the validity of the empirical enterprise itself. In 'Low-lands', at least one aspect of 'meaningful form' has been the 'relentless rationality' of Flange's everyday existence, and the turn to subterranean spaces (both actual and imagined) moves the narrative away from the surface world of domestic conformity. Flange's 'sustaining plasma' here echoes the 'irresponsible plasma of delusion' (*SL* 58) in which Geronimo Diaz floats. If the former is regarded as essential to continued human vitality, the latter signals the psychiatrist's mental instability, his complete enclosure in a world of fantasy. This shared vocabulary asks us to consider the (maybe permeable) border between an imagination that is insane and one that is artistic. Does a delight in stories, in the possibilities of fiction, act as an impediment to one's ability to function in the everyday? Flange's pleasure in narrative, and the potential for reinvention that it provides him, encourages us to read 'Low-lands' as an oblique commentary on the delights and perils of storytelling, of fiction as a response to the mundanity of the here and now. However, while this level of self-consciousness is undoubtedly at work in the story, the reader needs to be careful not to reduce 'Low-lands' to a straightforward paean to the creative imagination, as the final third of the narrative takes us deeper underground and into a space of fantasy that is ambiguously drawn. Woken from sleep by a girl's voice calling 'Anglo ... Come find me or I shall go away forever. Come out, tall Anglo with the golden hair and the shining teeth' (*SL* 72), Flange imagines that she is addressing his alter ego, 'that sea-dog of the lusty, dark Pacific days' (*SL* 73). Tempted outside, he knocks over a pile of tyres and loses consciousness. When he awakens once more, we have moved even further into a dream world, for the girl is described in terms that convey both perfection and strangeness:

> In the starlight she was exquisite: she wore a dark dress, her legs and arms were bare, slim, the neck arching and delicate, her figure so slender it was almost a shadow. Dark hair floated around her face and down her back like a black nebula; eyes enormous, nose retroussé, short upper lip, good teeth, nice chin. She was a dream, this girl, and angel. She was also roughly three and a half feet tall. (*SL* 73–4)

Intense beauty is combined here with something more insubstantial. Nerissa is a 'shadow' whose floating hair maintains the story's allusions to water. While there is a peculiar falling off in adjectival power (we move from the precision of an 'arching and delicate' neck to 'good teeth, nice chin'), nevertheless the passage asks us to regard this figure as 'a dream', an empty phrase but one which, in this case, might also literally be true. She takes him further into the heart of the dump to a refrigerator lying on its back, into which they both climb and descend 'down a gentle incline which must have run for a quarter of a mile'.[13] Flange finds himself in a second network of tunnels, like those used for smuggling under his own home, except this time their history is more politically radical in that they were constructed 'back in the '30s by a terrorist group called the Sons of the Red Apocalypse, by way of making ready for the revolution'. Economic insurrection in the 1920s under Flange's home makes way for political dissent a decade later in the bowels of the rubbish dump. Once the authorities had rounded up the troublemakers, Nerissa tells Flange, 'the gypsies had moved in' (*SL* 75).

The story concludes with the two characters arriving at Nerissa's room, where Flange meets her talking pet rat Hyacinth. (Hyacinth anticipates the rat Veronica in *V.*, and evokes T. S. Eliot's 'hyacinth girl' in 'The Waste Land' and maybe the character Hyacinth Robinson in Henry James's novel *The Princess Cassamassima* (1886), a figure similarly balancing the attractions of the aesthetic and the tangible). Nerissa is convinced that Flange will stay and marry her, and Dennis considers his options while watching her nurse her pet:

> And then: I wonder why Cindy and I never had a child.
>   And: a child makes it all right. Let the world shrink to a *boccie* ball.
> So of course he knew.
>   'Sure,' he said. 'All right. I'll stay.' For a while, at least, he thought.
> She looked up gravely. Whitecaps danced across her eyes; sea creatures, he knew, would be cruising about in the submarine green of her heart. (*SL* 76–7)

Between the expectations of a conventional marriage with Cindy and the fantasy family of a child-woman and a talking rat, Flange opts to remain in the dump, telling himself that it might only be a temporary arrangement, and alluding to Andrew Marvell's poem 'To His Coy Mistress' in the process ('Let us roll all our strength, and all / Our sweetness, up into one ball'). Nerissa offers what Mark Hawthorne has described as 'a fantasy space in which he [Flange] can play a heterosexual role without taking on its stereotypical demands'.[14] The final sentence keeps us connected to the metaphor of the sea in its explicit association of Nerissa with water, and 'whitecaps' and 'submarine' also echo Flange's idealised reconstruction of his navy past. Yet Nerissa takes him away from the homosocial world of male retreat, replacing it with a desexualised relationship and a ready-made family unit. The narrative provides a deceptive moment of revelation, 'So of course he knew', an epiphany about which Pynchon will teach us again and again in his work to be sceptical. This exclamation of decision is in fact a reaffirmation of passivity, a settling into fantasy (and maybe madness) that, from a certain perspective, might look less like liberation and more an alternative form of imprisonment. In its playful blurring of the boundaries between reality, imaginative creativity and solipsistic dreaming, 'Low-lands' is an early incarnation of Pynchon's continued interest in testing the narrative frameworks into which stories are placed by exploring some of the hidden passageways of fiction. As with the smuggling tunnels under Flange's house, some of these routes may lead to dead-ends by refusing to offer firm co-ordinates for interpretation. Others though, as we will argue, have the potential to recuperate possibilities of textual and political resistance.

Imaginary playmates: 'The Secret Integration'

In 1966 Pynchon turned to journalism and an illustrated piece published in the *New York Times Magazine* on the aftermath of the six-day riots in the Watts neighbourhood of Los Angeles in August 1965. While this article has generated relatively little critical attention, 'A Journey Into the Mind of Watts' is an explicit intervention in the politics of race during the Civil Rights Movement, and serves as a useful contextualising introduction to Pynchon's story of racial tension, 'The Secret Integration', published two years before. The one significant exception to this neglect is David Seed's account of the piece, a useful reading of its rhetorical strategies for generating readerly sympathy.[15] Of most interest to us here is Pynchon's early engagement with racial politics as viewed through the prism of the mass media and as articulated through waste, the latter, as we have seen, serving a frequent trope in his writing. While Pynchon presents the mutual mistrust and incomprehension to be found in Watts as the articulation of ingrained, automatic responses ('for every action there is an equal and opposite reaction'),[16] just as disturbing is his evocation of an absolute disparity between the landscape of the black suburb of Watts and that of downtown Los Angeles. Watts is characterised by particularity, a density of specification that, to Pynchon's mind, presents 'a pocket of bitter reality' against which the gleaming architecture of Los Angeles can only seem vacuous and sterile. Los Angeles, he writes,

> is basically a white Scene, and illusion is everywhere in it, from the giant aerospace firms that flourish or retrench at the whims of Robert McNamara, to the 'action' everybody mills along the Strip on weekends looking for, unaware that they, and their search which will end, usually, unfulfilled, are the only action in town.[17]

Corporate America, consumerist America, and military America (with the reference to President Nixon's Secretary of Defense McNamara) collide in this passage as white California conforms to expectations that can never be satisfied. Seed describes this as a process of 'collective self-mystification',[18] a useful phrase that underscores Pynchon's recognition of the power of organised happiness in the structuring of people's lives. Carefully policed and never satisfied, Los Angeles produces the ideal capitalist consumer. In Watts, however, white America appears as an invasive force, sending its bureaucratic authority into an environment that does not recognise its legitimacy and speaking a language of business that is bleakly humorous in its inappropriateness:

> Meantime, the outposts of the establishment drowse in the bright summery smog: secretaries chat the afternoons plaintively away about machines that will not accept the cards they have punched for them; white volunteers sit filing, doodling, talking on the phones, doing any kind of busy-work, wondering where the 'clients' are; inspirational mottoes like SMILE decorate the beaverboard office walls along with flow charts to illustrate the proper disposition of 'cases,' and with clippings from the slick magazines about 'What Is Emotional Maturity?'[19]

In contrast to such redundant gestures, Pynchon closes his piece by describing how the Watts riots have been commemorated by local artists at a festival held in honour of Simon Rodia, the architect who between 1921 and 1954 designed and built the Watts Towers, a collection of seventeen interconnected structures decorated with found objects and waste materials. The rational architecture of the urban metropolis is challenged by space that refuses to cohere into an abstract cartography. Whereas Los Angeles embodies corporate homogeneity, Rodia's architecture is the embodiment of the local environment. Thus it is fitting that Pynchon focuses on sculptures fashioned out of the debris of the riots: 'Exploiting textures of charred wood, twisted metal, fused glass, many of the works were fine, honest rebirths.'[20] In *Gravity's Rainbow* Pynchon would write of new consciousnesses being created out of the waste heaps, of minds 'kicking endlessly among the plastic trivia, finding in each Deeper Significance and trying to string them all together like terms of a power series ... to bring them together in their slick persistence and our preterition ... to make sense of, to find the meanest sharp sliver of truth in so much replication, so much waste' (*GR* 590). The final paragraph of 'Journey' details such an act of political and creative resistance that is so quintessentially Pynchonesque that one is tempted to question whether it is in fact an invention of the author:

> In one corner was this old, busted, hollow TV set with a rabbit-ears antenna on top; inside, where its picture tube should have been, gazing out with scorched wiring threaded like electronic ivy among its crevices and sockets, was a human skull. The name of the piece was 'The Late, Late, Late Show'.[21]

Making art out of a discarded television in this way represents, in concentrated form, an answer to Pynchon's frequently expressed concern about the dehumanising power of the mass media within American culture, a worry perhaps most explicitly articulated in his 1990 novel *Vineland*, although aspects of it can be traced throughout his work. Here television's deathly reach is itself terminated, and the media's culpability in perpetuating racial stereotyping of the kind that might perpetuate the tensions in Watts is both acknowledged and resisted.

'The Secret Integration' contains a passage which anticipates these observations on the pernicious blandness of much of the American urban experience. Pynchon describes the planned housing estates of the Berkshires as spaces of absolute transparency, where the chances of private or unconventional living are practically impossible in an environment of pure visibility:

> [T]here was nothing about the little, low-rambling, more or less identical homes of Northumberland Estates to interest or haunt ... no small immunities, no possibilities for hidden life or otherworldly presence: no trees, secret routes, shortcuts, culverts, thickets that could be made hollow in the middle – everything in the place was out in the open, everything could be seen at a glance; and behind it, under it, around the corners of its houses and down the safe, gentle curves of its streets, you came back and kept coming back, to nothing: nothing but the cheerless earth. (*SL* 158)

In this, Pynchon echoes the complaint that Henry James made of New York upon his return to that city after an absence of over twenty years. In *The American Scene* (1907), James writes with dismay of how

> it takes a whole new discipline to put the visitor at his ease in so merciless a medium; he finds himself looking round for a background or a limit, some localizing fact or two, in the interest of talk, of that 'good' talk which always falters before the complete proscription of privacy. He sees only doorless apertures, vainly festooned, which decline to tell him where he is, which make him still a homeless wanderer, which

show him other apertures, corridors, staircases, yawning, expanding, ascending, descending, and all as for the purpose of giving his presence 'away'.[22]

For James, the sheer accessibility of Manhattan (its 'doorless apertures') signifies its incorporation into the realm of business alongside its failure to generate the kind of civilising culture that, by implication in *The American Scene*, he associates with aspects of the Old World. Pynchon is less concerned with the notion of bourgeois civility (indeed in places he is sceptical of the very idea) than he is with the eradication of political possibility within America's spaces of late capitalism. As with his vision of white America in 'The Journey into Watts', Pynchon here describes a habitat that induces and controls a certain kind of behaviour: its panopticon-style openness ensures forms of self-policing that minimise the likelihood of dissenting or countercultural impulses.

'The Secret Integration', in its comic fantasy of children's attempts to rebel against a dominant white society, imagines a politics built around secrecy, espionage and private spaces. Telling the story of a children's gang led by Grover Snodd which sets out to undermine the structures of a white adult world through fostering rebellion in schools, planning sodium bomb attacks, and infiltrating parent–teacher meetings, the 'Inner Junta' (*SL* 161) have their hideout in a large house that had once belonged to King Yrjö, a 'European pretender' who had fled his 'hardly real shadow-state' during the political upheavals of the 1930s to purchase an estate in the Berkshires for 'a bucketful of jewels, [so] the yarn went' (*SL* 160). The hideout then is already established as a space of the imagination, part of a narrative the veracity of which is impossible to ascertain, but connected for the children to an exotic, mysterious Old World history that, like the Second World War, is comprehensible only as 'a kind of code, twilit, forever unexplained' (*SL* 161). Whereas the Northumberland Estates are exposing and homogeneous, King Yrjö's old house is replete with the unexpected and opaque, being full of

> mute injunctions: blind places you could be jumped out at from; stretches of warped floor that might suddenly open downward into dungeons or simple darknesses with nothing nearby to grab onto; doors that would not stay open behind you but were balanced to close quietly, unless you watched them. ... [D]oorways where old velvet hung whose pile was worn away into maplike patterns, seas and land masses taught in no geography their schools knew. (*SL* 164–5)

This is a space in which plots can be hatched and imagination can take flight; it also, Pynchon suggests, promotes a cartography that lies beyond the knowledge of established (and establishment) institutions of learning. The children, through the third-person narrative that is sympathetic to their experience, inhabit a realm in the 'Big House' (*SL* 164) in which adventure and danger are built into the fabric of the environment. As with 'Low-lands', this is a homosocial world of young male resistance to the demands and expectations of the adult world. (The one exception to this gender focus is a minor character, Kim Dufay, who, through being 'dolled up in her most sophisticated clothes and a size 28A padded bra she'd conned her mother into buying her', is able to do 'a pretty good job of passing' as an adult at a parent–teacher association meeting [*SL* 155]. As we will try to show, the reference to 'passing' is important in a story so concerned with the possibilities or otherwise of integration.) Pynchon's homosociality in the story, as David Seed has argued, is a careful blending of Mark Twain's sentimental romantic delight in childhood (in *Tom Sawyer* [1876]) *and* his critique of how such sentimentalism is exploited by adults (in *Huckleberry Finn* [1885]).[23] The story plays with the children's different levels of comprehension of the adult world – their confusion of the words 'cemetery' and 'symmetry' and 'arsenic' and 'arsenal' – and also combines moments of children's gleeful misbehaviour with serious, if at times oblique, social critique. Grover's response to being labelled 'uneducable' by the school principle is to get angry: 'it made him mad, it was like calling somebody a wop, or a nigger' (*SL* 150). Feeling a sense of injustice at the pejorative codes of the adult world, Grover aligns himself (as the Tom Sawyer-esque leader of the gang) with other targets of prejudice, and a racial tension that lies below the surface of the story and the conscious understanding of the boys.

The first mention of Grover's awareness of racial politics occurs in his response to reading volumes of the immensely popular *Tom Swift* series of boys' adventure stories, written under the pseudonym Victor Appleton. (Pynchon later gently parodies such narratives with the Chums of Chance in *Against the Day*.) Grover finds these books troublingly addictive, and worries about their eponymous hero:

> 'It's awful,' he said, 'the guy's a show-off, he talks funny, and he's a snob, and' – hitting his head to remember the word – 'a racist.'

'A what?'

'You know this colored servant Tom Swift has, remember, named Eradicate Sampson? Rad for short. The way he treats that guy, it's disgusting. Do they want me to read that stuff so I'll be like that?' (*SL* 144–5)

Grover feels the force of the injustice against Rad, even if he is less confident about the correct word by which it can be named. Significantly the responsibility for Grover's exposure to the corruptions of narrative lies with his parents. Instinctively he assumes that they share Swift's racism, and that the book is part of the adult world's plan to inculcate the same attitudes in its children. Tim, another member of the gang, then makes a key intervention: '"Maybe that's how," said Tim, excited, having figured it out all at once, "how they want you to be with Carl." He meant Carl Barrington, a colored kid they knew' (*SL* 145). The Barringtons have recently moved into a house in the Northumberland Estates, and their son, Carl, has been welcomed as a member of the gang. The matter-of-fact simplicity of the narrative's clarification of who Carl is negates adult fear of residential integration, or 'blockbusting' (*SL* 186), and indicates the children's lack of concern about racial difference. Significantly, too, Carl adds to the monotony of the Northumberland Estates, bringing a literal and an imaginative 'color' to the monochromatic landscape. Tim feels that Carl 'must somehow carry around with him a perpetual Berkshire autumn'; he 'brought with him a kind of illumination, a brightening, a compensation for whatever it was about the light that was missing' (*SL* 162). That the white children's parents are preoccupied with the social ramifications of this incursion of colour is apparent when Tim overhears his mother on the telephone, a sophisticated passage of writing that modulates with skill between the child's incomprehension and the adult's guilty exposure:

> There was a look on her face Tim had never seen before. A little – what do you call it, nervous? scared? – he didn't know. If she saw him there she gave no sign, though he'd made noise enough. The receiver stopped buzzing and somebody answered.
>
> 'You niggers,' his mother spat out suddenly, 'dirty niggers, get out of this town, go back to Pittsfield. Get out before you get in real trouble.' Then she hung up fast. The hand that was in a fist had been shaking, and now the other hand, once it let go of the receiver, started shaking a little too. She turned swiftly, as if she smelled him like a deer; caught Tim looking at her in astonishment.

'Oh, you,' she said, beginning to smile, except for her eyes.

'What were you doing?' Tim asked, which wasn't what he'd meant to ask.

'Oh, playing a joke, Tim,' she said, 'a practical joke.'

Tim shrugged and went on out the back door. 'I'm going out,' he told her, without looking back. He knew she wouldn't give him any trouble now about it, because he'd caught her. (*SL* 147)

Tim's attempts to read his mother are not entirely successful here. He is aware that she has been compromised by their encounter, but her face is, at least initially, difficult to read. The extremity of her reaction is captured by the detail provided by narrative voice, which has a degree of interpretative insight that is denied Tim. 'Spat', 'she smelled him like a deer', 'beginning to smile except for her eyes' – all manage to convey the disgust and subterfuge of the scene. Tim's response is to ask for clarification, but the question is different from the one he wants to ask (what that might be is left unclear). Playing a joke, something practised by children in the story, is offered as the reason for the mother's actions, suggesting the degree to which the moral authority of the adult world has been compromised. Tim, though, remains unaware of the full implications of what he has witnessed: his nonchalant shrug and exit, believing that he has won a minor victory over his parent ('he'd caught her'), are indicative of the story's general desire to signify the children's cloudy knowledge of racial politics.

While David Seed, for one, regards this reticence as a flaw in the text ('The problem here is that Pynchon devotes so much attention to the boys' games ... that the racial theme is virtually smothered'[24]), it seems more useful to suggest that 'The Secret Integration' choreographs strategies by which an awareness of race can be articulated not through explicit commentary but instead via imaginative appropriation, what William Solomon has characterised as the story's exploration of 'the persistent structure of feeling that drives the subject's movements toward and away from its Other'.[25] Adult racism is clearly depicted, however, and one scene in particular acts as a catalyst for the story's crucial revelation, a narrative pivot that, as we will show, allows the reader to reflect on the place of blackness within the white imaginary. As the gang approaches Carl's house they see that rubbish has been dumped on the front lawn. Looking through it they realise that it is refuse from their own homes, their own parents having participated in this symbolic act of white protest.

The children attempt to offer support to the victimised Barrington family but are asked to leave by Carl's mother. It is at this late point in the story that it becomes clear that Carl is in fact a figment of the boys' collective imagination, a member of the gang who is conjured up by them as an act of resistance to the racism of which the act of dumping rubbish is the story's most tangible instance. The narrative voice is responsible for alerting the reader to this structural shift in the story, and it comes as something of a surprise when we encounter the revelation:

> He [Carl] was what grown-ups, if *they'd* known, would have called an 'imaginary playmate.' His words were the kids' own words; his gestures too, the faces he made, the times he had to cry, the way he shot baskets; all given by them an amplification or grace they expected to grow into presently. Carl had been put together out of phrases, images, possibilities that grownups had somehow turned away from, repudiated, left out at the edges of towns, as if they were auto parts in Étienne's father's junkyard – things they could or did not want to live with but which the kids, on the other hand, could spend endless hours with, piecing together, rearranging, feeding, programming, refining. (*SL* 192)

Carl is imaginary and material, a mental fabrication and a robotic construction. This recalls the warning that Étienne's father gives, one which prevents him from participating in the racist behaviour the other white parents exhibit: 'why don't people stop worrying about Negroes and start worrying about automation' (*SL* 188). Carl is composed as a figure of preterition, which, as we have already noted, will become a characteristic designation in Pynchon's writing. Assembled from the marginalia of the adult world, he is another instance of the author's appropriation of waste to help elaborate a counter-narrative to the normative culture of white America. Moreover, Carl is doubly dangerous, being both black and mechanical. As Maureen Curtin has argued, 'Negroes and automatons exist on a continuum; that is, they are different in degree, not in kind, for Negroes, like automatons, of course, have been thought to usurp jobs and the threaten the economic livelihood of whites'.[26]

While the revelation of Carl's status is a tricksy effect in the narrative, it nevertheless allows the reader to consider how and why the white children choose to embody a figure that their parents have rejected. Solomon suggests that Pynchon's story plays out white fantasies of blackness that are consistent with the tradition of blackface minstrelsy, one of the key aspects of such a 'transgressive form of popular entertainment being that it unselfconsciously sensed and organized white tendencies to impersonate African Americans'.[27] He cites Eric Lott's influential contention that the imaginative inhabiting of African-America identity that the blackface tradition enacts has 'no coincidental relationship to the racial politics of culture in which it is embedded'. The assumption by white men of a black self, Lott argues, 'continues to occur when the lines of "race" appear both intractable and obstructive, when there emerges a collective desire (conscious or not) to bridge a gulf that is, however, perceived to separate the races absolutely'.[28] Refracted through the prism of children's consciousness of race, 'The Secret Integration' enacts such a version of blackface, for the collective construction and inhabitation of Carl becomes the story's most potent signifier of a desire to confront the segregationist prejudices of the adult world. Yet the story makes clear that the possibilities of interracial harmony may remain elusive, for parental power is always ready to reassert itself. The children begin to realise that their plotting and subversion will not succeed, for the energy required to maintain such acts of dissent will run down and dissipate as imaginative intent is obstructed by entropic reality (of which more in the next section of this chapter), 'something they could not be cruel to or betray ... would always be between them and any clear or irreversible step' (*SL* 188). While the children are unwilling to label this obstructive force parental 'love', it is clear that their acknowledgement that all of their adult targets also happen to be 'somebody's mother or father' is a recognition of the conformist pull that the family bond exerts. The 'reflex' of response that the children give to parental care takes over 'and made worthwhile anger with them impossible' (*SL* 189). The final paragraph of the story repeats this sober note, with Carl going into voluntary exile with the 'other attenuated ghosts' in King Yrjö's house, the only space that can contain him. The rest of the gang return to their homes and to the routines inculcated there, although the encounter with the ugliness of racial politics has left its mark: 'each finally to his own house, hot shower, dry towel, before-bed television, good night kiss, and dreams that could never again be entirely safe' (*SL* 193).

The single and unavoidable conclusion: 'Entropy'

'Entropy' is Thomas Pynchon's most anthologised work and has
come to be regarded as an early incarnation of many of the thematics that would go on to characterise his writing as a whole. In his
'Introduction' to *Slow Learner*, he is characteristically dismissive
of the story, pointing out what he regards as its central flaw – its
explicit theoretical premise. 'It is simply wrong to begin with a
theme, symbol or other abstract unifying agent,' he writes, 'and
then try to force characters and events to conform to it' (*SL* 12). As
this section of this chapter will argue, Pynchon's reader needs to
be always alert to those moments, of which there are many in the
'Introduction', when authorial judgement is apparently offered as
the last word in interpretative possibility. As we discuss shortly,
Pynchon's most explicit estimations of his work can also be read as
performances, participating in the construction of a character called
'Thomas Pynchon' who may be as fictitious as any of the author's
other creations. Yet while one might want to contest Pynchon's poor
opinion of the genesis and execution of the story,[29] his comments do
acknowledge the centrality of 'entropy' as a scientific and metaphorical phenomenon; the desire to construct a narrative around such
an organising trope lends it a formal tightness that complements
the story's exploration of the interplay between pattern and chaos,
plotting and randomness.

To begin with some definitions: the *Merriam-Webster Dictionary*
describes 'entropy' as

> a measure of the unavailable energy in a closed thermodynamic
> system that is also usually considered to be a measure of the system's
> disorder ... the degradation of the matter and energy in the universe
> to an ultimate state of inert uniformity ... a process of degradation or
> running down or a trend to disorder.

Derived from the second law of thermodynamics (that eventually all
natural processes result in decay), entropy refers to the increasing
dissipation of energy moving within a closed system, finally arriving
at total inertia. As Tony Tanner points out, it is centrally 'concerned
with the fate of energy – the individual's, society's, the world's – and
as such is well calculated to interest the novelist trying to discern
what patterns the released powers and vitalities of his age and
society are establishing'.[30] Pynchon acknowledges the importance

of two writers, Norbert Wiener (1894–1964) and Henry Adams (1838–1918), in his thinking on the topic, and it is worth outlining their ideas before exploring how 'Entropy' itself engages with them. Wiener's book *The Human Use of Human Beings* (first published in 1950, then revised in 1954) offers an important gloss on the possibilities that entropy offered to Pynchon. Wiener was a pioneer in cybernetics, and a strong advocate of the benefits that could be derived from increased automation in society. His book describes the surpassing of a Newtonian vision of physics (that is to say, the observation of smoothly running laws and scientific certainties from which might be extrapolated an analogous system for the universe) to acknowledge instead the presence of chance and contingency. Entropy figures for Wiener as the manifestation of contingency, the failure of systems to function coherently and productively. With the onset of entropy, he writes,

> the universe, and all closed systems in the universe, tend naturally to deteriorate and lose their distinctiveness, to move from the least to the most probable state, from a state of organization and differentiation in which distinctions and forms exist, to a state of chaos and sameness ... But while the universe as a whole, if indeed there is a whole universe, tends to run down, there are local enclaves whose direction seems opposed to that of the universe at large and in which there is a limited and temporary tendency for organization to increase. Life finds its home in some of these enclaves.[31]

It is in this advancing state of decline, as social order fractures and laws unravel, that Wiener suggests we become most conscious of our existence in a closed system. Once cracks appear in the structure of that existence, we begin to see the possibilities of alternative realities. As we have already noticed in 'Low-lands', and as 'Entropy' also explores, Pynchon describes possibilities of utopian spatiality unfettered by insistent entropic systems, but his narratives refrain from endorsing wholeheartedly the viability of these locations. Pynchon's 'enclaves' are precarious and often fantastical, and the reader is fully aware of their provisional and imagined status.

Wiener is explicit about the implications of entropy for writing itself, imagining a system of language that, through entropic decline, is less and less able to effect coherent communication. If 'messages are themselves a form of pattern and organization', then 'it is possible to treat sets of messages as having an entropy like sets of states of the external world'. For Wiener, the 'more probable' a message becomes, 'the less information it gives. Clichés, for example, are less illuminating than great poems'.[32] Message systems, then, also run down, exhibiting, as Stephen Schuber helpfully characterises it, 'decreasing differentiation and greater predictability' that mark the onset of entropy.[33] The importance of this for Pynchon will become clear as our readings of his work develop, but for now it is worth noting information decline as a possible result of our mass-media culture, a system of communication in which significant articulation becomes increasingly difficult in the face of linguistic vacuity. In novels such as *The Crying of Lot 49* and *Vineland* Pynchon is acutely aware of the political repressions that language systems are able to enforce, and both novels explore possible counter-reactions to such repression. An entropic language system, then, is one in which communication has become predictable and oppressive. Pynchon's preoccupation with espionage, with alternative plottings and imaginary possibilities, is indicative of the concern his narratives have with contesting entropy's disintegrative narrative, the sense of a culture's 'growing disarray', in Tanner's words.[34]

The other figure whose significance requires noting is the American historian Henry Adams, whose complex intellectual autobiography, *The Education of Henry Adams* (1907), describes the disruptive forces of contingency as they strike its author's well-ordered nineteenth-century mind. Prior to this revelation, Adams writes, 'man's mind had behaved like a young pearl oyster, secreting its universe to suit its conditions until it had built up a shell of *nacre* that embodied all its notions of the perfect. Man knew it was perfect because he made it, and loved it for the same reason'.[35] Such complacency is utterly destroyed in the face of the apparent randomness of science. 'For the first time', Adams opines, 'the stage-scenery of the senses collapsed; the human mind felt itself stripped naked, vibrating in a void of shapeless energies, with resistless mass, colliding, crushing, wasting and destroying what these same energies had created and labored from eternity to perfect'.[36] At the turn of the century, Adams struggles to make sense of newly observable forces of energy that, he laments, have fractured the secure narratives of eighteenth- and nineteenth-century America – 'in 1900, the continuity snapped'.[37] In a later text, 'Letter to American Teachers of History' (1909), he was even more explicit about the widespread impact of entropic forces of decline. Dissenting from a scientific exceptionalism popular in the United States at the time that held the view that

'Evolution must be upward', Adams instead applied the second law of thermodynamics to all processes and systems: 'the law of Entropy imposes a servitude on all energies, including the mental. The degree of freedom steadily and rapidly diminishes'.[38] As Matthew Taylor has recently noted, Adams rejected a belief 'in a telic progression of history – whether biologically or socially engineered', offering in its place 'an alternative, pessimistic account of humanity's past, present, and future' that exposes 'history's harmonious forward march as fantasy'.[39]

Adams's outlook is thoroughly pessimistic. Not for him the enclaves of resistance, those 'islands of locally decreasing entropy' that might, temporarily, offer refuge from the inevitable heat death of the universe.[40] Pynchon's story mediates between these two positions, between what one might call a pragmatic response to environments of dissipation and a defeatist one. 'Entropy' takes place in an apartment building in Washington DC and is split between two locations. In the lower one, Meatball Mulligan is hosting a party that, 'moving into its 40th hour' (*SL* 81), is becomingly increasingly chaotic and incoherent, exhibiting its own form of entropic decline. Upstairs Callisto and his girlfriend Aubade occupy a sealed room, protected from the contagions of the outside world. Callisto has created a space that, as Wiener posits, might offer some kind of resistance to the onset of heat death. 'It was a tiny enclave of regularity in the city's chaos,' Pynchon's narrator tells us, 'alien to the vagaries of the weather, of national politics, of civil disorder' (*SL* 83–4). Callisto's room, like Flange's underground world in 'Lowlands', represents a fantasy realm. Where Dennis's subterranean adventure may be a hallucinatory projection, Callisto's hothouse is a carefully constructed utopian space that Tanner sees as 'a dream of order' in the face of perceived external threats.[41] One of which, of course, is 'the hints of anarchy' (*SL* 88) embodied in the intrusive noise emanating from Mulligan's party.

While Callisto claims to understand the scientific definition of entropy ('which states that the entropy of an isolated system always continually increases' [*SL* 87]), his deployment of it as a trope in the story extends in more metaphorical directions. He finds the culture of the Eisenhower years – the story is precisely dated as February 1957 – one of increasing homogeneity, and, referring to himself in the third person (as does Henry Adams throughout *The Education*) he writes of how 'in American "consumerism"' he 'discovered a

similar tendency from the least to the most probable, from differentiation to sameness, from ordered individuality to a kind of
chaos' (*SL* 88). For Callisto, the effects of entropy are to be felt everywhere and at all levels: 'the isolated system – galaxy, engine, human
being, culture, whatever – must evolve spontaneously toward the
Condition of the More Probable' (*SL* 87). This final phrase resonates
in Pynchon's work more generally and encapsulates his interest in
the forms by which societies and cultures manufacture and police
visible structures of behaviour. With this in mind, setting the story in
the nation's capital is significant, for we are told that the Mulligan's
party is populated by American expatriates who work for a variety
of national bureaucracies – organisation men and women at the
heart of the government machine who might be thought to embody
the triumph of corporate America so lamented by William Whyte
in his book of 1956.[42] 'Entropy' posits possible locations of resistance (not just Callisto's room), and in a complex passage describing a Washington spring, Pynchon deploys musical terminology to
imagine such precarious spaces. Rapidly linking observations about
the weather, the movement of wind, and the notion that 'the soul ...
is nothing, substantially, but air', Pynchon writes:

> [I]t is only natural that warpings in the atmosphere should be reca-
> pitulated in those who breathe it. So that over and above the public
> components – holidays, tourist attractions – there are private mean-
> derings, linked to the climate as if this spell were a *stretto* passage
> in the year's fugue: haphazard weather, aimless loves, unpredicted
> commitments: months one can easily spend *in* fugue, because oddly
> enough, later on, winds, rains, passions of February and March are
> never remembered in that city, it is as if they had never been. (*SL* 83)

A 'stretto' is part of a fugue that tightens the musical theme, bringing together its component (and often counter-pointed) elements
to generate potentially new forms of experience. Here the '*stretto*
passage' forces consideration of invisible or unrecognised modes,
the contingencies of private experience that sit alongside more
authorised expressions. The regularity of public life, like the homogeneity of entropic decline, and indeed like the paranoid maintenance
of control in Callisto's room, is here countered by more unpredictable, contingent occurrences. Yet these possibilities, and the kind of
music they produce, are inaudible in Washington – or rather 'they
are never remembered'. Instead a different kind of fugue is endured,
one that is defined by the *Oxford English Dictionary* as 'a dissociative

reaction to shock or emotional stress in a neurotic, during which all awareness of personal identity is lost though the person's outward behaviour may appear rational'. Such a notion of fugue in this secondary sense, as a deadening neurosis that negates variety, sets the social and political standard in the nation's capital. Pynchon's story, then, sets in play a contrapuntal alternation between a view of the world as rational and contained (those 'arabesques of order' enjoyed by Callisto) and one that contains the possibilities of disruption and chance (the 'improvised discords' [*SL* 92] of Mulligan's party). The alternation might also be defined as one that mediates between an exceptionalist idea of the United States as isolated and an understanding of it as porous and pragmatically adaptable. As with the two-levelled house in 'Low-lands', in this story Pynchon is similarly interested in the distinctions – spatial and epistemological – that can be discerned between different visions of reality.[43]

Callisto's is a contrived and artificially sustained world, constituted as a response to the threat he sees posed by an outside environment where, 'despite the changeful weather, the mercury had stayed at 37 degrees Fahrenheit' (*SL* 85). This piece of information is crucial to his actions in the story but represents the culmination of a plan to create an environmental enclave that has taken him, we learn, 'seven years to weave together' (*SL* 83). His refuge is the ultimate closed circuit, but one which, in its enforced homogeneity, paradoxically works to repeat the entropic dynamic that it had set out to resist. Mulligan's party functions as a contrapuntal alternative to this fate. Significantly its members arrive and depart through open doors and windows, apertures which admit contact with a space beyond the walls of the building. But this half of Pynchon's story also explores an aspect of entropy that we have already mentioned, namely its adaptation within communication theory. Norbert Wiener's sense that informational entropy results in the failure of language to communicate effectively, and that linguistic precision gives way to static and cliché, is played out in some key exchanges in 'Entropy'. In one of these, we are introduced to Saul, a computer engineer whose marriage has recently ended due to what he calls 'a kind of leakage' in the system of communication established between him and his wife, Miriam. The disruptive word is crucial:

> Tell a girl: 'I love you'. No trouble with two-thirds of that, it's a closed circuit. Just you and she. But that nasty four-letter word in the middle,

that's the one you have to look out for. Ambiguity. Redundance. Irrelevance, even. Leakage. All this is noise. Noise screws up your signal, makes for disorganization in the circuit. (*SL* 90–1)

The presence of the signifier 'love' – that 'four-letter word' – introduces a note of incoherence into Saul's carefully ordered linguistic system. His dismissive aligning of love with 'redundance' and 'irrelevance' reminds us of Pynchon's continuing interest in the valuation we attach to waste and its synonyms. Here Saul dismisses the complexities of the word, concerned, like Callisto, to maintain a constant environment in which he can function. And, as with Callisto, the irony of Saul's desire to resist information entropy lies in the reader's growing awareness of his own entropic state – in this case, his failure as a communicator. His conversational tactics quickly descend into cliché ('It's a bitch, ain't it', 'The hell with it' [*SL* 91]), and their exchange breaks down in mutual incomprehension.

What options might be available then to counter the onset of entropic decline? Mulligan finds himself faced with two ethical possibilities as his party begins to spiral out of control and coherence: 'The way he figured, there were only about two ways he could cope: (a) lock himself in the closet and maybe eventually they would all go away, or (b) try to calm everybody down, one by one' (*SL* 96). While option (a) seems more appealing to him, Meatball decides to prevent his party 'from deteriorating into total chaos' by focusing on plan (b) – it 'was more a pain in the neck, but probably better in the long run'. Such a response is undoubtedly unheroic, with none of the romantic glamour associated with a defiant withdrawal into a self-constructed space. Yet in its piecemeal, pragmatic way, it might offer a genuinely resistant enclave (however fragile) against the larger, impersonal narrative of ever-increasing chaos. Yet Pynchon's narrative, typically, does not allow us to rest reassured in such a view, as 'Entropy' closes with a return to the upstairs apartment. Callisto has been trying to keep a sick bird alive by holding it against the warmth of his body, thereby offering evidence of his opposition to the gradual winding-down of the universe. However, in the entropic environment that Callisto has managed to construct, inevitably, the bird dies, Callisto's sense that he was 'communicating life to him' (*SL* 97) undone by the stasis and inertia of the space they inhabit. The final paragraph follows, as Aubade says 'I was just at the window':

He sank back, terrified. She stood a moment more, irresolute; she had sensed his obsession long ago, realized somehow that that constant 37 was now decisive. Suddenly then, as if seeing the single and unavoidable conclusion to all this she moved swiftly to the window before Callisto could speak; tore away the drapes and smashed out the glass with two exquisite hands which came away bleeding and glistening with splinters; and turned to face the man on the bed and wait with him until the moment of equilibrium was reached, when 37 degrees Fahrenheit should prevail both outside and inside, and forever, and the hovering, curious dominant of their separate lives should resolve into a tonic of darkness and the final absence of all motion. (*SL* 98)

On the surface of things, this passage seems to authorise Callisto's final acceptance of the inevitability of heat death. It reads Aubade's breaking of the window as an equalising act, one that acknowledges the futility of the enclave and, of course, of Mulligan's more modest gestures. The story ends by predicting entropic decay (with 'resolve' nicely punning between scientific and narrative conclusions). Yet the reader might wish to complicate such an interpretation by considering the possibility that the narrative at this point becomes a projection of Callisto's delusional consciousness. The 'single and unavoidable conclusion' is his own, imputed to Aubade; the phrase her 'exquisite hands' might also be said to ventriloquise Callisto's view; and the final melding of inside and outside in an anticipated vision of apocalypse so fully endorses Callisto's understanding of the entropic process that it is as if the narrative allows itself to become seduced by his vision. If Aubade's opening of the window is read as an act designed to negate entropy, as the introduction of outside influences into the sterility of Callisto's room, then these closing images of dissolution are misleading, playful poses on the part of the author who wishes to imitate the sanctity of a conclusion while still retaining the possibility that its certainties are fraudulent.

Everybody knows this: *Slow Learner*'s 'Introduction'

The issue of fraudulent authority extends to the 'Introduction' to *Slow Learner* that Pynchon added to the volume of his stories. It is a seemingly confessional text which offers itself as an honest, and frequently disparaging, reading by the older, celebrated Pynchon of his early authorial self. For a writer so careful to avoid the seductions of publicity, such an autobiographical statement at the outset of the volume is striking and unexpected, and for some critics these pages have been read as unmediated analysis: here at last is Pynchon revealing the secrets of his composition process and, furthermore, evaluating his first pieces of published writing from a position of retrospective achievement that sees them as inadequate and naïve. In a review of *Slow Learner* in the *Sunday Times*, Jonathan Raban eulogised the apparent honesty of Pynchon's voice: '[Pynchon] breaks cover for the first time with a remarkably openhanded portrait of the writer as a young man. Here is the sustained pleasure of watching a clever and talented young man struggling to find a style of his own. From such a reticent man it is a weirdly generous book.'[44] More recently, Avital Ronell has written that Pynchon, in the 'Introduction', 'relentlessly reviews the stupidity of the writer he was': 'As he reviews his writing, Pynchon admits to a puerility of attitude, his capacity for idiocy, and the problem of "adolescent values".'[45] This 'agony of avowal', Ronell argues, structures an autobiographical document that 'continues to haunt and heckle'.[46] While it may be interesting to examine Pynchon's 'Introduction' in the light of theoretical and philosophical considerations of 'stupidity' (i.e. how does one come to terms with one's own instances of imaginative or conceptual failure?), it is worth pausing to consider that in these opening pages Pynchon is fully aware of the kinds of expectations and exertions that authorial judgements have on readers, and that what he constructs here instead is a playful, tonally exaggerated persona whose estimations of his work, while occasionally insightful or provocative, are not intended to signify the last word in critical possibilities. Richard Poirier, in the *London Review of Books*, was tempted to admit the possibility that Pynchon was playing an elaborate game with the reader, but fell back on a reading of authorial intellectual exhaustion: Pynchon's 'jaunty complaints in the Introduction that the stories in *Slow Learner* fail to provide full, lifelike characters are ... so curious and irrelevant as to suggest either that he is kidding – and I'm afraid he isn't – or that he is tired'. Of course Pynchon's 'Introduction' establishes a temporal significance to the book's title: Pynchon is the 'Slow Learner', only now able to look back on his younger, apprentice self from a vantage point of canonical respectability and to see the foolishness of much of his early writing career.

If Pynchon is not 'kidding', then for Poirier the implications are more serious, for 'Pynchon does not want anyone to think that this volume in any way sufficiently represents him. Instead he suggests again and again, even by means of the title, that he has since learned to do things in an importantly different way'.[47] But what if we entertain the idea that Pynchon is indeed intent on 'kidding' the reader in his 'Introduction', so that its status as text is more uncertain than the reassurances of authorial design would suggest? Who is the author here, and what exactly is being written? In an occasionally theoretically opaque but nevertheless powerful reading of the 'Introduction', Alec McHoul and David Wills have countered the kinds of critical assurances that readers like Jonathan Raban assume by suggesting that uncertainties surround the status of Pynchon's first-person pronoun. 'We do not know', they write, 'whether to read this as genuine biography (where "I" slides easily from past to present verbs) or as fictional prose (where the "I" is much more problematic).'[48] Rather than granting the 'Introduction' a form of 'privileged insight', McHoul and Wills propose instead that it be read as 'no different from any other textual event or occasion'.[49]

Pynchon's opening paragraph establishes a tone of breezy informality, in which the reader is assumed to understand the author's dismay at looking over old work. Appealing to a shared sympathy, he claims that 'You may already know what a blow to the ego it can be to have to read over anything you wrote 20 years ago, even cancelled checks', where the bathos of the example works to unsettle the shattering seriousness of the affect. He tells us that he suffers 'physical symptoms' that 'we shouldn't dwell upon' as a result of reading his apprentice work, and that he is tempted to embark upon a Henry James-style rewrite to bring early Pynchon into happy consistency with his current sense of literary value. Instead such impulses 'have given way to one of those episodes of middle-aged tranquillity, in which *I now pretend* to have reached a level of clarity about the young writer I was back then' (my emphasis). Critical assertions are thus couched in the language of fiction, *as* fiction, and the dilemma in which Pynchon finds himself is exaggerated for comic effect as he wonders: 'how comfortable would I feel about lending him [his earlier self] money, or for that matter even stepping down the street to have a beer and talk over old times?' (*SL* 3).

The purpose of publishing this early material, Pynchon claims, is for it to serve as a warning to writers about the mistakes of tone and voice that they would do well to avoid. His stories exhibit 'typical problems in entry-level fiction' (*SL* 4) that, once revealed, can be

instructive to other young authors. The 'Introduction', then, plays
the bizarre role of rejecting in advance the five stories that are to
follow. It serves as a negative endorsement of Pynchon's status (he
is explicit about his failings), and, as such, is a playful variation on
the convention in eighteenth-century novels in which fictional cer-
tificates of authenticity are marshalled to support the verisimilitude
of the texts they introduce (e.g. Daniel Defoe's *Gulliver's Travels*
[1726] and *A Journal of the Plague Year* [1722]). In *Slow Learner*, the
prefatory material asserts an authorial figure whose often startling
comments on his work generate an inauthentic authenticity and
a confessional mode that obscures more than it reveals. Pynchon
makes some peculiar claims about his writing which start to unravel
once pressure is put upon them. Of 'Entropy' he writes, 'Because
the story has been anthologized a couple-three times, people think
I know more about the subject of entropy than I really do' (*SL* 12).
There is a strange logic at work here that equates the popularity
of this piece (its now canonical status within the tradition of the
American short story) with an increased danger that readers will
fail to discern Pynchon's apparent lack of scientific knowledge.
Would a less frequently anthologised 'Entropy' reduce that risk?
As Terry Reilly points out, Pynchon's self-evaluation here 'becomes
itself an entropic formula reconfigured ... as proportional relations concerned with anthologization, population, information and
knowledge'.[50]

Pynchon's account of the writing of 'Entropy' acknowledges the
importance of Henry Adams and Norbert Wiener to the intellectual
framing of the story, but is quick to judge his own deployment of
their ideas as 'mostly derivative', providing a 'distance and grandios-
ity' that 'led me to short-change the humans in the story' (*SL* 13), as
if Pynchon's now mature aesthetic chooses to privilege a model of
Jamesian interiority far removed from the apparently reductive simplicity of 'Entropy''s surfaces. In this he anticipates, through ironic
performance, the kind of critique that James Wood, in a reading
of Pynchon's recent work, levels at him. Wood coins the category
'hysterical realist' to describe a mode of postmodernist writing that,
in its exuberant expansiveness, ignores an idea of character as finely
wrought consciousness in favour of character as the ventriloquising
of a set of ideological positions. This kind of puppetry in the service
of an idea, Wood suggests, stems from a failure of empathy whereby
quirkiness is substituted for affect, and autonomy is replaced by

instrumentality. Wood's essay on Pynchon was collected in a book titled *The Irresponsible Self*, and it is the attainment of irresponsibility that best signals for Wood the success of a fictional character: one who exists for his or her own sake, not as vehicle for a set of discursive stances that the author may wish to delineate. Wood finds the most powerful examples of this kind of unfettered self in Shakespeare, whose characters 'feel real to us in part because they feel real to themselves, take their own private universes for granted, and in particular their memories and pasts'.[51] His target is the large, unruly novels of contemporary fiction (including Pynchon's *Mason & Dixon*), and his reading of them is a powerful instantiation of a strand of criticism that is sceptical of postmodernism's own scepticism of the structures of plot and character that preoccupy realist and modernist texts. One of the challenges (or 'awkwardnesses', as Wood terms it) of writing that is evaded in the narratives he discusses is 'an awkwardness about character and the representation of character in fiction, since human beings generate stories'.[52] He judges Pynchon (and Salman Rushdie, Don DeLillo, David Foster Wallace and Zadie Smith) as a writer of narrative that 'feels more like a fable than an exercise in verisimilitude'.[53] Certainly Pynchon is acutely aware of the artificiality of his fictional world. This is hinted at in his mock regret that 'Entropy' fails to render fully the human, or elsewhere in the 'Introduction' in his deceptively straightforward assertion that 'Today we expect a complexity of plot and depth of character which are missing' from 'Under the Rose' (*SL* 19). But the astute reader of Pynchon is aware that these are expectations that are continually contested or redefined across his writing career; they are not settled categories of literary value. Pynchon's revelling in artifice through self-conscious stylisation creates an exaggerated aesthetic, an artistic strangeness through which questions of, in the case of 'Entropy', containment and heterogeneity can be explored. But these explorations are undertaken within a fiction that challenges the assumptions of cognition, a fiction in which the delineation of a material world does not provide the substantial stability of realism and in which the representation of selfhood does not elicit the comforting psychological richness of a modernist aesthetic.[54]

Further instances of the playfulness of *Slow Learner*'s 'Introduction' abound. Writing of 'Low-lands', Pynchon assumes that 'Modern readers will be, at least, put off by an unacceptable level of racist, sexist and proto-Fascist talk throughout this story' (*SL* 11). Such a strong reading once more appears to narrow the room for readerly manoeuvre; it assumes that the story's unreconstructed politics damage our literary enjoyment of the story. But the playfulness here is noticeable in its implicit presumption that *acceptable* levels of such talk exist, raising the question of what such a level could possibly be, how it might be measured. This is not to say that the narrative Pynchon tells about himself in these pages is without value: his establishment of the political backdrop of the Cold War (*SL* 18–19) and the literary context of the Beat generation (*SL* 7–9) remains helpful in placing Pynchon's writing at this time. But this material helps to foster a deceptiveness that persuades the reader into believing that the 'Introduction' represents an authentic moment of autobiographical introspection. Instead, Pynchon presents us with a simulated author figure, one who articulates a series of opinions and offers snippets of biographical material in a complex amalgam of the historically plausible and critically perverse. At one point in his self-critique of one of the stories not discussed in this chapter, 'The Small Rain', Pynchon observes what he regards as an axiomatic rule for fiction: 'When we speak of "seriousness" in fiction ultimately we are talking about an attitude toward death – how characters may act in its presence, for example, or how they handle it when it isn't so immediate. Everybody knows this' (*SL* 5). While one might want to contest the premise upon which this evaluation of fiction is based (is literary 'seriousness' – and Pynchon's sceptical scare quotes should give us pause of thought – really only determined by how death is treated?), it is the throw-away expression 'Everybody knows this' that resonates. In its easy assertiveness it encapsulates the dominant tone of the 'Introduction', one that encourages us to succumb to passive reading. If the 'Introduction' is regarded as a refuge from the hard work of critical analysis, the reader has fallen into the trap its author has set.

Notes

1 David Riesman, *The Lonely Crowd: A Study of the Changing American Character* (1950), New Haven: Yale University Press, 1960, 22. For an excellent analysis of the class dynamics at work within the culture of conformity Riesman describes, see Andrew Hoborek, *The Twilight of the Middle Class: Post-World War II American Fiction and White-Collar Work*, Princeton: Princeton University Press, 2005. Joel Foreman's edited

volume *The Other Fifties: Interrogating Midcentury American Icons*, Champaign: University of Illinois Press, 1997 explores the transgressive racial, sexual and political undercurrents of the decade.

2 Riesman, *The Lonely Crowd*, 20.

3 C. Wright Mills, *White Collar: The American Middle Classes* (1951), New York: Oxford University Press, 2002, xii.

4 Timothy Melley, *Empire of Conspiracy: The Culture of Paranoia in Postwar America*, Ithaca: Cornell University Press, 2000, 53.

5 Bodine also makes an appearance in *Gravity's Rainbow* as a 'semi-AWOL' sailor from the 'U.S. destroyer *John E. Badass*' who persuades Tyrone Slothrop to break into the high-level peace conference at Potsdam dressed as 'Rocketman' to recover six kilos of 'top-grade Nepalese hashish' that has been buried there (*GR* 370).

6 Fiedler writes of 'the regressiveness, in a technical sense, of American life, its implacable nostalgia for the infantile, at once wrong-headed and somehow admirable. The mythic America is boyhood' ('Come Back to the Raft Ag'in, Huck Honey' (1948), in Steven G. Kellman and Irving Malin, eds, *Leslie Fiedler and American Culture*, Newark: University of Delaware Press, 1999, 26–34 [27]).

7 David Seed, *The Fictional Labyrinths of Thomas Pynchon*, Basingstoke: Macmillan, 1988, 26–7.

8 Seed, *Fictional Labyrinths*, 28.

9 John Dugdale, *Thomas Pynchon: Allusive Parables of Power*, London: Macmillan, 1990, 48.

10 Tony Tanner, *The American Mystery: American Literature from Emerson to DeLillo*, Cambridge: Cambridge University Press, 2000, 214.

11 David H. Evans, 'Taking Out the Trash: Don DeLillo's *Underworld*, Liquid Modernity, and the End of Garbage', *Cambridge Quarterly* 35.2 (2006): 103–32 (116).

12 Richard Patteson, 'Architecture and Junk in Pynchon's Short Fiction', *Illinois Quarterly* 42.2 (1979): 38–47 (39).

13 As Dugdale notes, there seems to be a conscious echoing and revision here of Lewis Carroll's *Alice's Adventures in Wonderland* (1865) as well as Washington Irving's fantastic tale of reinvention 'Rip Van Winkle' (1819) (*Thomas Pynchon*, 45); Seed prefers to consider Nerissa as a reworking of Miranda's effect on Ferdinand in Shakespeare's *The Tempest* (*Fictional Labyrinths*, 32–3).

14 Mark D. Hawthorne, 'Homoerotic Bonding as Escape from Heterosexual Responsibility in Pynchon's *Slow Learner*', *Style* 344.3 (2000): 512–29 (520).

15 See Seed, *Fictional Labyrinths*, 151–5. Less substantial accounts can also be found in Joseph Slade's *Thomas Pynchon*, New York: Warner Paperback Library, 1974 and William Plater's *The Grim Phoenix:*

Reconstructing Thomas Pynchon, Bloomington: Indiana University Press, 1978.

16 Thomas Pynchon, 'A Journey Into the Mind of Watts', *New York Times Magazine*, 12 June 1966: 34–5, 78, 80–2, 84 (82).

17 Pynchon, 'Journey Into the Mind of Watts', 78.

18 Seed, *Fictional Labyrinths*, 155.

19 Pynchon, 'Journey Into the Mind of Watts', 81.

20 Pynchon, 'Journey Into the Mind of Watts', 84.

21 Pynchon, 'Journey Into the Mind of Watts', 84.

22 Henry James, *The American Scene*, New York: Penguin Books, 1994, 126.

23 See Seed, *Fictional Labyrinths*, 63–6.

24 Seed, *Fictional Labyrinths*, 68.

25 William Solomon, 'Secret Integrations: Black Humor and the Critique of Whiteness', *MFS Modern Fiction Studies* 49.3 (2003): 469–95 (482).

26 Maureen F. Curtin, *Out of Touch: Skin Tropes and Identities in Woolf, Ellison, Pynchon and Acker*, New York: Routledge, 2003, 70. Curtin persuasively argues that Pynchon's story represents a response to the question of black invisibility posed in Ralph Ellison's novel *Invisible Man*. Stuart Barnett connects Carl as a preterite with other examples in Pynchon's work. See 'Refused Readings: Narrative and History in "The Secret Integration"', *Pynchon Notes* 22–3 (1988): 79–85.

27 Solomon, 'Secret Integrations', 482.

28 Eric Lott, 'White Like Me: Racial Cross-Dressing and the Construction of American Whiteness', in Amy Kaplan and Donald Pease, eds, *Cultures of United States Imperialism*, Durham: Duke University Press, 1993, 474–95 (475).

29 Gore Vidal (a generally unsympathetic reader of Pynchon), on the other hand, chose to concur with Pynchon's estimation, mocking a situation in which 'the imaginative writer can never be serious unless, like Mr. Thomas Pynchon, he makes it clear that he is writing about Entropy … and a number of other subjects that he picked up in his freshman year at Cornell' ('The Thinking Man's Novel', *New York Review of Books* 27.19 (4 December 1980): 10). See also Vidal's essay 'American Plastic: The Matter of Fiction', in *United States: Essays 1952–1992*, London: Abacus, 1997, 121–46.

30 Tony Tanner, *Cities of Words: American Fiction 1950–1970*, London: Jonathan Cape, 1971, 144.

31 Norbert Wiener, *The Human Use of Human Beings: Cybernetics and Society*, New York: Doubleday Anchor Books, 1954, 12.

32 Wiener, *The Human Use*, 21.

33 Stephen P. Schuber, 'Rereading Pynchon: Negative Entropy and "Entropy"', *Pynchon Notes* 13 (1983): 47–60 (49).

34 Tanner, *City of Words*, 180.

35 Henry Adams, *The Education of Henry Adams*, London: Penguin Books, 1995, 434.

36 Adams, *The Education of Henry Adams*, 276.

37 Adams, *The Education of Henry Adams*, 433.

38 Henry Adams, *The Degradation of the Democratic Dogma*, London: Macmillan, 1919, 251.

39 Matthew A. Taylor, 'The "Phantasmodesty" of Henry Adams', *Common Knowledge* 15.3 (2009): 373–94 (379, 380).

40 Wiener, *The Human Use*, 39.

41 Tanner, *Cities of Words*, 154.

42 See William H. Whyte, *The Organization Man* (1956), Philadelphia: University of Pennsylvania Press, 2002.

43 Dugdale explores the political resonances of this idea more thoroughly than most critics, drawing analogies between the entropic states conjured up in the tale and the global-political era of the Cold War: 'To read the text in this way is to take the disturbingly changeless temperature to be a "screen" figure for the atmosphere of the Cold War, itself a thermal or climactic metaphor, which has continued for the same seven years as Callisto's hothouse siege' (*Thomas Pynchon*, 65).

44 Jonathan Raban, 'Try, Try and Try Again', review of *Slow Learner*. *Sunday Times* (London), 20 January 1985: 44G.

45 Avital Ronell, *Stupidity*, Champaign: University of Illinois Press, 2002, 25, 26.

46 Ronell, *Stupidity*, 25, 28.

47 Richard Poirier, 'Humans', review of *Slow Learner*, *London Review of Books*, 24 January 1985: 18–20 (18).

48 Alec McHoul and David Wills, *Writing Pynchon: Strategies in Fictional Analysis*, Urbana and Chicago: University of Illinois Press, 1990, 141.

49 McHoul and Wills, *Writing Pynchon*, 144, 134.

50 Terry Reilly, 'A Couple-Three Bonzos: "Introduction", *Slow Learner* and *1984*', *Pynchon Notes* 44–5 (Spring–Fall, 1999): 5–13 (6).

51 James Wood, *The Irresponsible Self: On Laughter and the Novel*, London: Jonathan Cape, 2004, 21.

52 Wood, *The Irresponsible Self*, 169.

53 Wood, *The Irresponsible Self*, 170.

54 For an astute critique of Wood's reading of Pynchon, see Jeffrey Staiger, 'James Wood's Case Against "Hysterical Realism" and Thomas Pynchon', *Antioch Review* 66.4 (Fall, 2008): 634–54.

2

Convoluted reading: identity, interpretation and reference in *The Crying of Lot 49*

The Crying of Lot 49, Pynchon's second novel, was published in 1966. Although its initial critical reception was less universally positive than that which met the publication of his first novel, *V.*, it won the Richard and Hilda Rosenthal Foundation Award of the National Institute of Arts and Letters and quickly became one of his most popular and widely discussed works. As his shortest and (at least apparently) most accessible novel, it is also the one that tends most often to be held up by critics as representative of the difficulties of Pynchon's postmodern style. If *Gravity's Rainbow* has been read as Pynchon at his most challengingly postmodern, and the more than a thousand pages of *Against the Day* see him at his most encyclopaedic and widely ranging through space and time, *The Crying of Lot 49* presents through its tightly focused and concentrated narrative a no less complex and disturbing postmodern world, but does so in a considerably more intense and condensed manner than his longer works. Because of this, it frequently serves as emblematic of the complexities of Pynchon's prose, the key themes of his work, its contexts and main intertexts, and the problems of meaning and interpretation with which his writing confronts the reader. This makes good sense, and, despite the publishing chronology, it is the novel we have chosen to examine first as a vehicle to begin to explore these issues, and to set the scene for the analyses of the longer and more widely ranging novels that will follow in later chapters. Read alongside our previous chapter's discussion of the shorter fiction collected in *Slow Learner*, this chapter (as well as providing a detailed reading of the text) aims to set out the aesthetic and conceptual grammar with which Pynchon's works continue to play and to which our later chapters will often return.

A narrative in search of clues: reading *The Crying of Lot 49*

Despite its narratological, thematic and intertextual complexity, the impetus behind the plot of *The Crying of Lot 49* could hardly be more straightforward: the novel's protagonist, a housewife named Mrs Oedipa Maas, discovers that she has been made executor, or rather 'executrix', of the estate of an ex-lover, the 'California real estate mogul' Pierce Inverarity (*CL* 5). This unambiguous point of departure, however, soon gives rise to a quickly expanding fictional world of multiple plots, bizarre connections and increasing levels of complexity, confusion, self-doubt and paranoia on the part of both protagonist and reader. Travelling to the town of San Narciso, the centre of Inverarity's business interests, Oedipa encounters a range of intriguing characters, from the actor-lawyer Metzger who works as her co-executor and the sub-Beatles would-be rock band The Paranoids to the literary critic Emory Bortz and the philatelist Genghis Cohen, all of whom assist her in attempting to decipher and link together the many clues that her investigation of the estate throws up. This investigation continually generates series of strange signs, events and coincidences, including the sinisterly recurring image of a muted post-horn, the stories associated with a grisly collection of the skeletons of dead GIs that are used both for cigarette filters and as set dressing for scuba divers in Inverarity's Fangoso Lagoons development, an outrageously violent Jacobean play by Richard Wharfinger called *The Courier's Tragedy* that includes allusions to both the muted horn and dead soldiers in a lake, and the bizarre 'Nefastis Machine' that its inventor claims is capable of producing from nothing both energy and information and thus of violating the second law of thermodynamics. These encounters and events gradually lead Oedipa to the conviction that everything to do with the will, the people she has met, the town of San Narciso itself, the State of California, and even America as a whole, is in some way linked together: 'There was the true continuity, San Narciso had no boundaries. ... She has dedicated herself, weeks ago, to making sense of what Inverarity had left behind, never suspecting that the legacy was America' (*CL* 123). And at the heart of this America, as the novel's central enigmatic sign, lies a shady underground body that 'she was to label the Tristero System or often only the Tristero (as if it might be something's secret title)' (*CL* 29), the roots of which appear to trace back to sixteenth-century European conflicts about the delivery of mail, and which finds its most widespread modern instantiation in an alternative communication system used by those attempting to circumvent the US Postal Service.

As the novel progresses, clue builds upon clue, inference adds to inference, and apparent coincidence leads to echoing series of coincidences, to develop a complex and convoluted image of the nature of the Tristero as something between an anarchic alternative system of communication and a fully blown radical countercultural movement by which the otherwise dispossessed are able to exist within and resist the official order of the American state. But before the hints and clues Oedipa gathers can add up to any ultimate revelation or resolution, the novel ends: nothing finally is disclosed, there is no conclusive moment where the identity of the Tristero is revealed, and even Oedipa's despairing questions about whether everything she has encountered is no more than an elaborate hoax remain unanswered. The novel breaks off at the moment when Oedipa, attending an auction of Inverarity's possessions in the hope that a representative of the Tristero might come forward to bid for a collection of stamps that could just provide conclusive evidence for the existence of that organisation, 'settle[s] back, to await the crying of lot 49' (*CL* 127).

Summarised in this way, the plot of *The Crying of Lot 49* seems to follow closely the trajectory of a classic detective story: a mystery is presented to the protagonist, which it becomes their task to solve, and the narrative traces their adventures as they uncover and explore a range of clues, undergo a series of trials, see off threats from an enemy or enemies, and finally emerge triumphant as the 'answer' is revealed and the villains brought to justice.[1] For the reader, the narrative is frequently focalised from the point of view of the detective: the challenges faced by the protagonist are presented in a manner that allows readers to participate in their experiences of uncertainty, doubt, resolution and eventual triumph as the case is solved – especially if they manage to guess 'whodunit' before it is formally revealed. This is certainly true of the narrative structure of *The Crying of Lot 49*: Oedipa is the reader's point of access into the unfolding world of Inverarity's legacy, and the narrative encourages identification with her aspirations, suspicions, anxieties and frequent bafflement. And, as responses from reviewers and critics often demonstrate, it continually teases readers with suggestions, associations and half-clues that draw them into Oedipa's world of plots, conspiracies and paranoia. As many critics have noted, her name alludes to one of the very earliest detectives in world literature: Oedipus, the hero who found the solution to the riddle of the sphinx, became king of Thebes and was punished by the Gods when it became clear (on the basis of an investigation he himself insisted on launching) that he had married his mother and killed his father as foreseen by the Delphic Oracle. As Robert N. Watson indicates, the novel makes continual allusions to this story in its identifications of the protagonist:

> Perhaps Pierce Inverarity's mystery functions like the sphinx's and the oracle's, leaving Oedipa Maas (like Oedipus's mother) 'anxious that her revelation not … assume her to itself' [*CL* 115]. Oedipa guzzled 'bourbon until the sun went down and it was dark as it would ever get' and then 'drove on the freeway for a while with her lights out, to see what would happen.' The self-destructively extinguished headlights … allude to the guilt-racked Oedipus gouging out his eyes, an allusion reinforced two sentences later as she phones the Greek Way bar and her tears 'build up pressure around her eyes' [*CL* 122].[2]

Although, as the third section of this chapter will argue, it is somewhat too reductive of the novel's complex play of reference, allusion and intertexts to identify Oedipa straightforwardly and completely with Oedipus (or his mother), the introduction of this name for the protagonist and the many allusions that occur in the text hold out to the reader the suggestion of parallels between the novel and the classical Greek story about a detective-like search for answers. The parallels, and this is just one example of many, provide threads, trails of clues, for readers to follow as they progress through the novel's mysterious plot.

Midway through the novel, the text self-consciously refers to itself in terms drawn from the detective genre: 'Where was the Oedipa who'd driven so bravely up here from San Narciso? The optimistic baby had come on so like the private eye in any long-ago radio drama. … But the private eye sooner or later has to get beat up. This night's profusion of post horns, this malignant, deliberate replication, was their way of beating up' (*CL* 85). This self-reflective moment, the phrasing of which is directly interrogative of the reader, identifies the narrative generically (and yet also holds that genre at a distance: the 'long-ago' drama), indicates the point in the plot that has been reached, and holds out the expectation for those familiar with crime fiction of what sorts of events ought to follow. But if the

novel is identified generically as a detective story, it remains resolutely incomplete: Oedipa never fully recovers from this moment
of despair, the myriad clues fail to find resolution in an answer, and
in their frustration at the novel's lack of closure the reader has the
potential to feel as 'beaten up' as the protagonist.

An early and extremely influential discussion of the novel by
Edward Mendelson identifies 'mechanisms borrowed from the
detective story' being used to 'produce results precisely the opposite
of those in the model':

> Where the object of a detective story is to reduce a complex and
> disordered situation to simplicity and clarity ... *The Crying of Lot 49*
> starts with a relatively simple situation, and then lets it get out of
> the heroine's control: the simple becomes complex, responsibility
> becomes not isolated but universal, the guilty locus turns out to be
> everywhere, and individual clues are unimportant because neither
> clues nor deduction can lead to the solution.[3]

In response to what he identifies as the complexifying and univer-
salising movement of the novel, Mendelson's essay reads it in terms
of a somewhat problematic distinction between the sacred and
profane (which the final section of this chapter will return to) that
appears to require a leap of faith on the part of the reader if any
sense is to be made of the narrative. Irrespective, though, of whether
The Crying of Lot 49 is read as a text that remains incomplete in
terms of the production of answers or one that gestures beyond the
quotidian by breaking the generic frame to allude to some sort of
'higher' meaning, what is clear is that the apparent lack of closure,
the absence of the sort of straightforwardly revelatory resolution
provided by a detective's solution of the case, is a crucial element
of its narrative structure, the experience of reading the novel, and
something which requires analysis.

Recognising this process of raising and confounding generic
expectations is an important first step in beginning to understand
the ways in which Pynchon's work, and *The Crying of Lot 49* in particular, constructs its narrative, addresses the reader, and engages
more generally with contemporary culture and politics. The novel
presents a series of very precise problems of reading for the protagonist that, because of the focalisation of the narrative, produces
analogous difficulties for the text's readers. The next section will
explore the effect of these problems of focalisation, the ways in

which Oedipa's and other characters' identities become central to the generation of meaning in the narrative, and the consequences of this for the questions of interpretation and action that the novel poses to its readers.

Interpretation and implication: the world through Oedipa's eyes

The use of the narrative dynamics of the detective fiction genre, and the placement of a protagonist in the role of a detective who is unable to complete their case but nevertheless acts as a source of focalisation for the narrative, has been a common feature in much of Pynchon's work from the character of Herbert Stencil who searches the world for the enigmatic 'V.' in his first novel *V.* to Doc Sportello, the burnt-out hippy private eye investigating the mysterious Golden Fang in his recent one, *Inherent Vice*. However, it would be far too reductive simply to read Pynchon's work as just one more variation within the rules of that genre. In contrast to the standard trajectory of the detective story as a movement from mystery to revelation as the protagonist narrows down their search by finding and correctly interpreting clues, the narrative direction of Pynchon's work is, as Mendelson points out in his reading of *The Crying of Lot 49*, almost always the reverse as clue piles upon clue and interpretative decisions become increasingly impossible. And this makes all the difference to both the production of ideas in his texts and the experience of reading them.

The proliferation of meanings and possibilities frequently leads Pynchon's protagonists to some sort of breakdown: to being spiritually 'beaten up' and reduced to indecision and stasis. One of the most extreme cases of this in his work is instructive: Tyrone Slothrop, the central detective figure in *Gravity's Rainbow* who spends much of the novel searching an immediately post-Second-World-War Europe for traces of the ultimate V2 rocket, vanishes from the narrative as the novel moves towards its climax, becoming 'one plucked albatross. Plucked, hell – stripped. Scattered all over the Zone. It's doubtful if he can ever be "found" again, in the conventional sense of "positively identified and detained"' (*GR* 712). Slothrop, whose chameleon-like identity has continually changed (and often been forcibly changed) with each new encounter, finally evaporates, and one of the reader's central points of identification and coherence in the novel is removed. The loss of 'positive identity' he suffers as he is 'scattered all over the Zone', the world in which the characters of *Gravity's Rainbow* move, is an extreme but not atypical instance of another key narrative strategy in Pynchon's writing that it is helpful to introduce here: the refusal to close down the movement and play of signification by fixing or defining a true, real or actual meaning of, or even locus for, the events that occur. Throughout Pynchon's work the characters' and reader's ability to decide confidently between truth and falsity, reality and fantasy, comedy and tragedy, paranoia and the fact some 'they' really is out to get you, is thwarted at every point, making impossible the definition of ideas or events as literally true, metaphorically suggestive or deceptively false.

The developing bafflement of the protagonists in response to the worlds that unfold before them in Pynchon's texts places the problems of meaning and interpretation right at the heart of his work. Thomas Schaub describes the effect of this in the following manner:

> Pynchon's characters live in the conditional ground between the facts of their Situations and what the meaning of those facts may be. Readers of Pynchon's writing occupy that same uncertain ground because the stories he tells do not resolve in ways that align form with meaning. ... Meaning in Pynchon is always a medium, not an answer; his goal is to induce that medium, verging on psychosis, whereby the sterile and false world of 'official' forms is given the lie by a protective and inquisitive alertness, leaving an uncertain reality which both terrifies and releases.[4]

Schaub's sense of the slippery distinction between 'facts' and the 'meaning of those facts' is shared by the majority of critics of Pynchon's work.[5] And, as the final section of this chapter will attempt to demonstrate, the effect of this is simultaneously to 'terrify' and to (hold out at least the hope of) 'release'. This section, however, aims to explore the consequences of the idea of meaning as a 'medium' rather than an 'answer' in *The Crying of Lot 49*, exploring how this 'uncertain ground' is produced deliberately by the textual strategies employed in the novel, and how an explicit exploration of the problems of interpretation, truth and deception is fundamental to its narrative.

The terms 'cry' and 'crying' are continually invoked throughout the novel, and in many different ways: as formal proclamations, inarticulate sounds issuing from the night, expressions of emotion that lead to the production of tears, contextual and intertextual allusions to such themes as the suffering of Oedipus, and ultimately as the anticipated call for bids at the auction with which the novel closes. In one of the earliest references, the effect tears have on sight, and by extension on the focalisation the protagonist provides for readers, is explicitly addressed:

> Oedipa, perverse, had stood in front of the painting and cried. ... She could carry the sadness of the moment with her that way forever, see the world refracted through those tears, those specific tears, as if indices as yet unfound varied in important ways from cry to cry. (*CL* 13)

Viewing a picture by 'the beautiful Spanish exile Remedios Varo' at an exhibition in Mexico City to which she had been taken by Inverarity, Oedipa recognises that her previous life has been the equivalent of the women depicted in the painting as 'prisoners in the top room of a circular tower' and feels the overwhelming desire to escape, without being able to determine either from what or to where.[6] What this passage presents through the narrator's commentary is the singularity of perception: the 'sadness of the moment' could be carried by her 'forever', implying that her perception of the world will always be 'refracted through those tears' and thereby experienced in terms of a particular focus that itself contributes to and helps generate the truth of that perception. Unlike the rationalist ideal of the unemotional observer who judges entirely logically and objectively, Oedipa (and also, by extension, the reader) encounters the world as loaded with feeling and affect, altered and 'refracted' by the emotions that are brought to it in each act of perception. And, as the passage implies, each cry is 'specific', unique, and so perception and experience will necessarily vary 'in important ways from cry to cry', transforming perception from instant to instant as the world is 'refracted' in its own way by each cry. This sense that perception of the world is simultaneously reception of images and projection of feelings and ideas is, of course, far from unique to *The Crying of Lot 49*: it is central to modern and (in often very different ways) postmodern ideas of knowledge and art. In order to begin to understand Pynchon's complex play with this idea, it is helpful to briefly introduce it in more general terms.

For contemporary literary criticism, the idea of perception as both reception and projection was most clearly and influentially formulated in M. H. Abrams's agenda-setting 1953 study of English Romanticism *The Mirror and the Lamp*. Here Abrams argues that

towards the end of the eighteenth century a fundamental change
occurred in both philosophical ideas of perception and the vocabulary used to explain the processes of poetic composition:

> The change from imitation to expression, and from the mirror to the
> fountain, the lamp, and related analogues, was not an isolated phe-
> nomenon. It was an integral part of a corresponding change in popular
> epistemology – that is, in the concept of the role played by the mind
> in perception. ... The Copernican revolution in epistemology – if we do
> not restrict this to Kant's specific doctrine that the mind imposes the
> forms of time, space, and the categories on the 'sensuous manifold',
> but apply it to the general concept that the perceiving mind discovers
> what it has itself partly made – was effected in England by poets and
> critics before it manifested itself in academic philosophy.[7]

The claim about ordering in Abrams's account (whether poetry
precedes philosophy or not) is less important at this point in the
argument than the sense that modern thought and literature fundamentally change the ways in which experience is understood. The so-
called 'Copernican revolution' turns traditional ideas of perception in
which experience is simply the reception of external stimuli on their
head: pre-Kantian metaphysics reached an impasse in terms of its
inability to fully demonstrate that our perceptions of the world are
accurate, that we see the world as it truly is, and (in its most simple
terms) Kant's innovation was to assert that what is fundamental
to knowledge is the world as we experience it, whether or not that
experience is in any extra-experiential way 'true'. In other words,
instead of experience having to conform to objects (our perception
must allow us to experience objects as they really are; a proposition
the truth of which is impossible to verify), Kantian philosophy argues
that objects are experienced only through the constitution of the subject's perceptual capacities (objects appear to us in the ways in which
we are able to experience them; a proposition which self-evidently is
true). Ideas of perception and knowledge in the modern world – and
the Copernican revolution is frequently presented by philosophers
and theorists as a key moment in the inception of modernity – are
fundamentally different from pre- or early modern ideas in that
the modern subject plays an active role in *creating* rather than just
recording stimuli as they experience the world.[8]

This sense that perception is simultaneously the reception of
stimuli and the projection of interpretative schema that actively
make sense of the world, which Abrams finds in the 'Copernican

revolution' initiated in their different ways by Kant, Wordsworth, Coleridge and their contemporaries, is also important for understanding what is at stake in modern theories of reading, interpretation and criticism. Abrams sums up the consequences as follows: 'critical statements of fact are thus partially relative to the perspective of the theory within which they occur', which he argues is a positive thing as the fact that a particular theory 'in some degree alters the aesthetic perceptions it purports to discover ... may open [the reader's] senses to aspects of a work which other theories, with a different focus and different categories of discrimination, have on principle overlooked, underestimated, or obscured.'[9] In other words, the interpretative scheme that is brought to bear on an event, text or object projects its own set of values onto the 'aesthetic perception', and this has the potential both to 'alter' and de-objectify it and also to draw out ideas, associations and meanings that had hitherto been overlooked. Wordsworth puts this most succinctly in 'Tintern Abbey', where he describes perception as 'the mighty world / Of eye, and ear, – both what they half create / And what perceive', a process of continual interaction between projection and reception that generates experience and meaning.[10] Oedipa's process of investigating the estate and tracking down the Tristero partakes explicitly and very precisely of this duality of creation and perception.

Awareness that a procedure such as this occurs in perception and interpretation is crucially important for reading Pynchon, especially as his work relentlessly worries away at the problems this idea of experience and knowledge generates. While what is at stake in the differences between particular interpretative schemes tend within modern thought to be subject to analysis and debate which develops consensus about the truth and value of any particular claim, in Pynchon's work the stakes of such differences are transformed into fundamental and often irresolvable conflicts that foreground the impossibility of fully justifying one's choice of interpretative strategy in worlds that are shaped by crises of reception, projection, verification and paranoia. Such a world is presented in *The Crying of Lot 49*, as the novel is peopled by a range of active interpreters, each with her or his own system of knowledge that imposes rules on experience that to the non-believer can appear bizarre and arbitrary:

• Roseman, Oedipa's lawyer, refuses to distinguish between television and reality as he prepares his dossier *The Profession v. Perry*

Mason, A not-so-hypothetical Indictment and suspects her of being 'one of Perry Mason's spies' (*CL* 11–12);

- Mike Fallopian introduces her to the alternative delivery system that will become the Tristero, and interprets the world from the paranoid perspective of the ultra-right-wing Peter Pinguid Society's belief that the conflict between America and Russia, which can be traced back to a possible encounter between a Confederacy-supporting warship and the Russian Far East Fleet during the American Civil War, might 'today engulf us all' (*CL* 38);

- John Nefastis is 'impenetrable, calm, a believer', for whom the metaphorical 'Maxwell's Demon' that 'connects the world of thermodynamics to the world of information theory' is 'not only verbally graceful, but also objectively true' and can therefore be trapped in a sealed box to send revelatory messages from another world (*CL* 73);

- the Mexican anarchist revolutionary Jesús Arrabal, for whom real meaning resides in the cataclysmic, non-theological miracle of 'another world's intrusion into this one' that offers the possibility of 'revolution' and 'redemption', seems able to acknowledge that as a member of the anarcho-syndicalist movement he is 'a footsoldier' subject to the orders of the 'higher levels [who] have their reasons' that he has no need to know and yet at the same time able to believe that 'revolutions break out spontaneous and leaderless' without any sense of a contradiction (*CL* 83);

- Dr Hilarius is an ex-SS officer who had worked on 'experimentally-induced insanity' at the Buchenwald concentration camp and, as an act of denial, repentance or escape, chooses to believe entirely in 'Freud's vision of the world' that 'had no Buchenwalds in it' (*CL* 95), but ends up being carried off in a strait jacket after an armed siege at his clinic; and

- Oedipa's husband Mucho, tortured by the absence of anything to believe in at his car-lot job, becomes a disc-jockey who begins to be happy with his absence of faith but suddenly, once he becomes part of Hilarius's drug trial towards the end of the novel, acquires the ability to instantaneously 'break down chords, timbres, and words too into all the basic frequencies and harmonics, with all their different loudnesses, and listen to them, but all at once', grasping every sound he hears as an immediate comprehensible presence as if it was all 'the same voice', although only at the price

of 'losing his identity' by becoming 'less himself and more generic
... a walking assembly of man' (*CL* 97–9).

Each of these characters' systems of interpretation allows access
to a different sense of the world, produces alternative realities and
desires, and in most cases leads to some form of collapse: from
Roseman's never-completed lawsuit to Nefastis's fundamentalism,
or more destructively Hilarius's breakdown and arrest and Mucho's
loss of identity. Each system also competes to influence Oedipa,
offering her another possible means by which it might be possible
to discover the truth about the Tristero, adding elements to her (and
the narrative's) range of hermeneutic possibilities, and holding out
once more the promise of revelation, resolution and closure.

There is no space here to fully work through the consequences for
meaning and action of each of the different modes of understanding presented in the novel, but taking one example and exploring
how it contributes to the development of the narrative ought hopefully begin to illustrate what is at stake at the heart of the multiple
interpretative possibilities, and allow us to chart the ways in which
identity becomes increasingly implicated in knowledge as the plot
develops.

The dark machine: identity, perception and projection

Having watched a performance of Richard Wharfinger's *The
Courier's Tragedy* that contains a series of allusions to events and
names thrown up in the course of her enquiries, Oedipa goes
backstage to ask its director Randolph Driblette why he chose to
interpret the text's reference to Tristero in such a sinister manner.
Driblette's response presents a very precise version of an interpretative scheme:

> 'Why,' Driblette said at last, 'is everybody so interested in texts? ...
> Don't drag me into your scholarly disputes. ... You guys, you're like
> Puritans are about the Bible. So hung up with words, words. You know
> where the play exists, not in that file cabinet, not in any paperback
> you're looking for, but' – a hand emerged from the veil of shower-
> steam to indicate his suspended head – 'in here. That's what I'm for. To
> give the spirit flesh. The words, who cares? ... But the reality is in *this*
> head. Mine. I'm the projector at the planetarium, all the closed little
> universe visible in the circle of the stage is coming out of my mouth,

> eyes, sometimes other orifices also. ... Wharfinger supplied words and
> a yarn. I gave them life.' (*CL* 53–4)

For Driblette, speaking oracle-like from behind a 'veil of shower-
steam', the 'reality' of a work of literature is created not in the text,
but at its destination – in the mind of the reader, whose interpretation 'gives them life'. This is a complex claim. It is, first of all, a witty
send-up of the commonplace idea in 1950s and 1960s experimental
theatre and film theory of the director as *auteur*: the words of a
script, the actors, setting or location, and all other aspects of the production, are no more than suggestions and properties that permit
the real artist, the director, to produce his vision and 'give the spirit
flesh' as Driblette himself puts it in a hubristic invocation of divine
incarnation. At the same time, the evident solipsism and narcissism
of the claim is only an exaggerated form of the central premise of
the Copernican revolution of modern experience: where else could
meaning reside but in the receiving–projecting mind of the subject
whose perception also 'half creates'? It is also a direct contradiction
of the representatives of literary criticism in the text, Emory Bortz
and his students, for whom authors (and auteurs too, as we discover
Driblette's suicide in the same passage) are all 'dead' and the only
remains are 'Words ... Them, we can talk about' (*CL* 104). It is the
image of the projector in a planetarium, however, that becomes most
telling as the narrative develops. Driblette's metaphor presents the
ordering process of perception as delimiting from the infinite play
of the real universe of signification its own 'closed little universe' of
meaning 'visible in the circle of the stage': the reduction of the myriad
stars and galaxies to a comprehensible system of constellations that
'gives them life'. Interpretation in Driblette's solipsistic universe is
a wholly self-willed act of creation, projection and systematisation,
unconstrained by any prior meaning of the 'words, words'.

Despite its obvious problems, this interpretative method is not
one that can immediately be rejected as nonsensical as the novel
returns to revisit it more than once. Oedipa quickly assimilates the
metaphor of planetarium meaning-projection as an image for her
own procedure of ordering and organising the clues in her quest:

> it was part of her duty, wasn't it to bestow life on what had persisted,
> to try to be what Driblette was, the dark machine in the centre of the
> planetarium, to bring the estate into pulsing stelliferous Meaning, all
> in a soaring dome around her? ... Under the [muted post-horn] symbol

she'd copied off the latrine wall of The Scope in her memo book, she
wrote *Shall I project a world?* If not project then at least flash some
arrow on the dome to skitter among constellations and trace out your
Dragon, Whale, Southern Cross. Anything might help. (*CL* 56)

This repetition of Driblette's image contains subtle but informative
differences: 'bestowing life' has become a 'duty' that Oedipa only
feels able to 'try to' fulfil; the projector is transformed into the much
more menacing 'dark machine' which, instead of straightforwardly
projecting the 'closed little universe' into 'the circle of the stage',
Oedipa imagines 'flash[ing] some arrow ... to skitter among constellations' on a 'soaring dome' that surrounds her. Projecting a world is
entertained as a question ('Shall I ...?') that is immediately qualified:
it is no longer reducing the universe to the manageable sphere of
the stage, but becomes a gesture of reaching out into the infinite
in search of some flashes of meaning, order, 'Anything' that 'might
help'. This self-reflective doubt grows as the narrative progresses,
protecting Oedipa from the fatal consequences of the fundamental-
ist belief systems of characters such as Driblette and Hilarius, but
gradually leading to a loss of certainty and ability to decide or act.

While avoiding the outright narcissism of Driblette's self-con-
fident projections of meaning, Oedipa resolutely echoes his meth-
odological procedures and finds herself succumbing to a 'growing
obsession, with "bringing something of herself" – even if that something was just her presence – to the scatter of business interests
that had survived Inverarity. She would give them order, she would
create constellations' (*CL* 63). This process is not simply a matter
of re-ordering already given experiences to create a system of
meaning, but rather to 'give order' is to make possible the generation of experience itself: Oedipa 'had caught sight of the historical
marker *only because* she'd gone back, deliberately' owing to her
'obsession' (*CL* 62–3, italics added). The approach of 'bringing something of herself', if only 'just her presence', involves her intimately in
the meaning-production process and makes impossible the sort of
external objectivity demanded by modern rationalist analysis. As a
later passage on metaphor makes clear, interpretation is simultaneously 'a thrust at truth and a lie, depending where you were: inside,
safe, or outside, lost. Oedipa did not know where she was' (*CL* 89).
To approach the 'truth', one must do so from the 'inside' of personal
implication and involvement rather than viewing abstractly from a

critical distance 'outside' – the difficulty, it appears, lies in knowing in which position one is. Without her involvement, the investment of 'something of herself', in the quest for the will and the Tristero system there would neither be order and constellation nor any possibility of meaning or truth at all.

But what is this 'something of herself'? How does the novel present Oedipa as a 'self'?[11] For many readers Oedipa's identity, even her name itself, is just as much of a textual enigma as anything else in the novel, and it has been the subject of extensive critical interpretation (and sometimes a degree of projection). Watson's identification of 'Oedipa Maas' with both Oedipus and Oedipus's mother has already been cited, but the range of possible allusions to be discovered in her name has exercised critics since the novel's first publication. To mention just some of the myriad examples, while Tony Tanner mentions critics as having read her surname 'Maas' as 'suggesting Newton's second law of motion in which "mass" is the term denoting a quantity of inertia', Robert M. Davies identifies it as being Dutch for 'loophole', which suggests she might be some kind of a gap in signification (the 'dark machine' at the centre of the planetarium?), Cathy N. Davidson notes that Afrikaans has a slightly different meaning, 'web' or 'net', which alludes both to her task of fitting clues together (in an echo of the women weaving the tapestry in the Varo picture) and to the possibility of her being entangled in an inescapable mesh (being 'assumed' into 'the Tristero'?), and Judith Chambers notices that 'it refers to "Meuse", a French river', which is '[p]ronounced "my ooze"' and is thus 'very likely a homonym for "muse" and is, in fact, just one letter away from that word', perhaps suggesting her possible role as the inspiration for Inverarity's plot (if such a plot exists…).[12] Chambers also notes that Mucho affectionately shortens her name to 'Oed', 'the *Oxford English Dictionary* perhaps? The place to look up etymologies and chase down intricacies of meaning', which is what she sees Oedipa as spending much of the novel doing.[13] And, as a final example, Tanner approvingly cites Terry Caesar's argument that Pynchon 'is probably undermining and mocking the very act of naming … "Oedipa my ass"; she is no Oedipus at all': in other words, the name's most frequently noticed invocation is a lure, a red herring, a trap for the overly confident interpreter.[14] It is not a question, however, of choosing between these examples, of preferring Dutch, French or Afrikaans, profundity or humour. Oedipa, as the next section will attempt to argue, is all of them at once: each meaning is possible and opens different readings of and reactions to the text, projecting different worlds for Oedipa to interpret and inhabit, and the novel's narrative is structured in such a way as to keep this multiplicity in play throughout.

This necessity of involving herself in the world she projects, although it begins by holding out the promise that meaning might emerge, soon threatens to overwhelm her entirely: after the 'beating up', and faced with the appearance of one more potential clue, she finally 'left it alone, anxious that her revelation not expand beyond a certain point. Lest, possibly, it grow larger than she and assume her to itself' (*CL* 115). The threat here is the loss of self: Oedipa's being assumed or assimilated to the system itself if her interpretative quest requires her to give too much of her identity to the objects and events she seeks to understand.[15]

This sense of experience as a process of assimilation and self-projection, then, leads to its own series of problems that question quite profoundly the possibility of truth and verification for the modern subject. If sense-making is *active* and implicates the self in the objects of experience, *The Crying of Lot 49* asks, if the meanings of experience are actively *produced* by the ideas and desires of the subject or subjects, what guarantee can there be that the world is not simply a projection of one's own perversions or the product of a duplicitous plot launched by some sinister collection of other subjects intent on deceiving one and assimilating one to their nefarious projects? This, quite explicitly, is the realisation that stops Oedipa in her tracks towards the end of the novel:

> Either you have stumbled indeed ... on to a network by which X number of Americans are truly communicating while reserving their lies, recitations of routine, arid betrayals of spiritual poverty, for the official government delivery system; maybe even on to a real alternative to the exitlessness, to the absence of surprise to life, that harrows the head of everybody American you know, and you too, sweetie. Or you are hallucinating it. Or a plot has been mounted against you. ... Or you are fantasying such a plot, in which case you are a nut, Oedipa, out of your skull. (*CL* 117–18)

Soon after being told that arch-projector Driblette had simply 'walked out into the Pacific two nights ago. ... He's dead' (*CL* 105), Oedipa's own self-reflection presents her with four alternatives: (1) there really is a Tristero system, or (2) she has hallucinated its existence from a random collection of images and events, or (3) someone has faked the Tristero as part of a plot to delude her, or (4) she has fantasised such a plot. The novel allows Oedipa no way to decide between these four possibilities, and her personal collapse continues apace, manifesting itself in symptoms such as toothache, loss of concentration, 'nausea', 'headaches, nightmares, menstrual pains' (*CL* 118) – is her fear of assumption beginning to be realised in her physical disintegration?

Faced with the refusal to uncover the identity of the Tristero, to reveal the secrets of Inverarity's will, or even to disclose which of the four alternatives listed above is Oedipa's 'real' situation in the novel, readers are left with a profoundly ambiguous ending as the possibility of a 'correct' interpretation of the truth of her world is withheld. The question faced by critics of the novel is what to make of this: what are the consequences of the non-closure of the narrative? What does this refusal of meaning mean?

Repetition, reference and the refusal to end: the beauty of convolution

The first section of this chapter explored the way in which the focalisation of the narrative through Oedipa's eyes draws in the reader so that their experience of the development of meaning in the novel echoes her growing awareness of the Tristero. The second section discussed the ways in which Pynchon's writing self-consciously raises questions about meaning and interpretation more generally, and the third focused on a particular model of projection presented in the novel to analyse the ways in which Oedipa's attempts at interpretation bring her to the verge of collapse as the narrative nears its end. This final section will take a step back from the novel (at least to begin with) to examine the ways in which readers might be able to engage with its refusal to provide definitive answers to the questions it raises about representation and reality. By working through some exemplary critical approaches to the text, it will discuss how critics have argued about the ways in which *The Crying of Lot 49* addresses its readers, generates meanings and ideas to engage with the world, and sets it in the broader contexts of debates about modernism and postmodernism.

Pynchon's work is frequently read as an example of postmodern literature, and critics often cite it as an example of ironic, self-conscious, playful and disruptive writing that poses all sorts of problems of identification and comprehension for readers. It is, they often argue, writing that elicits questions about the methodologies and assumptions of critical practice and cries out for new modes of reading and analysis. Two critical analyses that have already been cited briefly in this discussion – Mendelson's, and Nicholson and Stevenson's – place Pynchon's challenge to critics at the centre of their readings, although each draws very different conclusions about the consequences for critical analysis that can be drawn from his work.

Mendelson's reading of the sacred and profane in *The Crying of Lot 49*, introduced in the first section of this chapter, identifies the Tristero system as an entity that transcends the convolution and fragmentation of the novel's narrative, and offers hope of some resolution and escape: 'The Trystero carries with it a sense of sacred connection and relation in the world, and by doing so it manifests a way of comprehending the world.'[16] This is a largely unquestionable assertion, as the novel undoubtedly refers continually to the pos- sibility of an escape from the problems of meaning it presents into a realm in which the protagonist and reader might finally recover 'the direct, epileptic Word, the cry that might abolish the night' (*CL* 81). As well as acting as the promise of freedom for its protago- nist, however, Mendelson's reading presents the idea that despite its incomplete narrative the novel as a whole gestures towards closure by invoking an extra-textual 'sacred' meaning:

> Pynchon uses religious terms and hieratic language not simply as a set of metaphors from which to hang his narrative, not merely as scaffolding (as Joyce, for example, uses Christian symbols in *Ulysses*). The religious meaning of the book does not reduce to metaphor or myth, *because religious meaning is itself the central issue of the plot.* ... The book offers the possibility that its religious metaphor is only metaphor: but if the book were founded on this limited possibility, the remaining portions of the book would make no sense, and there would be little reason to write it in the first place.[17]

The status of this claim is fundamentally different from the first one: to say that the novel includes a range of religious ideas and imagery is one thing, but to refuse to countenance the 'possibility that its religious metaphor is only metaphor' is to fail to recognise the complex and irreducible openness of the text. Faced with a passage such as 'Behind the hieroglyphic streets there would either be some meaning or only earth' (*CL* 125), this approach should immediately opt for the 'either'. However, this effectively refuses to take seriously Oedipa's dilemma of the four choices. For Mendelson, it is unquestionable that there really is a Tristero in the novel, otherwise 'the book would make no sense'. The ending of the novel is not the non-ending that this chapter has posited so far, but instead a gesture beyond the quotidian: in answer to his own question 'But why the *forty-ninth* lot?', Mendelson's argument responds 'Because Pentecost is the Sunday seven weeks after Easter – forty-nine days' and so 'the forty-ninth lot is the moment before a Pentecost revelation. ... This is why the novel ends with Oedipa waiting, with the "true" nature of the Trystero never established: a manifestation of the sacred can only be believed in; it can never be proved beyond doubt.'[18] In other words, once the interpretative scheme based on the idea that sacred revelation saves the novel from not making sense is brought to bear on the text, closure in the belief of an imminent 'manifestation of the sacred' can be achieved.

In contrast to Mendelson, Nicholson and Stevenson's '"Words You Never Wanted to Hear": Fiction, History and Narratology in *The Crying of Lot 49*' refuses to be drawn by the temptations of transcendence, and opts instead to focus on the novel's references to, and images and citations of, 'historical actuality':

> As readers, we are aware of the historical actuality of some of the novel's references in a way that Oedipa, part of the texture of the fiction, cannot be. Pynchon explicitly alerts us to this possibility in the passage ... where Driblette remarks the stamp collectors had told him that the Thurm and Taxis mail system did exist. The stamp collectors are right, of course. Not only did it exist, but it always delivered most of Europe's mail between 1290 and 1806. And this is far from being the only historical fact significantly reproduced in Pynchon's novel. Oedipa's unnerving descent into the historical penumbra of the Trystero closely parallels our own detection of a hidden history of actuality.[19]

This essay goes on to carefully trace the range of references in the novel to events from history including the conflicts in Europe that lead to the migrations that founded America and contributed to the California gold rush (which evokes the '49' of 1849 to suggest that the novel's 'crying' might also refer to the 'crying or suffering of those who arrived in California in 1849') to argue persuasively that 'Pynchon's historical figurations compel the reader's attention onto a problematic historical reality from which fiction is never allowed to be a complete refuge'.[20] In contrast to Mendelson's sense of a revelatory ending, for Nicholson and Stevenson the novel's unfinishedness is the key point as its complex referentiality gestures beyond the closure of the traditional novel into what they call the 'actuality of historical change', thereby directing the reader '"outside" into engagement with the nature and origins of the threats of contemporary history'.[21] Faced with the same passage as Mendelson, 'Behind the hieroglyphic streets there would either be some meaning or only earth' (*CL* 125), Nicholson and Stevenson would opt immediately for the 'or', though the 'earth' they chose as their focus would be very much more than '*only* earth'. Just as with Mendelson's reading, there is a belief structure here that, although coherent and compelling, is never entirely endorsed by the novel itself: the many historical references and intertexts embedded in the narrative can undeniably be verified in 'actuality' by the critic (in the way that Cohen and Bortz do for Oedipa's hints about the Tristero, for example), but the question of their meaning, effect, affect, and therefore their epistemological value, *within* the world of the novel remains open. In fact the relation between inside and outside, fiction and actuality, is precisely what remains in question: *The Crying of Lot 49*'s 'acts of metaphor' are 'a thrust at truth and a lie, depending where you were: inside, safe, or outside, lost' (*CL* 89). And, like Oedipa, we cannot finally be sure from which of these positions, inside or outside, we are reading.

These two readings have been chosen because of their lucidity and influence, and as a means of demonstrating the fundamentally different approaches to its meaning which the text's ambiguity and convolution makes possible. In relation to the discussion of perception and interpretation as partaking simultaneously in reception and projection, though, the suspicion remains that these essays find precisely what they are looking for: the transcendent moment of the awaited Pentecost in a reading focusing on the sacred in the former, and the radicalism of opening to 'historical actuality' generated by the materialist approach of the latter. *The Crying of Lot 49* contains both of these possibilities, as well as many more, and this multivocality is essential to its reading.

In their very different ways, both Mendelson and Nicholson and Stevenson read *The Crying of Lot 49* as a novel that problematises modernist fiction without fully breaking from it, an approach to the text which is contextualised and developed by Brian McHale's influential organisation of Pynchon's early novels in terms of a relation between the modern and postmodern in his book *Postmodernist Fiction*. McHale provides a detailed and noteworthy analysis of the move from modernist to postmodernist fiction, arguing that it is marked by a change from a focus on epistemological issues to an exploration of ontological questions. By this he means that modern fiction asks about how a world can be interpreted or changed, and is interested in questions of truth and knowledge – in other words, in epistemology. The most familiar and straightforward example of this is the one with which we began: the literary detective who sifts the evidence presented in order to discover who committed the crime. McHale argues that postmodernist fiction, on the other hand, raises questions about the very status of reality and the world: 'What is a world?; What kinds of world are there, how are they constituted, and how do they differ?; What happens when different kinds of world are placed in confrontation, or when boundaries between worlds are violated?'[22] In other words, according to McHale postmodernist fiction confronts the reader with questions about what sort of world is being created at each moment in the text, and who or what in a text they can believe – in questions of ontology. On the basis of this distinction, he reads *The Crying of Lot 49* as a transitional text that marks Pynchon's movement from the epistemologically dominant modernism of *V.* to the fully fledged ontological uncertainty of postmodernism in *Gravity's Rainbow*.[23] In the passage below, he compares the novel to the modernism of Henry James's *The Turn of the Screw*:

> As in *The Crying of Lot 49*, the reader is forced to hesitate between an explanation in terms of epistemological categories – the governess's vision of events is distorted from within, she is hallucinating the apparitions – and one which posits an alternative ontology – there are other orders of being, the ghosts really exist, this is a case of 'another world's intrusion into this one.' Also as in *Lot 49*, there is finally no way to decide between the alternatives. ... The difference between *The Turn of the Screw* and *Lot 49* – and it is a crucial difference – is, of course, that James's governess is herself unaware of the alternatives, believing in the 'ghostly' explanation from the outset ... [w]hereas Oedipa is only too aware of her alternatives. ... [S]he understands the ambiguity of her situation as clearly as her readers do. ... The dead-ending of epistemology in solipsism can be transcended, but only by

shifting from a modernist poetics of epistemology to a postmodernist poetics of ontology, from Oedipa's anguished cry, 'Shall I project a world?,' to the unconstrained projection of worlds in the plural.[24]

On this reading, the complex allusive structure of the text with its invocations of the transcendent running alongside its references to history refuses the 'dead-ending of epistemology in solipsism' by continually projecting new and multiple worlds, worlds that are continually 'refracted through [Oedipa's] tears, those specific tears, as if indices as yet unfound [that] varied in important ways from cry to cry' (*CL* 13).

This commitment to openness and multiplicity is stated explicitly at the very end of the text: 'She had heard all about excluded middles; they were bad shit, to be avoided; and how had it ever happened here, with the chances once so good for diversity?' (*CL* 125). The 'law of the excluded middle', a central premise of philosophical logic that can be traced back to Aristotle's *Metaphysics*, can be summarised as the idea that any proposition must be either true or not true; it cannot be both or neither. And yet this is what Pynchon's writing in the novel resolutely attempts to resist: by refusing to resolve its images, ideas and action into a straightforward either/ or of truth/untruth (or any of the other oppositions presented in the text such as sacred/profane, literal/metaphorical, reception/ projection, and so on), it seeks to retain the 'chance' for 'diversity'. For Stefan Mattessich's resolutely postmodernist reading, this refusal is precisely the point as, in offering no possibility of escape from the convoluted cycle of repetitions its narrative produces, the novel's presentations of resistance and community remain ambivalent and open:

> *The Crying of Lot 49* does not choose one or the other of the possibilities confronted by Oedipa at the 'crying of lot 49'; it chooses the impasse as such, it presents the tautological circle of that double bind as the vehicle for its escape. This elliptical and repetitious textual ambivalence signals a desire that includes the world and refuses its own exemption or election in it, a 'preterite' desire that takes the world as its object in all its 'promise, productivity and betrayal'. ... Pynchon attempts to write the displacement of the difference between the real and simulacral, and as such to imagine the America that follows from the displacement of both in its vitiating effects and its desiring modes. Only through this attempt does the 'community' of 'the people' who 'communicate' through WASTE come into being.[25]

For Mattessich, the novel's refusal to choose between possibilities is the source of its radicalism: 'it chooses the impasse ... as the vehicle for its escape'. The novel's postmodern play with ontological uncertainty and its parody of our day-to-day sense-making processes open a fictional space where the choice of 'either/or' is put in abeyance, and other possibilities of meaning and signification are gestured towards through a process of self-consciously ironic repetition and convolution.

During his first meeting with Oedipa in the Echo Courts motel, Metzger makes the following claim: 'our beauty lies ... in this extended capacity for convolution' (*CL* 21). 'Convolution', the action of rolling or twisting together of elements so that something turns in on and folds into itself to produce a complex self-relating structure, is central to the form of the novel, the way its narrative develops, and, if we extrapolate from Metzger's claim, its 'beauty' and the pleasure it produces for the reader. The complexities, intertextualities, referentialities and self-referentialities of Pynchon's narrative tease the reader with promises and possibilities of meaning, suggestions of knowledge and insight that, on a second glance, seem to have disqualified, withdrawn or undermined themselves. Pynchon's writing is playful, engaging, exciting and fun. It is also at times disturbing and deadly serious. Running alongside the invocation of convolution's beauty, there is a parallel and much less positive echo: the 'Endless, convoluted incest' (*CL* 8) of Mucho's experience of the continual round of selling and buying that made up his work at the car lot, and drove him gradually to despair and intolerable nightmares: 'it was', he says, 'the sign in the lot, that's what scared me. ... We were a member of the National Automobile Dealer's Association. NADA. Just this creaking metal sign that said nada, nada, against the blue sky. I used to wake up hollering' (*CL* 100). It is this doubly significant sense of convolution as beauty and horror that achieves what Schaub in the passage cited earlier describes as Pynchon's 'goal': 'to induce that medium, verging on psychosis, whereby the sterile and false world of "official" forms is given the lie by a protective and inquisitive alertness, leaving an uncertain reality which both terrifies and releases.'[26] Reading Pynchon's elusive narratives is a process of engaging with this convolution of meaning, appreciating the joys of his writing without flinching from its invocations of violence and atrocity, remaining open to the pluralities of experience and affect his texts produce, and beginning to explore the alternative possibilities they offer for thinking about identity, interpretation, history and politics.

Notes

1 Tony Tanner relates Pynchon's novel to the more precisely defined California private eye sub-genre as practised by Raymond Chandler, Ross MacDonald and Erle Stanley Gardner (whose detective Perry Mason is invoked on more than one occasion in the text). See Tanner, *Thomas Pynchon*, London: Methuen, 1982, 56.

2 Robert N. Watson, 'Teaching Crying: General Education, the 1960s, and *Lot 49*', in Thomas H. Schaub, ed., *Approaches to Teaching Pynchon's* The Crying of Lot 49 *and Other Works*, New York: Modern Language Association, 2008, 14–15.

3 Edward Mendelson, ed. *Pynchon: A Collection of Critical Essays*. New Jersey: Prentice Hall, 1978, 123. For an alternative version of Oedipa as an 'anti-detective', see Stefano Tani, 'The Dismemberment of the Detective', *Diogenes* 120 (1982): 22–41.

4 Thomas H. Schaub, *Pynchon: The Voice of Ambiguity*. Urbana: University of Illinois Press, 1981, 103–4.

5 There are too many different approaches to this problem of meaning in Pynchon, but an excellent source that offers a range of ways in which Schaub's distinction can be approached is Patrick O'Donnell's edited collection *New Essays on* The Crying of Lot 49, Cambridge: Cambridge University Press, 1991, which (alongside other excellent readings) includes Bernard Duyfhuizen's influential '"Hushing Sick Transmissions": Disrupting Story in *The Crying of Lot 49*' (79–96) and N. Katherine Hayles's brilliant '"A Metaphor of God Knew How Many Parts": The Engine that Drives *The Crying of Lot 49*' (97–126).

6 This episode is central to readings of the novel by a range of critics, and its possible meanings are the subject of a good deal of debate. A particularly detailed reading of the place of the painting in the novel that takes seriously the fact that the picture described is the central frame of a triptych is developed by Stefan Mattessich in *Lines of Flight: Discursive Time and Countercultural Desire in the Work of Thomas Pynchon*, Durham: Duke University Press, 2002, especially 49–56.

7 M. H. Abrams, *The Mirror and the Lamp: Romantic Theory and the Critical Tradition*. Oxford: Oxford University Press, 1953, 57–8.

8 This reference back to Romanticism and the idea of a Copernican revolution in philosophy and poetry that sets the scene for modernity is, as we shall attempt to show, important for exploring what might be at stake in the very common identification of Pynchon as a 'postmodern' writer. Two of the most influential theorists of the distinction between

modernity and the postmodern locate the transformation in philosophy
developed in Kant's work as fundamental to understanding the two con-
cepts. Jürgen Habermas argues that 'In Kant's concept of a formal and
internally differentiated reason there is sketched a theory of modernity',
characterised by the 'renunciation of the substantial rationality of inherited religious and metaphysical worldviews' in favour of a 'procedural
rationality' in which meaning are truth must be arrived at by consensus
('Philosophy as Stand-in and Interpreter' in K. Baynes, J. Bonham and T.
McCarthy, eds, *After Philosophy: End or Transformation?* Cambridge, MA:
The MIT Press, 1987, 296–315 [298–9]). Jean-François Lyotard identifies Kant as crucial for both movements: his work 'marks at once the
prologue and the epilogue of modernity. And as the epilogue to modernity, it is also the prologue to postmodernity' (*The Lyotard Reader*, ed.
Andrew Benjamin. Oxford: Blackwell, 1989, 394).

  9 Abrams, *The Mirror and the Lamp*, 4–5.
10 William Wordsworth, 'Tintern Abbey', lines 104–6, in R. L. Brett and
    A. R. Jones, *Wordsworth and Coleridge: Lyrical Ballads*, 2nd edition.
    London: Routledge, 1961, 116.
11 This problem of the self is seen by Mendelson as a key moment where
    Pynchon breaks from modernist literature because of his 'refusal to
    dwell on psychological drama or domestic detail. ... In his books, char-
    acter is less important than the network of relations existing either
    between characters, or between characters and social and historical
    patterns of meaning.' (Mendelson, *Pynchon*, 4–5). Colin Nicholson and
    Randall Stevenson in their important essay '"Words You Never Wanted
    to Hear": Fiction, History and Narratology in *The Crying of Lot 49*'
    (*Pynchon Notes* 16 [1985]: 89–109) cite and endorse this claim, but (as
    the final section of this chapter will attempt to show) draw very differ-
    ent conclusions about its consequences.
12 Tanner, *Thomas Pynchon*, 60; Robert M. Davis, 'Parody, Paranoia, and the
    Dead End of Language in *The Crying of Lot 49*', *Genre* 5 (1977): 367–77
    (373); Cathy N. Davidson, 'Oedipa as Androgyne in Thomas Pynchon's
    The Crying of Lot 49', *Contemporary Literature* 13 (1977): 38–50 (43);
    Judith Chambers, *Thomas Pynchon*. New York: Twayne, 1992, 101.
13 Chambers, *Thomas Pynchon*, 100.
14 Tanner, *Thomas Pynchon*, 60. Tanner does not give a reference for
    Caesar's claim.
15 This, in essence, is what seems to happen to Slothrop in the passage
    from *Gravity's Rainbow* cited above.
16 Mendelson, *Pynchon*, 119
17 Mendelson, *Pynchon*, 119–21.
18 Mendelson, *Pynchon*, 135.
19 Nicholson and Stevenson, 'Words You Never Wanted to Hear', 93.

20 Nicholson and Stevenson, 'Words You Never Wanted to Hear', 97 and 106.
21 Nicholson and Stevenson, 'Words You Never Wanted to Hear', 108.
22 Brian McHale, *Postmodernist Fiction*. London: Methuen, 1987, 10.
23 McHale's much more extended account of the postmodern narrative complexities of *Gravity's Rainbow* is key to our argument (and discussed in some detail) in chapter 5.
24 McHale, *Postmodernist Fiction*, 24–5.
25 Mattessich, *Lines of Flight*, 63–4.
26 Schaub, *Pynchon: The Voice of Ambiguity*, 104.

3

Disappearing points: *V.*

V., Thomas Pynchon's first novel, was published in 1963. It was received by critics with a good deal of acclaim, and not a little bafflement: an often-cited review in *Time Magazine* describes it as a 'likable, mad and unfathomable first novel' that 'sails with majesty through caverns measureless to man', and concludes that '[f]ew books haunt the waking or sleeping mind, but this is one'; and George Plimpton's review for *The New York Times*, while not describing much more than a sense of enjoyable confusion with regard to the plot, notes that Pynchon is certainly 'a young writer of staggering promise' and relates *V.* to the 'picaresque' fiction of important writers of the period such as Saul Bellow, Jack Kerouac and Joseph Heller.[1] Almost all of the early reviewers of the novel were quick to recognise Pynchon as a major new force in American fiction, and *V.* was nominated for the 1963 National Book Award as well as receiving the William Faulkner Award for the best debut novel of that year. The first readers and reviewers more or less unanimously detected in the work a complex and original creative voice that was capable of integrating into the text a vast range of literary and non-literary styles as well as allusions to a great many canonical texts while managing to retain its own unique and sometimes genuinely quirky outlook on the contemporary world. The aim of this chapter is to explore the novel in terms of some of the key categories critics have assigned to it, in particular to read it as engaging with the ideas of modernism, postmodernism, intertextuality and parody with which Pynchon's early work has so frequently been associated.

'Events seem to be ordered into an ominous logic': *V.*'s plots

Plots and ideas of plotting are central to *V.* Or, more precisely, the novel focuses continually on the possibilities of plot: whether the stories told and schemes launched by its many characters are meaningful, effective, coherent, accidental or even entirely pointless; what potential consequences are entailed by the various plans and projects initiated; what sorts of secret intrigues and conspiracies are taking place behind the characters' backs to shape their actions and experiences; which modes of language can give order to events; and even whether the events and experiences are susceptible to being brought under the auspices of a plot in any comprehensible manner. Ranging across the world and throughout the twentieth century, the various narrative threads that make up *V.* hold out the possibility of some deeper, possibly entirely malign, plot while simultaneously straining at the limits of connection and coherence to raise questions about whether there is any order or plan shaping the events of the novel at all.

In the simplest terms, *V.* is made up of two apparently distinct but subtly interwoven and thematically integrated narratives. Since Joseph Slade's early discussion of the novel, critics have commonly noted that one of the novel's central oppositions, that which is set up between the contrasting perspectives of its two protagonists, at first sight seems very closely to echo the narrative dynamic of 'Entropy', which we discussed in the first chapter.[2] The presentation of Benny Profane and Herbert Stencil mirrors the opposition between Mulligan and Callisto: the chaotic and never fully engaged wandering of Profane through the alienated present-day of the novel's 1950s America contrasts with the obsessively ordered 'hothouse' of Stencil's relentless collection of apparently unconnected anecdotes and stories drawn from the margins of many of the twentieth century's key events as he builds his search for the strange and elusive figure known only as 'V.' For other critics, the contrast between these two protagonists anticipates Oedipa Maas's internal struggle with the central paranoid question of meaning she faces in *The Crying of Lot 49*: is the world made up of a series of random and ultimately meaningless coincidences that bounce us from place to place without adding up to any greater significance as Profane seems to find, or are all occurrences 'ordered into an ominous logic' (*V.* 449), a hidden plot to be unravelled, a secret that once revealed would uncover to Stencil 'The Big One, the century's master cabal' (*V.* 226)?[3] This is a key question the novel poses for its readers, and, being by Pynchon of course, resolutely refuses to finally answer. While this comparison with texts discussed in the previous two chapters might help begin to locate some of this novel's concerns, it is important to state at the outset that *V.* is neither simply 'Entropy' bulked out and extended to a story of almost 500 pages, and nor is it just a dry run for Oedipa's internalised conflict of belief in *Lot 49*. Rather, the apparently simple opposition that frames the novel's plots and points of focus is one that is continually transformed, problematised and reworked as the narrative progresses: the range of images, ideas, intertexts and cultural and historical resonances is considerably vaster than either of the shorter texts, and the questions it poses to the reader turn out to be quite different. The world produced by the novel's plots, just like the elusive titular figure, remains just at the limits of what can be grasped, drawing the reader further into a complex web of coincidences and obsessions. Even though events of *V.* may *seem* to be 'ordered into an ominous logic', the meaning of this appearance is impossible to fix: the phrase 'repeated itself automatically and Stencil improved on it each time, placing emphasis on different words – "events *seem*"; "seem to be *ordered*"; "*ominous* logic" – pronouncing them differently, changing the "tone of voice" from sepulchral to jaunty: round and round and round' (*V.* 449). And what they circle is the novel's central enigma, the continually just out-of-reach feminine figure, at once ominous and seductive, V.

The opening pages of the novel introduce Benny Profane, a sailor discharged from the US Navy who wanders 'up and down the east coast like a yo-yo' (*V.* 10) without any apparent motive or aim, taking on various jobs including road builder, night-watchman at a research institute that uses robots to test the effects of accidents such as car crashes and radiation leaks, and hunter of albino crocodiles that have escaped into the New York sewer system. Profane refers to himself throughout the novel as a 'schlemihl', a slang term derived from Yiddish for an unlucky, ineffectual and incompetent person who is a dupe or victim, and he reacts to everything he encounters in terms of this persona. Throughout his many adventures during the novel, he remains largely unaffected by his surroundings or the other people he meets: near the beginning the reader is told that 'Profane hadn't changed. ... Road work had done nothing to improve the outward

Profane, or the inward one either. Though the street had claimed a big fraction of Profane's age, it and he remained strangers in every way. Streets ... had taught him nothing' (*V.* 36–7), and at the end of the novel his final line, a response to the question 'Haven't you learned?', reprises this idea: '"No," he said, "offhand I'd say I haven't learned a goddam thing"' (*V.* 454). In this sense, Profane disappoints the expectations of the reader familiar with the typical *Bildungsroman* form of the modern novel: rather than a narrative charting the protagonist's growth, learning and coming to maturity, Profane's is a picaresque story of continual change without any real sense of development or progress. Like the 'yo-yo' that he often evokes, his movement through the text is entirely subject to the whims of others: charming and funny, he is a fascinating figure through whose eyes we experience a strange, amusing and often disconcerting post-war world that has been stripped of any deeper sense of meaning or significance; he goes everywhere and yet gains nothing.

Soon after his arrival in New York, Profane falls in with a group of dissolute and ineffectual artists and intellectuals who call themselves the Whole Sick Crew. In contrast to the adventurous political activism of the range of early twentieth-century avant-garde figures evoked in many of the historical chapters (of which more in a moment), the Crew is presented as thoroughly disengaged from the world and irrelevant to the wider context of political and historical struggle as they produce little other than clichéd discussion at their seemingly endless round of parties: 'the Whole Sick Crew had nothing to offer. ... The pattern would have been familiar – bohemian, creative, arty – except that it was even further removed from reality, Romanticism in its furthest decadence; being only an exhausted impersonation of poverty, rebellion and artistic "soul"' (*V.* 56). This decadence is later described in the following terms: the 'Crew does not live, it experiences. It does not create, it talks about people who do. ... It satirizes itself and doesn't mean it' (*V.* 380). Everything for the Crew is second-hand: there is no originality, inspiration, achievement; only pretension, impersonation and exhaustion. Cooper is not alone among critics in seeing them as exemplary of *V.*'s entropy: 'the spiritual heat death into which the Whole Sick Crew is drifting' (*V.* 86). *V.* is a novel of artists, activists and intellectuals, with narratives focusing on key moments of early twentieth-century artistic innovation and explorations of the aesthetics and politics of poetry, painting, music and dance, but it depicts a present where avant-garde experimentation appears to have exhausted itself entirely and descended into non-productive hedonism and solipsism.

Among the non-creating artists, inactive activists and unengaged intellectuals of the Crew, one figure quickly comes into focus as the novel's second protagonist: the obsessive seeker after order, truth and the mysterious figure 'V.', Herbert Stencil. Profane first meets Stencil at one of the Crew's parties: 'Young Stencil the world adventurer, seated on the sink, waggled his shoulderblades like wings. ... Born in 1901, the year [Queen] Victoria died, Stencil was in time to be the century's child' (*V.* 52). This opening image is focalised through Stencil's own eyes and in his own voice, despite the grammatical third-person from which his dialogue never strays and which forms the basis of what he calls his 'Forcible dislocation of personality' (*V.* 62) through which he takes on a repertoire of identities to aid him in his quest. The idea of the 'world adventurer', identification with Victoria and sense of a relation to the twentieth century as the 'century's child' are all crucial aspects of the self-image he develops as the novel progresses, and also suggest a broader cultural, political and historical resonance for his actions that he himself never acknowledges. These, when taken together with the description of the shoulder blades 'waggled' like wings, present Stencil's persona and quest as something of more than individual human significance, even perhaps evoking the sort of image made familiar to modern critics by the German philosopher Walter Benjamin's figure of the 'Angel of History' in his 'On the Concept of History': 'His face is turned towards the past. Where a chain of events appears before *us*, *he* sees one single catastrophe, which keeps piling wreckage upon wreckage and hurls it at his feet.'[4] The Angel bears witness to the disasters of history, experiences them as something present rather than past as they are hurled at his feet, and in many ways this is precisely Stencil's role in *V.* The past is his milieu: Stencil collects and retells tales from the first half of the twentieth century, forming narratives which make up the entirety of five of the novel's sixteen chapters as well as being significant aspects of many of the others, and have often been the main focus of critical responses to the text. In direct contrast to Profane's apparently aimless drifting, Stencil is relentlessly driven onwards from clue to clue in a quest for meaning and truth. The novel's most succinct description of his character captures this single-mindedness: 'he was quite purely He Who Looks for V.' (*V.* 226).

In contrast to Benjamin's Angel, however, Stencil demonstrates no desire to 'stay, awaken the dead, and make whole again what has been smashed', but displays an attitude so obsessively focused on a single figure that all other events, even those involving the most extreme suffering and horror, appear only on the sidelines, as set dressing for the attempted discovery and identification of V.[5] Developing his fixation from evidence he inherited from notebooks left by his father Stanley, a spy for the English government, he links together a series of events in which the figure V. appears to play an active or walk-on part: a competition between secret agents during the conflict about the control of Africa played out between the European powers in 1898 that became known as the 'Fashoda Incident'; an attempt to steal Botticelli's *Birth of Venus* that gets caught up with Latin American politics and revolutionary rioting in Florence in 1899; a decadent party taking place against the backdrop of the genocidal reaction to a native uprising in southwest Africa by the German colonists in 1922; a confessional diary kept by a would-be modernist poet detailing the experience of intensive air raids during the siege of Malta in the 1940s; and the seduction and death of a young dancer in an avant-garde ballet in the Paris of 1913. Each of these episodes is 'Stencilised': traced, patterned, ornamented and coloured by Stencil's obsession so that around each one 'developed a nacreous mass of inference, poetic license, forcible dislocation of personality into a past he didn't remember and had no right in' (*V.* 62).

Because of this continual process of 'Stencilisation', the forms and meanings of the historical events presented in *V.* are complicated, and the novel is, somewhat like *The Crying of Lot 49*, as much an interrogation of the possibility of historiographical understanding and order as it is a straightforward depiction of any sort of historical 'fact'. Comparing the narratives of Pynchon's short story 'Under the Rose' (collected in *Slow Learner*) with Chapter Three of *V.*, both of which share the same plot depicting struggles between spies during the Fashoda Incident, David Cowart argues that Stencil has 'a poor sense of history ... [as] he tends to be rather careless about detailing the activities of *V.*'s supporting cast', which leaves the chapter 'fragmented and decidedly unclear' when compared with the omniscient narration and coherent focalisation of the short story.[6] This is probably overstating the case slightly, as the novel raises important questions about violence, colonial exploitation, war and culture by way of its depictions of historical conflict, but Cowart's assertion of the complexities of focalisation and voice in the various episodes is important. Each of the 'historical' episodes of *V.* is subject to the process of 'Stencilisation' in some way or another: focuses shift, paranoia reigns and the narrative voices introduce speculations, allusions and suggestions into the texts to continually draw the eye towards a mysterious figure at the limits of perception. Historical material may form the basis of Stencil's stories, but 'the rest was impersonation and dream' (*V.* 63). This is not, of course, to say that the presentation of historical order in *V.* is irrelevant or wholly incoherent: according to Tony Tanner, if Stencil is 'the "century's child", then he is by the same token searching for the century's "mother" or, more generally, who or what it was that gave birth to the twentieth century and caused it to move so rapidly towards world wars, genocide, nuclear bombs – a whole arsenal of events and inventions, dehumanizations – which would indeed seem to be accelerating the approach of total entropy'.[7] The impetus that drives Stencil's quest for this figure, who may or may not have been his literal mother, is at once a personal obsession and also a more universal drive to discover an order and a reason at the heart of the century's violence. *V.* engages with this violence, exploring its origins and consequences through the complex links between the various plots that make up the novel, invoking a range of narrative modes and intertexts in which it can be figured, as the next section of this chapter will attempt to show, and returning frequently to its dehumanising effects in the novel's present in ways which the final section will explore. The novel does this most explicitly by centring its focus on a continually elusive and disappearing point: V.

Questions of whom or what V. might be, what her wider significance is, and even whether or not she actually exists, pervade Stencil's parts of the novel: V. 'yielded him only the poor skeleton of a dossier. Most of what he has is inference. He doesn't know who she is, nor what she is. He's trying to find out' (*V.* 155). In each of his narratives, a different incarnation of V. appears as a protagonist. She is first introduced as Victoria Wren, the naïve young girl abroad in the 1898 and 1899 episodes, at first appearing as a benign figure subjected to the male desire of the spies and agents, although her fascination with the violence of the riot at the end of the Florence chapter (*V.* 209) suggests a loss of innocence and prefigures the sadistic proclivities of her later associations. She reappears in the characters of both Vera Meroving and Hedwig Vogelsang, fellow guests that sexually pursue and are pursued respectively by the increasingly delirious narrator Kurt Mondaugen during the 'siege party' in 1922 southwest Africa. She then becomes the sinister 'Bad Priest' in Second-World-War Malta, a mysterious and malign figure associated with betrayal, suffering and death, who is finally trapped, stripped and 'disassembled' by a gang of children playing among the ruins. Finally, in the France 1913 episode, she transforms into 'the lady V. of Stencil's mad time-search', a figure who has become anonymous as 'No one knew her name in Paris' (*V.* 406), and seduces the girl-dancer Mélanie l'Heuremaudit who, having been forcibly changed into V.'s fetish, dies as she is impaled on a spike during the first performance of the new ballet. During this last episode, the question of the continuity between V.'s identities is explicitly raised: 'perhaps, if she were in fact Victoria Wren ... that Victoria was being gradually replaced by V.; something entirely different, for which the young century had as yet no name' (*V.* 410). The conditionals here, 'perhaps' and 'if', refuse any definite connection between V.'s incarnations, even in Stencil's obsessively ordering mind, but hold out the possibility of an order and logic to her appearances that is irresistibly 'ominous'.

If V. were simply the female figure recurring in Stencil's stories, her identity and influence might be comparatively easy for critics to pin down: similar to the Trystero in *Lot 49*, the central question of who she might be would focus on whether she was real or the projection of Stencil's paranoid imaginings, and the novel would follow closely the questions of narrative truth and identification we explored in Chapter Two. In *V.*, though, she overflows this part of the text, appearing not just in the historical chapters but also as a figure associated with other people, places and ideas in both the novel's past and 1950s present-day: the V-Note, a jazz bar that is the scene of a number of key episodes; the Virgin Mary, who is evoked incessantly throughout the novel, often in the most apparently inappropriate places; Vheissu, a strange hidden realm that holds out either hope for future salvation or utter despair and a descent into madness; Veronica the sewer rat, 'a kind of voluptuous Magdalen' whom the deranged Father Fairing, who has escaped from Malta to found a rodent congregation in the New York sewer system, believes will 'head the list' for 'canonization' as 'the only member of his flock ... to have a soul worth saving' (*V.* 121); as well as Venus,

Venezuela, Queen Victoria, the Vatican, and a whole host of other figures and signs whose relation to the letter 'V' grants them a suggestive power and resonance within the text.

Although she acts as the figure towards which the narrative of *V.* is driven, the multiplication of personalities, associations and significances places V. just out of reach, as a continually shifting figure marking the disappearing point lying at the horizon of the narrative gaze. Towards the end of the novel we are told: Stencil 'had left pieces of himself – and V. – all over the western world. V. by this time was a remarkably scattered concept' (*V.* 389). In order to understand just how scattered, and how resonant, a concept V. becomes in the novel, it is useful to explore the way *V.*'s extensive use of intertexts produces further suggestions of meaning and significance for both Stencil and the reader.

'... a remarkably scattered concept': a novel of intertexts

After the manner adopted by the early reviews cited in the introduction to this chapter, the most frequent line of analysis taken by critics has been to continue to explore the novel's range of adopted voices, vastly expanding the number of possible intertexts for *V.*; and the detection, tracing and analysis of allusions and references in the novel is certainly the most significant strand of its critical reception. In fact, from the earliest journalistic reviews to the most recent critical-theoretical analyses, the assertion of *V.*'s open and enigmatic character has gone hand in hand with the discovery of further echoes, allusions and suggestive references. To work through the whole range of these is beyond the scope of this chapter, but focusing closely on one important series of discussions will help locate some key ideas and themes developed in the novel.

A series of influential readings of *V.* take their point of departure as the identification of Pynchon's parodic response to the literary, artistic and political ideas associated with modernism in many of the book's historical episodes, and explore that as a crucial factor in the development of its narrative. Many of these also identify and explore *V.* as, in some sense, a postmodernist novel, which is an important category for this chapter's analysis. This approach is perhaps most succinctly summed up in Maarten Van Delden's reading of the novel as not only a 'dark parody [of] the modernist vision of higher forms of coherence' but a rejection of the values associated with the idea of

modernism presented by the dominant mode of critical reading that
Pynchon would most likely have encountered as a student of English
at Cornell University in the late 1950s, which Van Delden identifies
as New Criticism: 'to the extent that Pynchon aims his satire of the
rage for order at the modernist conception of myth, his work reflects
an understanding of modernism that has been strongly influenced
by the New Critics', and in particular their insistence on the 'theory
of the autonomy of art'.[8] He asserts that the extreme complexity of
the novel's narrative structures and intertexts explicitly refuses to
'culminate in the discovery of a higher unity' of the sort often associated with New Critical modernism's 'rage for order', and argues that
the 'proliferation of associations makes it impossible to formulate
a clear set of alternatives within which the meaning of V. may be
contained'.[9] In other words, for Van Delden, there is no solution to
the novel's questions, no restorative gesture of coherence or closure,
and the narrative thus 'points the reader towards something else
altogether: the arbitrary playfulness of the novelist'.[10] This reading
helpfully locates *V.* in literary history: it identifies the novel not as an
outright rejection of modernist aesthetics, but as a disruption of the
image of modernism's conceptions of 'autonomous art' and the 'rage
for order' propagated by the New Criticism that was prevalent in
North American academia during the period in which Pynchon was
studying. It sees *V.* as a continuation of modernism's radical formal
experimentation that critiques, disrupts and refuses the political
investments of much modernist art, and identifies it in terms of a
'postmodernism' that is 'neither entirely continuous nor fully discon-
tinuous with modernism'.[11] The sort of postmodernism Van Delden
is invoking with his notion of the 'arbitrary playfulness of the novelist' is the playful pastiche identified by Fredric Jameson: rather than
modern parody, which gains its critical edge by sending up things
'insofar as they ostentatiously deviate from a norm which then reas-
serts itself', pastiche assumes no such order, and the postmodern
'disappearance of the individual subject' as the basis for judging
norms and standards leads to a proliferation of imitative voices and
possibilities 'without any of parody's ulterior motives, amputated of
satiric impulse ... and of any conviction that alongside the abnormal
tongue you have momentarily borrowed, some healthy linguistic
normality still exists'.[12] For Jameson, such pastiche lacks any critical
edge, and is potentially reactionary as well as 'devoid of laughter',
which is certainly not Van Delden's claim (or, in terms of humour,

true of any of Pynchon's works, all of which contain passages that are *extremely* funny), but this notion of postmodern pastiche does capture quite clearly the playfulness and refusal of closure that he identifies in the novel. And, perhaps most importantly, it prepares the formal ground for the development of an understanding of the critical and political investments of the intertextuality of *V.* in particular and Pynchon's work more generally, as well as setting the scene for the challenges to modern identity in the novel which will be the subject of the final section of this chapter.

This sense of a sceptical and interrogative attitude towards its literary predecessors is developed further, and in a more immediately political direction, by John Dugdale's argument that

> *V.* speculatively restages key moments in *fin de siècle* or Modernist art, seeking to discover the reality behind the scenes and images it invested with mystique: the dancer and the 'terrible beauty' of violence in Yeats; the acrobats of Picasso and Rilke; the rose garden, the hyacinth girl and the journey on the underground in Eliot. Imagining actual instances of apocalyptic crisis, military destruction, rape or sacrifice in the appropriate period, it interrogates the use made of such phenomena in Modernist fictions.[13]

Beginning from a similar premise, but perhaps more politically pointed than Van Delden's view of *V.* as a rejection of a form of modernist writing, Dugdale presents the novel as a trenchant critique of the historical and political violence that lies beneath the 'mystique' of the modernist image. Dugdale's reading traces the allusions to familiar modernist tropes and explores the ways in which Pynchon deploys them to explore the cruelty at their base: by taking them as 'veils and disguise', *V.* 'strips them away to reveal the real entities they purport to represent'.[14] So, for example, the figure of the dancer, which Dugdale identifies as 'the Modernist image par excellence', is embodied in Chapter Fourteen, 'V. in Love', as an actual young girl, Mélanie l'Heuremaudit, a child-star whose sexuality is exploited by all who come into contact with her: her father, her choreographers and the mysterious woman V. who turns her into a fetish object. Her fate, being impaled during the riotous opening night of a performance that very closely echoes the premiere of Stravinsky's *Rite of Spring* (*Le Sacre du printemps*), works, according to Dugdale, as 'the simulation of Mélanie's death leading to her actual death; and it shows artistic simulation of apocalypse occurring the summer before the cataclysm of 1914. As it holds the mock-*Sacré* responsible for Mélanie's fate, so it holds the art it epitomises responsible for collusion in the cultural drive towards war.'[15] In other words, *V.* indicts modernism for its complicity with exploitation, violence and totalitarianism by ironically reproducing modernist images and ideas in a manner that makes explicit the 'reality behind the scenes' and the ever-present threat of the imminent world war. This is a powerful and persuasive reading of the use of intertextuality in the novel, and gets to grips very well with episodes such as that set in Paris and, perhaps even more disturbingly, the episode covering the siege party and genocide in southwest Africa.

Dugdale's reading draws out a political edge to the novel's parodies of modernism, presenting *V.* as postmodern not in Jameson's sense mentioned above, but much more in the manner of the mode of parodic critique presented by Linda Hutcheon's analysis of postmodern art:

> Contrary to the prevailing view of parody as a kind of ahistorical and apolitical pastiche, postmodern art ... uses parody and irony to engage the history of art and the memory of the viewer in a re-evaluation of aesthetic forms and contents through a reconsideration of their usually unacknowledged politics of representation. ... Parody can be used as a self-reflexive technique that points to art as art, but also to art as inescapably bound to its aesthetic and even social past. Its ironic reprise also offers an internalized sign of a certain self-consciousness about our culture's means of ideological legitimation.[16]

Read in this light, *V.*'s parodies of modernist art are immediately political: they open up familiar historical ideas, forms of art and cultural norms to self-reflexive critique as familiar intertexts and allusions are presented in new and sometimes intensely disturbing lights. In this sense, Dugdale's and Hutcheon's analyses of parody present *V.*'s postmodernism as a critique of modern politics and art.

Important and insightful as Dugdale's reading is, however, there is a sense in which his approach overstates its case by focusing so exclusively on modernism, which, although clearly significant in the novel, is just one of the sets of references and allusions opened up in *V.* It is not just modernism that Pynchon takes up as intertexts in the novel: critics have been quick to identify and explore the vast array of philosophical, scientific and cultural references and allusions ranging from Ludwig Wittgenstein's *Tractatus logico-philosophicus* to the mythological theories of J. G. Frazer and Robert Graves, from contemporary developments in robotics to the ability of a ship's radar to cook raw meat with microwaves, and from the classical beauty of Sandro Botticelli's *Birth of Venus* to experimental jazz and the drunken hilarity of Botticelli as a name-guessing game for the Crew's parties. References to so-called 'high art' and 'popular culture' are treated with equal seriousness (or, more often, with an equal lack of reverence) in the novel, and there is little sense at any stage of a simple opposition or hierarchy between the two. This refusal of discrimination opens *V.* up to reading from the perspective of another influential account of postmodernism: Andreas Huyssen's analysis of art and mass culture in *After the Great Divide: Modernism, Mass Culture, Postmodernism.* Here, Huyssen argues that 'modernism's running feud with mass society and mass culture', its elitism, or what Van Delden refers to as the New Critical assertion of the 'autonomy of art', has run its course and the 'pedestal of high art and high culture no longer occupies the privileged space it used to'.[17] Breaking down the 'great divide' between art and the masses, Huyssen argues that postmodernism has the capacity to resist both the de-politicisation of art that treats it as a separate sphere that transcends the ideological interests of historical contexts and also the 'anything goes' of commodification where the only value of a work is the price it can achieve. A work's eclecticism, intertextual play and irreducibility to pre-established sets of aesthetic criteria serve to disturb and disorientate the reader or viewer by refusing to play by established rules, surprising them into questioning the meanings and intentions of the allusions they spot: the point of such postmodernism, Huyssen claims, 'is not to eliminate the productive tension between the political and the aesthetic, between history and text, between engagement and the mission of art. The point is to heighten that tension, even to rediscover it and bring it back into focus in the arts as well as in criticism.'[18] It is this heightening of tension that becomes apparent when one takes as seriously the play of popular-cultural allusions and intertexts in the present-day chapters of *V.* as one does the more literary and high art aspects of the historical chapters. As with the analysis of the specific engagements with modernism, however, questions of how these more widely ranging allusions and references are deployed in *V.*, to what ends, and what the consequences of recognising them might be for an appreciation of the novel's meaning, suggest a range of possible readings of the text.

In his 'Introduction' to *Slow Learner* Pynchon himself mentions a whole series of non-high-art influences on his early work, which chiefly comprises a list of early and mid-twentieth-century British thriller writers such as John Buchan, E. Phillips Oppenheim, Helen MacInnes and Geoffrey Household, whose racy adventure stories explored the sorts of crime, intrigue and international espionage depicted in some of the historical chapters of *V.* He also refers to another key intertext for the novel: the travel guidebooks published from the nineteenth century onwards by Karl Baedeker. In the ironically self-denigrating tone of the 'Introduction' that we explored in the first chapter, Pynchon describes the origin of his story 'Under the Rose' (which, substantially reworked, became Chapter Three of *V.*), in terms of 'literary theft': 'Karl Baedeker, whose guide to Egypt for 1899 was the major "source" for the story. ... Loot the Baedeker I did, all the details of a time and place I had never been to, right down to the names of the diplomatic corps' (*SL* 17–18). Taken together with the thriller writers, Pynchon claims that the 'net effect was eventually to build up in my uncritical brain a peculiar shadowy vision of the history preceding the two world wars' (*SL* 18), which 'shadowy vision' provides the complex historical and political background to many of the events of *V.*

Recognising both high-modernist works and popular-cultural references, Tony Tanner offers an extensive (though, by his own admission, still far from exhaustive) list of the novel's literary intertexts:

> [W]e can find echoes, allusions to and parodies of many other genres and writers in it. Spy novels, adventure novels, historical and political novels, romantic and pornographic or perverted novels – all are invoked; and one can detect traces of Conrad, Lawrence Durrell, Evelyn Waugh, Melville, Henry Adams, Nathaniel West, Djuna Barnes, Faulkner, Dashiell Hammett and many others, not to mention works like *The Golden Bough* and *The White Goddess*. But it is not merely a clever exercise in collage.[19]

This last phrase of this passage is crucial: *V.* is not simply a 'collage' of these sources, nor was Pynchon uncritically indulging in the 'literary theft' of which he accuses himself in *Slow Learner*, and neither indeed do Dugdale's 'parody' nor Van Delden's 'satire' cited in the passages above sum up completely the stakes of the novel's intertextuality (though, as we have tried to show, the broader analyses presented in their readings are extremely suggestive). Allusion and intertextuality are not sub-textual structures that the narrative seeks to hide, but are rather explicitly presented on the surface of the text. The references to Baedeker are, for example, frequent and explicit, producing a notion of the 'Baedeker land' of tourists and vagrants that organises the writing of the earlier historical sections of the novel (Chapters Three and Seven in particular) to provide a lens through which the events can be viewed. If Pynchon really had set out to be the literary criminal that *Slow Learner* presents, he would be an absurdly inept one whose continual explicit admissions to the 'theft' in the novel make almost redundant any critic-detective's work in tracking him down. Not only the narrative voice but a significant number the characters themselves appear aware of their implication in a field of prior texts and contexts that shape both the reader's and their own experiences of the events of the plot. Intertextuality thus produces, organises and presents the novel's narrative: it is not a background to the plot, but is rather *is* the novel itself, its milieu, medium, style, and the source of its search for the central, titular enigmatic figure, V. herself. In fact, V.'s identification as the twentieth century's 'master cabal' and subsequent transformation into 'a remarkably scattered concept' is a direct function of her implication in the rapidly multiplying range of intertextual suggestions and allusions that make up the novel's plots and its identification of the twentieth century.

This self-consciously intertextual, parodic and playful narrative style, which readily adopts immediately recognisable generic traits and explicitly draws its material from high and popular culture alike, continually multiplies possibilities of meaning and interpretation to leave the plot's central question, 'who or what is V.?', finally open. This openness does not, however, make the question pointless or irrelevant. The continual refraction and refocusing of events in the narrative through lenses of rapidly transforming modes of literary style, whether of styles adopted from the avant gardes or the modernists in Stencil's 'forcible dislocations of personality' or the popular comic modes taken on in the present-day narratives that follow Profane's picaresque wanderings, explicitly evoke questions of referentiality, knowledge and truth. And it is to these questions and the problem of the human that we will turn in the next section.

'Humanity is something to destroy': V.'s postmodern transformations

One recurring theme in *V.* anticipates a series of central debates in postmodern theory with particular force: the transformation, or even destruction, of the idea of the human. This idea crops up throughout the novel in a wide range of contexts and forms, each of which presents a challenge to those Enlightenment and modern humanist philosophies that identify the subject's individual consciousness as foundational for knowledge, morality and experience. While the most explicit expression of this might occur during the 'Fashoda Incident' chapter when, in response to the naïve question 'what is humanity?, one of the more sinister of the secret agents responds with 'You ask the obvious, ha, ha. Humanity is something to destroy' (*V.* 81), images of this destruction are so ubiquitous in the novel that it is not too much of a stretch to claim that *V.* is the imagining and narrating of the death, or at least transformation, of the human as it is played out during the twentieth century.

Similar challenges stand at the core of much postmodern theory, presenting the demise of the humanist subject as a crucial symptom of contemporary changes in technology, politics, knowledge and power. For Jameson, postmodernism marks 'the "death" of the subject itself – the end of the bourgeois monad or ego or individual'.[20] Similarly, in his *The Postmodern Condition*, Jean-François Lyotard describes the technological developments of postmodern capitalism as 'a vanguard machine dragging humanity after it, dehumanising it in order to rehumanise it at a different level of normative capacity'.[21] In each case, the humanist subject that acted as the guarantor of truth and experience, a subject such as the 'thinking being' produced in Descartes' philosophy that becomes the source of morality and knowledge as it initiates and judges actions undertaken in the world, is stripped of its foundational status and changed into something produced and continually transformed by a complex array of external forces – for Jameson and Lyotard, forces such as contemporary capitalism, technological and scientific development, modern multi-channel media, globalisation, and so on.

As we shall try to show in this section, a key aspect of the challenge to humanism in *V.* emerges from the novel's explorations of gender and desire. *V.* narrates the problematic pursuit of the feminine, in such guises as the desired but seemingly interchangeable waitresses of the opening bar scene; the more complexly drawn characters such as Paola and Fina, who flirt with Profane; and especially the continually transforming, impossible to identify or capture figure of V. herself, who is the object of Stencil's interminable quest. Focalised almost entirely from a male perspective, women in *V.* are objects of surveillance, desire, suspicion and fear. In an approach to this disruption of humanist subjectivity in postmodernism that usefully opens up such questions about gender, Alice Jardine argues that in postmodern theory there is a 'slippage in male philosophical discourse from the *feminine* (anonymity, passivity, and so on) to women (as metaphorically opposed to men) and, finally, to "we" ("we Westerners")': the 'delegitimation' of the subject, 'experienced as crisis, is the loss of the paternal fiction. ... The [postmodern] discussion of the loss of authority inevitably comes around to women, who return, empirically, as among those principally to blame for the loss.'[22] For the mode of feminist philosophy on which Jardine is drawing here, the humanist subject is invariably conceived as masculine, active, and the feminine 'other' is reduced to being a passive object of his knowledge and desire: this is the ontological structure of modern gendered identity. And, in ways which hopefully will become apparent, this reduction and the problems for the 'paternal fiction' it generates are crucial to *V.* The aim of this section of the chapter is to explore the ways in which *V.* stages, first, the disintegration of the humanist subject and, second, the crises of identity, gender and knowledge that emerge from this process, and, finally, to examine the ways in which these challenges are present at the conclusion of the novel's narrative.

The potential for the transformation of the human is apparent from the opening pages of the novel, and is explicitly tied to the titular figure. The first invocation of V. in the novel occurs in quite different circumstances from the incarnations discussed in the previous sections of this chapter, but its importance for an understanding of the ways in which *V.* explores identity should not be underestimated. In a passage depicting Profane's arrival on East Main Street in Norfolk, Virginia on Christmas Eve 1955 with which the narrative opens, V. appears as a perspectival sign for the disappearance into distance of another of the novel's key tropes, the 'Street':

Profane had grown a little leery of streets, especially streets like this. They had in fact all fused into a single abstracted Street, which come the full moon he would have nightmares about. ... Dog into wolf, light into twilight, emptiness into waiting presence, here were your underage Marine barfing in the street, barmaid with a ship's propeller tattooed on each buttock, one potential berserk studying the best technique for jumping through a plate glass window (when to scream Geronimo? before or after the glass breaks?), a drunken deck ape crying back in the alley because the last time the SPs caught him they put him in a strait jacket ... overhead, turning everybody's face green and ugly, shone mercury-vapor lamps, receding in an asymmetric V to the east where it's dark and there are no more bars. (*V.* 10)

The recurring motif of the 'Street' becomes the locus for the novel's action, and is later figured explicitly as 'The street of the 20th Century, at whose far end or turning – we hope – is some sense of home or safety. ... a street we must walk. It is the acid test. ... this is 20th Century nightmare' (*V.* 323–4). In both passages, the Street is presented as the site of a 'nightmare' journey along which the narrative must travel towards a 'far end', either to 'home or safety' or a place where 'it's dark and there are no more bars'. And this journey is lit by the forbidding mercury-vapour lamps forming an 'asymmetric V' that shed a malign light over proceedings, 'turning everybody's face green and ugly'. This 'V' figures the experience of the process of narrative unfolding itself: a perspectival narrowing towards a horizonal point at which some revelation or resolution may perhaps be possible draws the reader on with a promise that might or might not eventually be fulfilled. And the green and ugly tinge it spreads is just the first suggestion of its capacity for dehumanising transformation.

Besides the introduction of the idea of the 'Street' and the first suggestion of a malign V. figure colouring experience, there is a good deal more going on in this passage that is important for an understanding of the novel's production of identity. A gallery of characters is presented, each isolated in their own secluded misery or madness, at once comic and disturbing, and caught up in the opening figures of transformation ('Dog into wolf, light into twilight, emptiness into waiting presence') as they weep, barf, bare their buttocks or plan a leap through a window. Each in its own way is isolated, on the edge, another misfit in the novel's world of misfits. Another 'street' passage that occurs towards the end of the opening chapter echoes and develops these ideas of nightmare, transformation and identity further, concluding a comic account of a dream where Profane discovers and removes a screw from his belly button only to find that, when he stands up, 'his ass falls off':

> To Profane, alone in the street, it would always seem maybe he was looking for something too to make the fact of his own disassembly plausible as that of any machine. It was always at this point that the fear started: here it would turn into a nightmare. Because now, if he kept going down that street, not only his ass but also his arms, legs, sponge brain and clock of a heart must be left behind to litter the pavement. ... This was all there was to dream; all there ever was: the Street. (*V.* 40)

That this passage immediately follows the broad humour of the belly-button joke exemplifies *V.*'s continual and radical shifts of tone: the joke loses its humour as its implications dawn on Profane, and the journey along the Street is refigured as a movement of disassembly and destruction. His body, in its disintegration, is transformed from living flesh to mechanism and object: the belly-button screw, as well as the 'sponge brain and clock of a heart' become inanimate objects as Profane's life ebbs away. Indeed, J. Kerry Grant argues that 'No other word of comparable significance appears as often in *V.* as does the term "inanimate"', citing 'over sixty occurrences in the novel' and identifying it as lying at the heart of 'one of the main thematic threads that runs throughout'.[23] The fear, the nightmare, in this passage is the reduction of Profane's living body to inanimate and disconnected matter: the loss of his human self. This threat is reiterated during Profane's work as a night-watchman for Anthroresearch Associates (a subsidiary of Pynchon's commonly evoked fictional company Yoyodyne) looking after two 'synthetic human' robots used to test the effects of accidents and violence, one of whom appears to speak to him and tells him that they are 'Nearly what you are', almost human, and in fact are 'what you and everybody will be someday' (*V.* 284–6), the next inevitable stage in human-machine evolution, the *telos* of twentieth-century innovation and change. Whether these words are simply Profane's projection of identity onto the mannequins or whether they actually speak to him is left undetermined, but the uncanniness of this episode is echoed throughout the novel in recurrent instances of bodily change and the disintegration of humanist identity.

The process of human transformation is not therefore simply a threat in Profane's imagination, but is a trope that recurs and is refigured continually in a range of modes and moods. Examples abound, too many to cite here, but key instances include: the cyborg human-machine innovations of characters such as Fergus from the Whole Sick Crew who turns himself into 'an extension of the TV set' by placing electrodes in his arm to act as a 'sleep switch' (*V.* 56), which echoes the spy Bongo-Shaftsbury's attempt to terrify the young Victoria Wren with a switch in his arm supposedly connected to his brain that he claims alters the way he acts when flicked (*V.* 80–1); the various surgical transformations including the reconstruction of Evan Godolphin's face, which takes place after his plane is shot up in the war and he is turned into 'the worst possible travesty of a human face lolling atop an animate corpse' (*V.* 98–9), in which his nose cheek and chin are replaced with artificial pieces made of ivory, silver and celluloid respectively, which in turn finds its own echo in the gruesomely detailed chapter-long account of Esther getting a nose job in the novel's 1950s present that depicts the operation as at once grotesquely violent and suggestively erotic (*V.* 95–110); the gradual transformation of V. from the innocent and wholesome young Victoria in the earlier historical episodes, via Vera Meroving and her artificial eye with its 'delicately-wrought wheels, springs, ratchets of a watch, wound by a gold key' that cause its 'white' to 'show up when in the socket as a half-lit sea green' (*V.* 237) that is eerily reminiscent of the colour cast by the opening V of the streetlights, to the disassembly of V.'s incarnation as the 'Bad Priest' during the siege of Malta where false hair, foot, navel, teeth and glass eye are removed from the stripped and dying body by the local children (*V.* 341–4); and finally to Stencil's imagined contemporary incarnation of V. as entirely machine:

> Skin radiant with the bloom of some new plastic; both eyes glass but now containing photoelectric cells; connected by silver electrodes to optic nerves of purest copper wire and leading to a brain exquisitely wrought as a diode matrix could ever be. Solenoid relays would be her ganglia, servo-actuators move her flawless nylon limbs, hydraulic fluid be sent by a platinum heart-pump through butyrate veins and arteries ... even a complex system of pressure transducers located in a marvellous vagina of polyethylene (*V.* 411)

In Stencil's overheated imagination, the present-day V. has become completely artificial; but has, crucially, lost none of her allure, and remains for him a feminine object of desire.

Desire is central to *V.*, and is continually focalised through the
male characters' pursuits of the females around them. Catharine R.
Stimpson identifies a tendency in Pynchon's earlier work towards
the stereotypical presentation of women as objects of a masculine
gaze and male desire that she sees as emerging from his 'sexual
conservatism, which pervades the early fiction' and finds its most
extended series of examples in *V.*: although the other women in *V.*
'lack the elusiveness of V. that arises from Stencil's faulty perceptions
... [they all] are judged according to the degree they resemble V. The
more like her they are, the worse they are'.[24] This is a persuasive
claim, and certainly examples of such a reduction of women abound
in *V.*, often quite blatantly in characters such as the interchangeable
barmaids all named Beatrice, descriptions of the girls surrounding
the Crew as 'silent. They were camp followers of a sort and expend-
able. Or at least could be replaced' (*V.* 57), or Profane's unchallenged
belief that 'woman is only half of something there are usually two
sides to' (*V.* 18). However, it is perhaps worth noting that this sexism
is almost certainly far from inadvertent as the numerous presentations of gendered relations in the novel are, generally speaking,
ironic and knowing. This is not, of course, to deny Stimpson's claim
of conservatism, but it is possible to suggest that one might read the
overt objectification of women in such passages as interrogative
of the sexual values and stereotypes of the period in which it was
written. In fact, Jardine's characterisation of V. as a fetishistic deconstruction of the 'paternal fiction' identifies this reduction of the
women in the novel with the reader's desire as she or he is caught up
in the unfolding narrative:

> Slowly the reader begins to realise that V. herself is nothing more than
> a 'fetish-construction' – an 'inanimate object of desire' 'beyond' the
> merely human. She is what man will always search for, without ever
> knowing why. ... For V., as object, is never to be found – not by histori-
> cal man, twentieth-century man, or the reader. Stencil disappears into
> the next to last chapter of V.; Profane into the Maltese night; the reader
> into the circular interpretative machine of his or her own invention.[25]

For Jardine, *V.* confronts the reader with their own interpretative
inadequacy by using the figure of V. as a means to make explicit the
power and gender relations in the modern humanist discourses that
criticism (and in particular the New Critical and modernist modes
of reading identified by Van Delden and Dugdale in the last section

of this chapter) has tended to deploy: the novel's parodies of high modernist and contemporary popular culture, fragmented voices and changes of tone present the human as a category in crisis as the 'paternal fictions' of modernity begin to collapse in on themselves.

There is, however, a final reference back to, and parodic echo of, modern narratives of identity at the novel's conclusion. Profane, having been deserted by both Stencil and Paola who he arrived in Malta with, runs into an entirely new character, Brenda Wigglesworth, who is a student and, like him, a drifter. She recites one of her poems to him, which includes the line 'I am the twentieth century' but quickly and emphatically dismisses it as 'a phony college-girl poem. Things I've read for courses', or in other words a pastiche of the sort that *V.* itself might be, and discovers in return from Profane that in all his travels he hasn't 'learned a goddam thing' (*V.* 454). Together, as Jardine notices but does not explore, they step out into the Maltese night:

> Later, out in the street, near the sea steps she inexplicably took his hand and began to run. ... Hand in hand with Brenda whom he'd met yesterday, Profane ran down the street. Presently, sudden and in silence, all illumination in Valetta, houselight and streetlight, was extinguished. Profane and Brenda continued to run through the abruptly absolute night, momentum alone carrying them toward the edge of Malta, and the Mediterranean beyond. (*V.* 455)

This passage, Profane's exit from the novel, echoes the ending of a key modern text that forms one of the central pillars of modern humanist literature, John Milton's *Paradise Lost*:

> In either hand the hastening angel caught
> Our lingering parents, and to the eastern gate
> Led them direct, and down the cliff as fast
> To the subjected plain; then disappeared.
> ....
> Some natural tears they dropped, but wiped them soon;
> The world was all before them, where to choose
> Their place of rest, and providence their guide:
> They hand in hand with wandering steps and slow,
> Through Eden took their solitary way.[26]

Having eaten from the Tree of Knowledge and been expelled from Eden, together, hand in hand, Adam and Eve journey out to the 'subjected plain' of the temporal world. Profane and Brenda, having

learned nothing from their travels, move beyond the V of streetlights, and away from the street itself to disappear into the night,
leaving the suggestion of the possibility that they might in some way
represent the new possibilities for existence that follow on from the
novel's relentless dislocation of twentieth-century humanity.

Notes

1 Anon. 'A Myth of Alligators', *Time*, 15 March 1963. George Plimpton, 'The
   Whole Sick Crew: *V.* by Thomas Pynchon', *The New York Times*, 21 April
   1963.
2 In an early discussion of Pynchon (first published in 1974) that structures its reading into chapter-length studies of Profane's and Stencil's
   plots framed in terms derived from the idea of entropy, Joseph Slade is
   one of the first critics to make the connection between *V.* and 'Entropy',
   and also presents one of the most detailed and fascinating introductions
   to the novel. See Slade, *Thomas Pynchon*, New York: Peter Lang, 1990,
   esp. 31–106.
3 A particularly insightful comparison between Stencil/Profane and
   Oedipa is produced in a discussion of the epistemology of Pynchon's
   work in Peter L. Cooper, *Signs and Symptoms: Thomas Pynchon and the
   Contemporary World*, Berkeley: University of California Press, 1983,
   131–52.
4 Walter Benjamin, 'On the Concept of History', in *Selected Writings*:
   Volume 4, *1938–1940*, ed. Howard Eiland and Michael W. Jennings,
   Cambridge, MA: Harvard University Press, 2003, 392.
5 Benjamin, 'On the Concept of History', 392.
6 David Cowart, *Thomas Pynchon: The Art of Allusion*, Carbondale:
   Southern Illinois University Press, 1980, 66–7. This sort of exploration
   of the meaning of rewriting in *V.* forms the core of an outstanding essay
   on the Southwest Africa chapter (Chapter Nine: Mondaugen's Story)
   that explores the changes between early manuscript and final version
   to draw out the politics of race, colonialism and sexuality in the novel
   in an extremely insightful manner: Luc Herman and John M. Krafft,
   'From the Ground Up: The Evolution of the South-West Africa Chapter in
   Pynchon's *V.*', *Contemporary Literature* 47.2 (Summer, 2006): 261–88.
7 Tanner, *Thomas Pynchon*, 45.
8 Maarten Van Delden, 'Modernism, the New Criticism and Thomas
   Pynchon's *V.*' *NOVEL: A Forum for Fiction* 23.2 (Winter, 1990): 117–36
   (120–1).
9 Van Delden, 'Modernism', 122.
10 Van Delden, 'Modernism', 122. In this sense, Van Delden's approach

to *V.* directly rejects the most fundamental premises of another fairly common sort of approach to the novel: one that resolutely attempts to decipher and fix an identity for the mysterious *V.* and thereby achieve narrative closure. What is perhaps the most explicitly determined example of this type of reading can be found in Kenneth Kupsch's 'Finding *V.*', *Twentieth Century Literature* 44.4 (Winter, 1998): 428–46.

11 Van Delden, 'Modernism', 134.
12 Fredric Jameson, Postmodernism, or, The Cultural Logic of Late Capitalism, London: Verso, 1991, 16–17.
13 Dugdale, *Thomas Pynchon*, 105.
14 Dugdale, *Thomas Pynchon*, 106.
15 Dugdale, *Thomas Pynchon*, 97.
16 Linda Hutcheon, *The Politics of Postmodernism*, 2nd edition, London: Routledge, 2002, 96–7.
17 Andreas Huyssen, *After the Great Divide: Modernism, Mass Culture, Postmodernism*, Basingstoke: Macmillan, 1986, 218–19.
18 Huyssen, *After the Great Divide*, 221.
19 Tanner, *Thomas Pynchon*, 40.
20 Jameson, *Postmodernism*, 11.
21 Jean-François Lyotard, *The Postmodern Condition: A Report on Knowledge*, trans. Georges Van Den Abeele, Manchester: Manchester University Press, 1984, 63.
22 Alice Jardine, *Gynesis: Configurations of Woman and Modernity*, Ithaca: Cornell University Press, 1985, 66–7.
23 J. Kerry Grant, *A Companion to V.*, Athens and London: The University of Georgia Press, 2001, 10.
24 Catherine R. Stimpson, 'Pre-Apocalyptic Atavism: Thomas Pynchon's Early Fiction', in George Levine and David Leverenz, eds, *Mindful Pleasures: Essays on Thomas Pynchon*, Boston: Little, Brown, 1976, 31–47 (38–9).
25 Jardine, *Gynesis*, 250, 252.
26 John Milton, *Paradise Lost*, ed. Alastair Fowler, 2nd edition, London: Longman, 2007. Book 12, lines 637–40; 645–9.

4

'A progressive *knotting into*': power, presentation and history in *Gravity's Rainbow*

A 'new form of fiction'? *Gravity's Rainbow* and the problems of reading

Published in 1973, *Gravity's Rainbow* has frequently been described by critics as Pynchon's most complex, challenging and experimental novel. Due at least in part to the byzantine nature of its plotting, and the demanding variety of its formal and stylistic modes of presentation, it has provoked wildly differing reactions from readers, ranging from adulation to disgust. On the one hand, it has been hailed as his masterpiece, and indeed *the* masterpiece of twentieth-century American literature by critics such as Tony Tanner, who declares that 'Pynchon has created a book that is both one of the great historical novels of our time and arguably the most important literary text since *Ulysses*.'[1] And yet, on the other, for a reader such as Norman Mailer it has proved impossible: asked in a 1980 interview by Michael Lennon how he rated Pynchon as a novelist, Mailer declared that he was either 'a genius or vastly overrated. I've never been able to get through the bananas in *Gravity's Rainbow*', a comment which, considering the banana episode happens in the first dozen pages of a novel of over seven hundred, suggests a less than rapt engagement with the text.[2] These entirely opposite responses from two serious and respected literary figures are indicative of the range and polarisation of reactions the novel generates. In fact, it is probably safe to say that *Gravity's Rainbow* has produced more polarised responses of love or detestation, and left readers with less middle ground, than any of Pynchon's preceding works: its complexity, mixture of rough humour and outright horror, explicit depictions of perverse sexuality, and often disorientating narrative style make it a novel that takes a serious effort to engage with at all, let alone complete, as it challenges the reader at every level.

On publication, *Gravity's Rainbow* quickly became the subject of intense critical argument: in particular, it proved especially controversial with the judging panels of the various literary awards for which it was nominated, provoking widely varying responses from three different bodies. In 1974 it was co-winner of the US National Book Award and was elected but then rejected for the Pulitzer Prize, and in 1975 Pynchon was offered the Howells Medal of the American Academy of Arts for the novel but turned it down. The Pulitzer non-award became a scandal: the fiction panel's judges recommended *Gravity's Rainbow*, but the overall board for the prize declared the book 'obscene' and 'unreadable', and refused to allow it to go forward, which meant in the end that no award was made for that year. Not even the prizes that were awarded went without incident: notoriously reclusive, Pynchon sent a comedian named Professor Irwin Corey to pick up the National Book Award in his place, who delivered a mock acceptance speech that sent up both the idea of awards and the more general culture of literary celebrity; and declined to accept the Howells Medal at all in a letter containing the following comments:

> The Howells Medal is a great honour, and, being gold, probably a good hedge against inflation too. But I don't want it. Please don't impose on me something I don't want. It makes the Academy look arbitrary and me look rude. ... I know I should behave with more class, but there appears to be only one way to say no, and that's no.[3]

These incidents, on the one hand, contribute to the 'elusive Pynchon' mythology that we discussed in the introduction and, on the other, also begin to indicate the extremely challenging and controversial nature of a novel which continues to confuse, disturb and frustrate readers and critics.

That Mailer and the Pulitzer committee can reject *Gravity's Rainbow* so decisively, and that the former is prepared to admit publically to not being able to read it at all, might of course be taken to say a good deal about their respective failings, but is also more widely significant as it begins to indicate the sheer complexity of the work itself. Michael Wood sums up this difficulty most succinctly in an early review of the novel for the *New York Review of Books*: '*Gravity's Rainbow* is literally indescribable, a tortured cadenza of lurid imaginings and total recall that goes on longer than you can quite believe. ... It is crowded, technical, serious, self-indulgent, frivolous and very heavy going. It doesn't let up.'[4] Even in comparison to the sophisticated and sometimes difficult Pynchon narratives we have discussed so far, *Gravity's Rainbow* is a text that continually undermines the expectations of a reader familiar with realist or modernist novels and takes narrative experimentalism to a completely new level, providing what Tanner calls 'an exemplary experience in modern reading. The reader does not move comfortably from some ideal "emptiness" of meaning to a satisfying fullness, but instead becomes involved in a process in which any perception can precipitate a new confusion, and an apparent clarification can turn into a prelude for further difficulties.'[5] In other words, rather than gradually unravelling a series of clues to reach clarity and closure, the novel piles complexity upon complexity to generate what the opening moments of the narrative refer to as 'not a disentanglement from, but a progressive *knotting into*' (*GR* 3) the confusion of the novel's world.

For many critics, *Gravity's Rainbow* marks a significant development from Pynchon's earlier work. In the epilogue to *Thomas Pynchon: Allusive Parables of Power*, an insightful text that we have cited a number of times in the preceding chapters, John Dugdale explains how the 'sheer scale and multifariousness' of the novel indicates a break with Pynchon's previous writings in a way that, although there are of course continuities, marks it out as something quite new:

> The major discontinuities are obvious, and are regularly remarked in criticism: the 'polyphonic' organisation, involving several principal centres of narration; the single historical setting (1944–5), rather than the multiple, variously-dated scenarios of *V.*; the emergence of a narrative voice – by turns comic, darkly prophetic, taunting or lyrical – which is frequently completely detached from character-perspective; the exploitation of the text's spaciousness to accommodate both a new expansiveness of style and an 'encyclopaedic' abundance and diversity of information.[6]

Like Wood, Dugdale produces lists of descriptions in his effort to get to grips with the novel's narrative strategies and styles: this 'encyclopaedic polyphony' guarantees that there is no possibility of a single 'correct' interpretation of the novel's themes or even comprehensive drawing of its multiple strands together, no sense of a coherent development of a central character or idea, and no chance of conclusion or closure at the novel's end. In a similar vein, Kathryn

Hume argues that many readers encounter *Gravity's Rainbow* as 'a new form of fiction': it 'seems bent on rendering problematic all the discourses we associate with traditional and modernist fiction and presents us with an unknowable reality by means of an almost unknowable text. ... Even our attempts at interpretation are discredited as a form of paranoia, as an open admission of the terror we feel when confronted by chaos.'[7] The novel provides, then, a serious, relentless and inescapable challenge to the familiar sense-making processes of reading and criticism, and, in Wood's phrase, it 'doesn't let up'.

However, *Gravity's Rainbow*'s complexity is not simply a case of arbitrary stylistic playfulness or just a result of authorial pretension. Rather, as Hume and Tanner suggest, it serves a purpose: to confront the reader forcefully with the terrible chaos of modern existence by refusing to allow the possibilities of plot and meaning to settle down into a clear, definable and determined structure that resolves the problems introduced during the narrative. By putting at stake the very possibility of reading and by presenting interpretation as a mode of paranoia, the novel confronts readers with a broader challenge about the possibility of making sense of the contemporary world. It is for these reasons that Brian McHale in a pair of important discussions collected in his influential book *Constructing Postmodernism* identifies *Gravity's Rainbow* as the paradigmatic postmodern novel, presenting it as a text that, perhaps more profoundly than any other, challenges and disturbs the 'discourse of critical interpretation' associated with modernist criticism, which still remains a default mode of approach to literary interpretation for the contemporary reader.[8] McHale argues that the complexity of *Gravity's Rainbow* stems first of all from its rapid shifts of narrative register that call for a continual reassessment by the reader of the state of the novel's referents, thereby raising questions about whether any particular passage is taking place in a reconstruction of our historical 'real world', the novel's made-up 'real world', a fantasy world associated in some way with one or both of these, a particular character's fantasy or psychosis, the fantasy of some other voice within the text that cannot be associated with one of its protagonists, or even just emerging from the reader's current misunderstanding of the 'reality' or 'fantasy' that will later be corrected by further information. This often causes the meanings of key episodes to be retrospectively transformed by subsequent revelations that generate what McHale calls a 'recurrent concretization–deconcretization structure'.[9] The complexity is enhanced further, he argues, by the frequency with which the narrative's focalisation follows characters' mystical or magical modes of extra-sensory perception (such as the ability of a character named Pirate Prentice to inhabit and re-create the fantasies of others, the witchcraft of Geli Tripping that may or may not motivate some of the plot's connections, or the journeys to the 'Other Side' undertaken by spiritual mediums such as Carroll Eventyr and Peter Sachsa), and this leads to the 'growing suspicion that any character in this novel can be analogically related to almost any other character – to raise for us the demoralizing prospect of free and all but unmanageable analogical patterning' taking place throughout and between each of the novel's narrative layers.[10] Moreover, McHale also highlights *Gravity's Rainbow*'s continual and disturbing use of what appears to be the direct interpolation of the reader by means of the recurrent use of the word 'you', arguing that the identity of the addressee of this word is often irreducibly ambiguous, and critical identifications of who 'you' might be have a tendency to 'prejudge the case' on the basis of the assumptions they bring to the text rather than allowing the multiplicity of possible readings of 'you' to remain open and accept the complexity of the reader's experience of the unfolding of meaning in the novel. McHale concludes that by 'confronting us with irreducibly ambiguous, or, better, multiguous features such as the second-person pronoun [as well as the 'recurrent concretization–deconcretization structure' and 'all but unmanageable analogical patterning'], Pynchon compels us to reflect upon our own critical practices, inviting us to become metareaders, readers of our own (and others') readings – and, more to the point, of our own inevitable *mis*readings.'[11] He concludes that *Gravity's Rainbow* is ultimately unreadable, if by 'reading' one means finding a comfortable and consistent understanding of the novel's meaning, focus, mode of address to the reader and form of engagement with history, politics and the 'real world'.[12] McHale's stress on the complexity of the narrative structure of the novel has been questioned and even rejected by a number of critics as leading 'only to the conclusion that we simply don't know what is happening in *Gravity's Rainbow*'.[13] However, this seems to over-state the problem: as a reader one might never be finally *certain* what is happening, but one's striving to know is a fundamentally important aspect of the aesthetic pleasure gained from reading the novel – as McHale describes it in a phrase borrowed from the Romantic poet John Keats, it is the pleasure of 'negative capability', of 'being in uncertainties, Mysteries, doubts'.[14] This is what is at stake in the process of a 'progressive *knotting into*' the novel's multiple worlds, which, as we shall try to show in the following sections of the chapter, is so crucial to gaining a sense of what might be at stake in its explorations of modern identity, society and politics.

How, then, will this chapter begin to approach this 'unreadable' novel? There are simply too many strands to *Gravity's Rainbow*'s plot, too many characters and events, and too much complexity to its narrative structure to provide a comprehensive reading here, and that will not be the aim of this chapter.[15] Rather, picking up from the critical and theoretical approaches set out in our discussions in the last three chapters, this chapter sets out to explore Pynchon's critique of the anti-foundationalism of contemporary culture and identity, and examine the uses *Gravity's Rainbow* makes of multiple modes and genres of representation, from slapstick and pornography to scientific discourse and astrological mysticism, to produce a narrative form that simultaneously constructs, embraces and challenges the disorientation of postmodern experience.

'Scattered all over the Zone': agency, identity and transformation

The majority of the events of *Gravity's Rainbow* take place in London during the closing days of the Second World War and mainland Europe in its immediate aftermath, and concern the efforts of a number of individuals and groups to gain control of the technology associated with the German V2 rocket. The V2, developed by Wernher von Braun and a team of scientists and engineers working on the island of Peenemünde in the Baltic Sea, was the first long-range ballistic missile to be used in combat when it was deployed towards the end of the war and fired at London from the autumn of 1944 up until just before the German surrender. The V2 provided the model for the post-war development of the rocket propulsion systems that drove technologies and people into orbit in both the American and the Russian space programmes, as well as being the basis for the intercontinental ballistic missiles which, when fitted with nuclear warheads, were the weapon-of-last-resort that maintained the 'balance of terror' between East and West by threatening devastation during the Cold War.[16]

In *Gravity's Rainbow*, the V2 rocket takes on for each character and group an almost (and occasionally literally) mystical significance: 'It comes as the Revealer. Showing that no society can protect, never could – they are as foolish as shields of paper ...' (*GR* 728). Shattering the ideas of natural order, physical cause and effect, and social organisation held by many of the characters at the novel's opening, the rocket forms the hinge between an apparently familiar and understandable pre-war old-world stability, and a future that, depending on the particular character's point of view, promises or threatens to be radically different and strange. One of *Gravity's Rainbow*'s chief recurring themes is the violent competition to control the post-war world, and each character finds her- or himself at the mercy of forces of change and transformation that they struggle to understand, negotiate with or resist. The novel concludes by invoking this dual possibility: a single rocket, the quasi-mystical '00000' is fired into orbit containing only a single sacrificial victim by one of the chief Nazi rocket scientists before the Allies' victory and, apparently simultaneously but clearly many years later in the 'present day' of the reader directly addressed as 'you', another or somehow and impossibly the same rocket descends to impact upon the roof of a movie theatre where 'old fans who have always been at the movies (haven't we?)' (*GR* 760) await the beginning of a film. As the ultimate object of both terror and desire lying at the heart of the novel, the opening and closing agent of the narrative's movement, the rocket takes on a vast range of meanings, associations and significations that tie together the multiple plots, characters and events without ever quite allowing them to cohere into a single explicable order.

The narrative opens with an account of an evacuation which will always have been too late by the time the rocket's 'screaming comes across the sky' in the novel's much-analysed opening line because, as the V2 travels faster than the speed of sound, it will already have hit its target before it is heard (one of the many apparent reversals of causality in the novel). It is, like the ending, 'all theatre' (*GR* 3), and in fact rapidly changes narrative level and register to transform into a dream of such an evacuation, as the novel then goes on to introduce the groups and individuals struggling to understand, locate and lay claim to the rocket technology.[17] The first of these to appear are the Allies' Special Operations Executive groups, which go by a series of acronyms including ACHTUNG (Allied Clearing House, Technical Units, Northern Germany) and PISCES (Psychological Intelligence Schemes for Expediting Surrender), a loose collection of scientists, statisticians, Pavlovian psychologists, mystics, spiritualists and others experimenting to find new and different ways to 'expedite surrender' – though 'whose surrender is not made clear' (*GR* 34). Based in London, the various members of these groups compete with each other and the security services to locate and salvage material from the rockets that hit the capital, and as the narrative develops the myriad jealousies, intrigues, affairs, plots and counter-plots of the central figures of these groups remain a continual point of focus, developing finally into an underground conflict between two parties: one named simply 'The Firm', a shady organisation appearing at the edges of the narrative that appears to be made up of the agents of the governments and international corporations taking control of the post-war world (which the novel usually evokes simply with the epithet 'They'), and another more loosely affiliated group made up of a number of the novel's protagonists that gives the final section of the story its title, 'The Counterforce'.

Key among the characters introduced in the opening pages is an American Lieutenant, Tyrone Slothrop, who comes as close as anyone in the novel to being the main protagonist. Slothrop is a figure cast from the same mould as *V.*'s Benny Profane: a chubby, comical anti-hero fascinated by women, drugs, comic-books and loud clothing, and apparently largely uninterested in the wider political struggles of his time, who drifts around the city between (possibly imagined) sexual encounters that he records on a map of London, which draws the attention of the various competing groups and agencies because each star on the map appears to anticipate the location of a rocket attack, and he is therefore assumed to have a unique psychic link to the V2. A possible explanation for this co-incidence of sex and rocketry is suggested later in the novel when Slothrop discovers a reference to his childhood that mentions psycho-sexual conditioning experiments undertaken on him by the plastics scientist and soon-to-be rocket developer Laszlo Jamf for the company IG Farben, to whom he suspects he may have been sold 'like a side of beef', which link sexual arousal with 'the smell of Imipolex G' (*GR* 286), a key component of the rocket.[18] In terms of his erections, and also his actions and character more generally, Slothrop becomes what James Earl identifies as the site at which the 'struggle between freedom and determinism is played out large in *Gravity's Rainbow*' as both The Firm and The Counterforce struggle to identify, influence and control his wanderings around war-torn Europe.[19] He is a figure through whose eyes we experience a good deal of the novel's world, and yet we are unable to be certain quite who he is or to what extent he is even in control of his own thoughts and desires.

Following the opening section in London, the novel's focus moves to mainland Europe in the direct aftermath of the war, first to the 'Casino Hermann Goering', which the Allies have taken over as a base of operations from the defeated Germans (though without yet having got around to changing the name). Here, Slothrop is re-programmed and encouraged to learn all he can about V2 technology before his identity is stripped from him as his identification papers and clothes are stolen, and he is sent out into the 'Zone' in search of the secret of the rocket. From this point onwards, he undergoes continual alterations of identity, taking on the names and personas of, for example, the English war correspondent Ian Scuffling, the comic-book-style characters Rocketman and Plasticman, the actor / porn star Max Schlepzig and the pig-god Plechazunga, until finally 'he has become one plucked albatross. Plucked, hell – *stripped*. Scattered all over the Zone. It's doubtful if he can ever be "found" again, in the conventional sense of "positively identified and detained"' (*GR* 712). Slothrop is gradually stripped of his identity and scattered, losing whatever coherence, agency and sense of self he might once have had as he fades out of the narrative's focus. Although never 'found' again in 'the conventional sense' in the novel, he is recalled very close to the end in a retrospective story, invoked perhaps by a traumatised soldier recovering from the fighting in contemporary (1970s) Vietnam:

> There is also the story about Tyrone Slothrop, who was sent into the Zone to be present at his own assembly – perhaps, heavily paranoid voices have whispered, *his time's assembly* – and there ought to be a punch line to it, but there isn't. The plan went wrong. He was broken down instead, and scattered. (*GR* 738)[20]

In its presentation of Slothrop's possible fate, this passage captures a number of key aspects of the novel that are important to discuss if a clear sense of its presentation of the post-war world is to emerge: the continual possibility of a meaning or relevance beyond the knowledge of narrator, characters and reader ('perhaps ... *his time's assembly*'); the possibility of a shadowy presence controlling the novel's events and characters (Slothrop was 'sent', but by whom?); the sense of paranoia as a crucial mode of experience and knowledge; the lack of closure and resolution that might have been made possible had there been a 'punch line'; and also the image of the 'Zone', which is the locus for much of the novel's action. We shall begin by exploring this last aspect first, before discussing paranoia in more detail in the next section.

The location named 'the Zone' denotes the part of mainland Europe in which the final battles of the Second World War were fought, and is a vast area of movements, interconnections and anarchic struggles for control of the technologies of the future that take place between the various survivors of the war. According to Joseph Slade, the Zone is 'an Oz where "categories have been blurred badly" ([*GR*] 303) and where ghosts of the victims of the war rub shoulders with the living ... a cloud chamber in which human particles are erratically visible ... an "interregnum" ([*GR*] 294), a moment in time when no government has control, a power vacuum.'[21] As quickly becomes apparent, there is no law in the Zone, and little order; rather, it is presented as an anarchic space of possibility and competition from which the new, post-war world will be born. Besides Slothrop, numerous other individuals and groups move in and out of focus as the narrative develops and they criss-cross the Zone searching for rocket technology, lost relatives, drugs, sexual fulfilment, revenge or just freedom from the past. Key among these is the Schwarzkommando, a group of rocket-troops from the German colony in southwest Africa, led by Oberst Enzian, who is trying to re-assemble the rocket, or, more precisely, to assemble the '00001' a replica of the mysterious '00000' rocket with the firing of which the novel ends. Enzian is being pursued by his half-brother, a Soviet intelligence officer named Vaslav Tchitcherine, who is in the Zone under orders to gather 'technical intelligence. But his real mission ... is private, obsessive': a personal 'need to annihilate the Schwarzkommando and his mythical half-brother' (*GR* 337–8). A third significant group that is actively searching the Zone is a company of United States Marines calling themselves 'Marvey's Mothers', 'the meanest-ass technical team in the whole fuckin' Zone' (*GR* 287), led by the rabidly racist Major Marvey, who seeks not just to commandeer rocket technology but also to eliminate the Schwarzkommando and get his revenge on Slothrop, who was present when Marvey was flung from the roof of a moving freight-train by Enzian. These three groups, active seekers after rocket technology and each other's downfall, are complemented by a range of other 'citizens of the Zone': the faded movie stars, drug runners, pleasure seekers, anarchists, abandoned children, witches, lemmings, light-bulbs that have achieved states of consciousness, and displaced persons of all varieties who make up the supporting cast of the novel, each with their own story and perspective that contribute to the reader's sense of a vast, chaotic and out-of-control world.

As well as being a post-war wasteland, the Zone also comes at times to symbolise a place of hope and transformation: the cradle of a range of possible new orders of existence. For a group of Argentinian anarchists who, in a darkly comical inversion of the escape of high-ranking Nazis to Latin America at the end of the war, have hijacked a German U-boat and sailed it back across the Atlantic to 'seek political asylum in Germany', the Zone promises the potential of 'openness' and a space for resistance to the 'System'. Squalidozzi, their leader, puts it in the following terms:

> In ordinary times ... the centre always wins. Its power grows with time, and that can't be reversed, not by ordinary means. Decentralising, back towards anarchism, needs extraordinary times ... this War – this incredible War – just for the moment has wiped out the proliferation of little states that's prevailed in Germany for a thousand years. Wiped it clean. *Opened it.* ... We want to leave it open. We want it to grow, to change. In the openness of the German Zone, our hope is limitless. ... So is our danger. (*GR* 264–5)

The suspension of law and national sovereignty in the Zone 'opens' the possibility of alternative modes of existence that resist central systematic organisation and hierarchy. The only market in the Zone is a black market, a pleasure boat cruises the Zone's rivers as the setting for a continual orgiastic party, a small community returns to its roots to celebrate the return of Plechazunga their Pig-Hero-God, the light-bulbs plan a revolution to break away from human tyranny: each micro-community is able to create its own rituals and relationships, to live for a moment by its own individual rules and beliefs, as it is set free from the centre's control. The threat of a return to control and national or international systems of order continually hovers over the proceedings, but the containment never, at least within the scope of the novel's narrative, manages to become total.

Even at the moment that this 'openness' is produced, however, its collapse is immediately evoked, and it is not just the containment by the 'System' that threatens: anarchy itself contains the seeds of its own ruin. Enzian grasps this most succinctly: 'Separations are proceeding. Each alternative Zone speeds away from all the others, in fated acceleration, red-shifting, fleeing the Center. Each day the mythical return Enzian dreamed of seems less possible' (*GR* 519). The disorder dreamed of by the anarchist Squalidozzi is less a liberation here than a collapse of meaning and sense: the Zone fractures (just as the narrative structure of the novel seems to do at this point) with each moment, group and possibility of an alternative future flying away from the others at astronomical ('red-shifting') speeds to produce a galaxy of separate and disconnected worlds; and any hope of communication, co-operation or consensus between them, any 'mythical return' to order or community, threatens to vanish. All that seems to remain is incessant and apparently random movement and separation from sense, self and other at an increasingly accelerating pace. Like Slothrop, meaning itself is 'plucked', 'stripped' and 'scattered all over the Zone'.

'The detritus of an order': preterition and paranoia

Just as it is to the characters existing in the Zone, the idea of movement – physical, metaphorical, symbolic and narratological – is central to the reader's experience of *Gravity's Rainbow*: nothing in the novel stays fixed as focalisation, voice, context and style shift registers from paragraph to paragraph, even at key points within sentences, and characters fade in and out of the action as the narrative constructs identities that are then transformed, decomposed and scattered, leaving little to grasp or comprehend. In a breathtaking passage (metaphorically, but also literally due to the length and complexity of the sentences that make it up) which describes the migration of people across the Zone, Pynchon places the image of relentless, unstoppable and chaotic movement at the centre of the novel's world:

The Nationalities are on the move. It is a great frontierless streaming out here. Volksdeutsch from across the Oder, moved out by the Poles and headed for the camp at Rostock, Poles fleeing the Lublin regime, others going back home, the eyes of both parties, when they do meet, hooded behind cheekbones, eyes much older than what's forced them into moving, Estonians, Letts, and Lithuanians trekking north again ... Sudetens and East Prussians shuttling between Berlin and the DP camps in Mecklenburg, Czechs and Slovaks, Croats and Serbs, Tosks and Ghegs, Macedonians, Magyars, Vlachs, Circassians, Spaniols, Bulgars stirred and streaming over the surface of the Imperial cauldron, colliding, shearing alongside for miles, sliding away, numb, indifferent to all momenta but the deepest, the instability too far below their itchy feet to give a shape to ... caravans of Gypsies, axles or lynchpins failing, horses dying, families leaving vehicles beside the roads for others to come live in a night, a day ... so the populations move, across the open meadow, limping, marching, shuffling, carried, hauling along the detritus of an order, a European and bourgeois order they don't yet know is destroyed forever. (*GR* 549–51)

Gravity's Rainbow depicts the mass migrations taking place at the end of the War as an index of the destruction of a whole order of existence, and this is what stirs up the novel's sense of a chaotic 'instability too far below ... to give a shape to': the reader is confronted with a list of names of nationalities, some still familiar but others now consigned to history as the maps of Europe are redrawn in the post-war world. These refugees making their way across the Zone are as yet unaware of this change in the structure of their world and cling to the 'detritus of an order' that has already passed away. Like the evacuees in the novel's opening dream-description, they are 'too late', and any broader significance to their journey (to many of the journeys in the novel) is refused as 'it's all theatre' (*GR* 3). The passage from which this pan-European 'great frontierless streaming' is taken, much too long to quote in its entirety, captures at once the sheer scope of the novel's historical and political ambition and its key point of focus: these dispossessed groups, the refugees, evacuees and newly stateless who have been impoverished and cast adrift by the war to be lost in the new world that is beginning to emerge are, like practically every character that the reader encounters throughout the novel, in the process of becoming, to employ a term that *Gravity's Rainbow* invests with a great deal of energy and power, the 'preterite' of the post-war order.

The idea of preterition that Pynchon draws upon in the novel derives from Calvinist theology, specifically as it was manifest in the New England Puritanism of the seventeenth century, and indicates the negative side of a binary opposition with election: for this version of Puritan theology, the elect are those who are predestined to be saved, God's chosen people, and the preterite or reprobates are the rest, those who, as the grammatical definition of the term 'preterition' suggests, are passed over, omitted and neglected; those who, in short, are consigned to a future of eternal damnation. An explicit reference to its Calvinist theological usage occurs in the invocation of one of Slothrop's early relatives, a seventeenth-century 'first American ancestor' named William Slothrop who published a tract entitled *On Preterition* in which he argued for the 'holiness' of the preterite, 'without whom there'd be no elect ... And it got worse. William felt that what Jesus was for the elect, Judas Iscariot was for the Preterite ... [so] we have to love Judas too. Right?' (*GR* 555).[22] In William's text, the possibility of election and salvation rests on its opposition to preterition, and for either side of this opposition to function its relation to the other is necessary: without the presence of preterition nobody could hope to be saved, and therefore the preterite were just as central to salvation and God's plan as the elect minority. This sacrilegious idea is immediately rejected by William's peers ('You can bet the Elect in Boston were pissed off about that' [*GR* 555]), his book is burned, and the claim fades into historical insignificance. However, recalled in the openness of the Zone, it appears to take on a new significance as the 'Slothropite heresy'. The response of the narrator (focalised at this point through Slothrop) is important:

> Could he have been the fork in the road America never took, the singular point she jumped the wrong way from? Suppose the Slothropite heresy had had the time to consolidate and prosper? Might there have been fewer crimes in the name of Jesus, and more mercy in the name of Judas Iscariot? It seems to Tyrone Slothrop there might be a route back ... maybe for a little while all the fences are down, one road as good as another, the whole space of the Zone cleared, depolarized ... without elect, without preterite, without even nationality to fuck it up ... (*GR* 556)

The idea here of an alternative history in which the dispossessed preterite people of America and the world might have been instilled with some form of value, Judas's mercy rather than Jesus's crimes becoming the guiding light of politics and progress, shines out in the anarchy and openness of the Zone as an opportunity for change in the present: a chance for the opposition of election and preterition to be broken open. However, like the other alternative orders 'opened' by the chaos of the Zone, this possibility remains continually just out of reach.

We have already noted the interest in the excluded at the centre of Pynchon's work, which ranges from the populations of rubbish dumps and targets of racial prejudice in *Slow Learner* to the dispossessed masses of *Lot 49* and the violently supressed colonial subjects of *V.* A number of critics have taken the possibility presented in the passage cited above of a world 'without elect, without preterite' as the position adopted by *Gravity's Rainbow*, and even Pynchon's writing as a whole, towards the idea of preterition. Michael Berubé, for example, asserts that 'the novel *is* beyond elect and preterite', at least in what he calls the 'cultural' field, in that unlike *The Crying of Lot 49* 'in which America's preterite seem to be unproblematically valorised' there is little sense of a redemptive possibility in the novel.[23] Although interesting and suggestive, this seems, however, only to be partially correct. Clearly, there is a difference between the presentations of preterition in the two novels, but Berubé's argument is too optimistic about the political possibilities of deconstructive reading presented in the novel: the key difference between it and the earlier novel is more to do with focalisation than valorisation. *Lot 49* differs from *Gravity's Rainbow* in that it presents the possibility that the reader might have the capacity to experience the elect/preterite opposition from both sides, from the side of the dispossessed who make use of the WASTE system as well as that of the bourgeois users of the US Postal Service, but leaves in question which might be the 'true' perspective taken by the narrative: as we attempted to show in Chapter Two, Oedipa sees both the official and the underground networks at work, and is confronted with the question of whether some form of transcendence of the apparent randomness of the surface reality is possible or not, which means that the central question with which we are left is which possibility of meaning, sacred or profane, the novel presents. The reader, in other words, is left uncertain of their position in relation to election. In a similar manner, in *V.* the question of the relation between order or connection and chaos or chance is presented as a coherent (albeit finally irresolvable) opposition between Stencil and Profane. In contrast, the perspective from which all of the action is presented in *Gravity's Rainbow* is irreducibly preterite. As Louis Mackey argues, 'In *Gravity's Rainbow* we see the divine decree of predestination from a new angle ... we are treated to the view from below. The Elect experience their election as the consciousness that all things, even tribulations, conspire together for their good. For the Preterite this converts to the strong suspicion, bordering on conviction, that "they're out to get me."'[24] It is not that the opposition between election and preterition is deconstructed, transcended or obliterated; rather, from the preterite perspective of all of the novel's voices, the position of the elect is present only as a paranoid projection of an undefinable and inaccessible 'They' who might or might not be determining the meaning of the events depicted in the novel as well as the identities, and even existence, of its preterite characters.[25]

The preterite focalisation of the narrative in *Gravity's Rainbow* gives rise to its major tone, one that almost all of the novel's critics have taken note of as a central category in their readings: paranoia. Relatively close to the beginning of the narrative, a link between preterition and paranoia is suggested: 'it's a Puritan reflex of seeking other orders behind the visible, also known as paranoia, filtering in' (*GR* 188). This idea that there might be 'other orders behind the visible' is continually gestured towards throughout the novel, holding out the possibility to characters and readers alike of hidden meanings that, should they ever finally surface, might explain and resolve the tensions in the text, and lead either to resolution, completion and closure, or perhaps to absolute despair. These 'other orders' are presented as plural: the binary structure of the oppositions between sacred and profane that we noted in *The Crying of Lot 49* and the choice of a Stencilised or a Profane history in *V.* is not what is at stake in the paranoid worlds of *Gravity's Rainbow*. Instead, one is faced with the sort of potentially infinite multiplication of identities, worlds, meanings and orders that McHale's argument about the novel's unreadability evokes. Leo Bersani traces out the implications of this paranoid sense with great acuity:

> The 'orders behind the visible' are not necessarily – are, perhaps, not essentially – orders *different from* the visible; rather, they are the visible *repeated as structure*. Paranoid thinking hesitates between the suspicion that the truth is wholly obscured by the visible, and the equally disturbing sense that truth may be a sinister, invisible design *in* the visible. ... Paranoia repeats phenomena as design. What you

thought was a chance juxtaposition may turn out to be a deliberate coupling.[26]

In other words, the problem presented by paranoia is that of verification: the 'truth' or 'reality' of experience (the 'visible'), its potential meaning and design, is continually a subject of suspicion and fear. Is a given experience real or imagined or some combination of the two that is incomprehensible? Is something that happens mere chance or has someone or something organised it? Is there a larger plan of which I am a part while remaining unaware of my place and purpose? Is there a 'They' that is out to get me? These questions confront each of the novel's characters at different times and in different manners, shaping their engagements with each other and the world. They also confront the reader as she or he tries to make sense of what *Gravity's Rainbow* is itself about so that, as Hume argues, the reader's 'attempts at interpretation' are frequently themselves 'discredited as a form of paranoia'.[27]

This challenge is central to understanding what is perhaps the most frequently cited idea of paranoia in the novel, where Pynchon defies it in the following terms: 'it is nothing less than the onset, the leading edge, of the discovery that *everything is connected*, everything in the Creation, a secondary illumination – not yet blindingly One, but at least connected, and perhaps a route In for those ... who are held at the edge' (*GR* 703). The paranoid desires and draws up connections, relates events to each other to generate meanings, but can never be certain of their ontological force. It is in this manner that the members of PISCES use all means at their disposal to track Slothrop, whose sexual conquest chart's convergence with the V2 strikes leads them to believe he has a special connection with the rocket that will somehow illuminate its ultimate truth. Similarly, Enzian, Tchitcherine and Marvey each believes the others have some secret connection to the rocket or power more generally, which each feels they must seek out, interpret and steal in order to gain the upper hand. In fact, practically every character who appears is subject to the paranoid suspicion that others have access to some meaning or truth that eludes them but that might, should it be revealed, serve as a 'route In' to the truth.

Slothrop, in particular, sees connections everywhere and between almost everyone and everything, while all the time remaining entirely conscious of his own paranoid compulsion to invent links that might not actually exist. In fact, midway through the text he actually embraces this idea: 'If there is something comforting – religious, if you want – about paranoia, there is still also anti-paranoia, where nothing is connected to anything, a condition not many of us can bear for long. ... Either They have put him here for a reason, or he's just here. He isn't sure he wouldn't, actually, rather have the *reason*' (*GR* 434). This is the same choice that is placed on any interpreter of the novel: one must either invest the text with connections, no matter how bizarre or absurd some appear, in the fashion of a paranoid, or refuse that mode and give up on finding any sense of connection and coherence in the novel at all – which would, of course, be to find its meaninglessness unbearable. There is no getting out of paranoia in *Gravity's Rainbow*: the novel's preterite characters and voices continually suspect plots are in operation behind their backs but cannot verify their existence, and as readers we share their vision of the novel's worlds and their paranoia about meaning so that we are compelled, as McHale argues in the passage we cited earlier, continually to 'reflect upon our own critical practices ... to become metareaders, readers of our own (and others') readings – and, more to the point, of our own inevitable *mis*readings.'

   The impossibility of escape from the paranoia of one's preterite position in relation to the novel's meaning that is staged by the narratives of *Gravity's Rainbow* refuses the possibility of a resolution or 'disentanglement from' the text's myriad suggestions, allusions and contradictions, and forces the reader to follow a path of 'progressive *knotting into*' its worlds. And, as we shall attempt to show in the final section of this chapter, this irreducibly multiple connectedness is crucial to the novel's exploration of contemporary identity, history and politics.

'The Rocket-state': crises of history and truth

Within the novel's fragmenting worlds and zones, between its transforming and disappearing character identities, through its preterite and varyingly paranoid narrative voices, *Gravity's Rainbow*'s depictions of identity, war, desire and the possibility of a radically different future challenge many of the systems of political and historical sense-making which readers, even those familiar with Pynchon's earlier works, might recognise. It is not simply a novel that plays with literary conventions, but one that is fundamentally interested in understanding the complexities and contradictions of the power structures of the post-war world. This is not to argue that it is a novel with a straightforward political programme or message for readers; rather, the complex narratives that make it up explore the possibilities of power, control and resistance in the contemporary world that are products of the development of rocket technology and the social, political and market structures that accompany it. Even though the majority of its actions take place in the closing days of World War Two, the thematic and critical focus of *Gravity's Rainbow*'s narrative frequently falls explicitly on the consequences of these actions for the future of that world, and the development of a new post-war order: the 'System' as defined by the various paranoid narrators' images of 'They' – the shady cartels of industrialists, scientists, military technicians, bureaucrats, secret-service agents and assorted other figures who flit across the landscape without ever quite coming into focus. This idea of the 'System' is continually evoked as a guiding thread connecting the plots of the various agencies involved in the search for rocket technology, and is on several occasions in the novel explicitly named the 'Rocket-cartel' or 'Rocket-state': '*A Rocket-cartel*. A structure cutting across every agency human and paper that ever touched it ... a State begins to take form in the stateless German night, a State that spans oceans and surface politics, sovereign as the International or the Church of Rome, and the Rocket at its soul ... this meta-cartel which has made itself known tonight, this Rocket-state' (*GR* 566). The aim of this section is to explore the depiction of this 'Rocket-state' and examine how its projection sets the political and historical stakes of the novel.

Recent criticism of *Gravity's Rainbow* has come to focus more and more on its proleptic suggestions of a future order, and thus its engagement with the politics of the Cold War and, in particular, the 1960s and 1970s America in which it was being written. From this perspective critics often assert that developing an understanding of Cold War America is just as important for grasping the novel's politics as having a sense of what is at stake in its depictions the Second World War. Eric Meyer in an essay entitled 'Oppositional Discourses, Unnatural Practices: *Gravity's* History and the 60's' was one of the first to argue that the novel is essentially a 'text of "The 60's"' because 'anxieties of an America at War both at home and abroad' that were prominent during the era of the Vietnam conflict run through it at all levels.[28] In a similar fashion, Jeffrey S. Baker asserts that the novel 'echoes an escalating countercultural critique of the Establishment's repression at home and murderous imperialism abroad', and that examining 'the analogies that the 1960s radicals made between American imperialism at home and abroad and the German Reich's earlier imperialism ... helps to place Pynchon's novel in the context of that time and that ideology'.[29] Similarly, David Cowart identifies a particular 1960s element in the novel's plot when he claims that 'Pynchon transforms the counterculture of those years into the Counterforce that he imagines as coming into existence at the end of World War II'.[30] Although Cowart does not follow up the implications of this analogy for thinking through the political stance of the novel as a whole, it ought quickly to become clear from the later stages of the text that the ineffective nature of the Counterforce's various modes of resistance to the System (Roger Mexico's rebellion, for example, amounts to nothing more than breaking up a party by causing mass vomiting among the guests and interrupting an official meeting by urinating on the table and his fellow participants) suggests, at the very least, a scepticism about the efficacy of the carnivalesque 'happenings' of the 1960s counterculture rather than an endorsement of any form of hippie revolution – a scepticism that is expanded upon in Pynchon's other writing, especially the California novels *The Crying of Lot 49*, *Vineland* and *Inherent Vice* (see our discussions in the chapters on these texts).[31] Clearly, then, *Gravity's Rainbow* is not just a celebration of the playful radicalism of 1960s countercultural politics; its approach to politics is more nuanced than simple affirmation of a particular system.

Understanding the novel's approach to history and politics is not, therefore, only a question of drawing a straightforward parallel between the Second World War and Vietnam. If war is central to the novel, and of course it is, *Gravity's Rainbow* does not simply paint a historically accurate (or even wildly inaccurate) picture of the last days of a World War Two that now lies securely in the past, but rather insistently puts the question of what modern war might actually be, how its consequences shape the world of the 1960s and 1970s in which the novel was written, and encourages critical speculation about how these consequences might continue to influence and structure the present-day world in which it is read. The disruptions of linear time produced by the faster-than-sound rocket and insisted upon by the novel's narrators, the 'opening' of identity and history in the anarchic spaces of the Zone, and the multiplication of worlds and counterfactual possibilities refuse any fixing of the war's events as unproblematically past, completed or closed. To grasp the novel's political engagement, it is vital to explore its presentation of the relationship between the various historical moments of narration and reading. In a sophisticated discussion of history and trauma in *Gravity's Rainbow*, Paul Crosthwaite argues that,

> The emphasis on inscription [in the novel] also invites the reader to reflect on the 'time of writing' – the present of the text's composition – a moment itself imperilled by a looming threat of instantaneous devastation. This ... along with the oblique allusions to Vietnam and the space race, again place strain upon the spatio-temporal integrity of the text, causing it to gesture, in accordance with the logic of trauma, not simply towards the privations and convulsions of the Second World War, but towards the geopolitical conflicts of the 1960s, the fetishized core 'object' of which – the nuclear warhead, descendent of the 'German rocket' – threatens a catastrophic fusion of signification with the Real, even as such an occurrence remains, in its perpetual deferral, 'fabulously textual'.[32]

Crosthwaite's analysis of the explicitly self-conscious and self-referential modes of narration that generate the sorts of complexity we have explored in earlier sections of this chapter draws attention to the processes of the novel's inscription in a manner that makes the reader immediately conscious of its textuality: the multiple levels of reality-presentation from documentary realism to dream-like disconnection, the exploitation of different media from the lyrics of popular songs to the film and comic-book modes that are used to narrate particular passages, the mixture of sophisticated specialist languages such as the discourses of mathematics and engineering as well as mystical lexicons drawn from tarot and spiritualism that present ideas in their own terms without 'simplifying' them for the non-specialist, all serve to draw the 'convulsions of the Second World War' into the reader's present by setting out a quite disorientating range of possible connections, analogies and levels of potential meaning. The implications and effects of the rocket in its 'perpetual deferral' from presence in the text connect it to everything (in the truly paranoid fashion evoked by the narrative), transforming it from a particular piece of military hardware into a mystical point of origin for the future 'Rocket-state' of Their 'Rocket-cartel', which is, of course, the post-war world of the novel's production and consumption.

The link between 'cartel' and 'state' in the description of the post-war world is made more than once in the novel, and is important: for *Gravity's Rainbow*, war is inseparable from capitalism. Wider than just being an exploration of two of the United States' military conflicts during the twentieth century, *Gravity's Rainbow* presents, as Steven Best and Douglas Kellner argue, the inextricable interrelations of war, markets, identity and politics in a postmodern era of seemingly endless capitalist and technological transformation: they read the novel as the paradigmatic literary engagement with what they call the 'postmodern adventure', a situation emerging after the Second World War in which 'the future of humanity and other complex life-forms is being mortgaged to a rampaging capitalism and profit-driven science and technological development'.[33] This postmodern situation is, they assert, the world projected as the 'Rocket-state' in which international business cartels (the true elect of the novel's post-war world) take control.

Threaded through the novel's various narratives, relations between myriad fictional and real-world corporations (such as Shell, ESSO, Krupp, Siemens and, most frequently, IG Farben) are constructed, fragmented and rearranged to form the System of an elect business, political and military cartel that is the paranoia-inducing 'They' of the narrative's preterite voices, the 'meta-cartel' envisaged by Tchitcherine of the 'Rocket-state whose borders he cannot cross ...' (*GR* 566).[34] To cite one version of this by way of example, the historical figure of Walter Rathenau (the German Jewish industrialist, intellectual and statesman who was assassinated in 1922, soon after having been made Foreign Minister for the Weimar Government) is introduced in a manner that carefully collapses the two world wars and the future Cold War together into a vision of the 'cartelized state':

> Rathenau – according to the histories – was a prophet and architect of the cartelized state. From what began as a tiny bureau at the War Office in Berlin, he coordinated Germany's economy during the World War, controlling supplies, quotas and prices, cutting across barriers of secrecy and property that separated firm from firm – a corporate Bismarck. ... Walter was more than another industrial heir – he was a philosopher with a vision of the postwar State. He saw the war in progress as a world revolution, out of which would rise neither Red communism nor an unhindered Right, but a rational structure in which business would be true, the rightful authority. (*GR* 164–5)

Historically located in the 1920s, the language of this passage with
its deliberately imprecise references to unspecified 'World War' and
'postwar' suggest both a pre-history to the Rocket-cartel and a vision
of the novel's post-Second-World-War 'present' in which the 'rightful
authority' over human destiny has been assumed by the markets.
This account of Rathenau's vision is presented as the 'official version',
but the suggested consequences go significantly further: it 'might
almost – if one were paranoid enough – seem to be a collaboration
here, between both sides of the Wall, matter and spirit. What *is* it they
know that the powerless do not? What terrible structure behind the
appearances of diversity and enterprise?' (*GR* 165). The preterite
paranoia that there is an elect market plan for everything in existence, 'matter and spirit', is never finally confirmed in the novel, but
echoes as a possibility throughout the narrative.

Towards the beginning, we are reminded that 'the real business of
war' is 'a celebration of markets':

> Don't forget the real business of the War is buying and selling. The
> murdering and the violence are self-policing, and can be entrusted to
> non-professionals. The mass nature of wartime death is useful in many
> ways. It serves as spectacle, as diversion from the real movements of
> the War. ... The true war is a celebration of markets. Organic markets,
> carefully styled 'black' by the professionals, spring up everywhere.
> Scrip, Sterling, Reichsmarks continue to move, severe as classical
> ballet, inside their marble chambers. But out here, down among the
> people, the truer currencies come into being. So, Jews are negotiable.
> Every bit as negotiable as cigarettes, cunt, or Hershey bars. (*GR* 105)

This passage goes right to the heart of *Gravity's Rainbow*'s political
engagement by forging a link between war, capitalism and spectacle.
The 'official' histories of the war as battle and death are a 'diversion'
from its 'real movements': the movements of the nations across
the Zone that we discussed in the last section, and the experience
of war generated 'down among the people' in which everything –
'Jews', 'cigarettes', 'cunt', 'Hershey bars' – is reduced to currencies
and commodities for exchange. If everything is connected for the
paranoid narrators, everything also has its price and place in the
System. And the Rocket itself, the ultimate object of desire for many
of the novel's chief protagonists, becomes the central principal of
exchange: at once commodity and mystical totem, the 'Rocket has
to be many things, it must answer to a number of different shapes in

the dreams of those who touch it – it must survive heresies shining, unconfoundable. ... It comes as the Revealer' (*GR* 727–8).

This infinite transformability is the basis of the dual rocket with which the novel closes, and which ties together history and future, 1940s and 1960s, in a convoluted present that is governed by the trajectory of the rocket's flight. The final section of the novel focuses on the firing of the 00000 rocket at the end of the war, the adapted V2 that has become a prototype space rocket with its single, sacrificial human cargo, but ends in a cinema in the 1970s where the audience, 'we', await the revelation:

> The screen is a dim page spread before us, white and silent. The film has broken, or a projector bulb burnt out. It was difficult even for us, old fans who have always been at the movies (haven't we?) to tell which before the darkness swept in. ... And in the darkening and awful expanse of screen something has kept on, a film we have not learned to see. ... And it is just here, just at this dark and silent frame, that the pointed tip of the Rocket, falling nearly a mile per second, absolutely and forever without sound, reaches its last unmeasurable gap above the roof of the old theatre. (*GR* 760)

Gravity's Rainbow grinds to a halt, caught between the broken film or process of projection and the apocalyptic imminence of the Rocket's explosion over our heads, and yet something 'has kept on', even if we haven't yet learned to see it. As Smith puts it, 'When the "film" breaks in the novel's final scene, it is an indication of what ... we will see once our eyes are opened to the true nature of power. But by then, Pynchon suggests, it will be too late for us to escape our collective fate. ... Pynchon's "film" suggests that we, its "audience" have surrendered any control over, or responsibility for, the history we witness. [*Gravity's Rainbow*] is his warning to us to take back this control before it is too late.'[35] If we are passive viewers of the development of a new international order, a Rocket-state, then the threat of the annihilation that post-war rocketry has brought to bear in the mutually assured destruction of the Cold War system of the Rocket-cartels is presented as an inescapable fate. But, as *Gravity's Rainbow* continually suggests, there are possibilities of resistance: not, perhaps, the organised but finally ineffective countercultural Counterforce of the final section, but the continual disruptions of order and system that occur in the Zone and can be spotted fleetingly in the interstices of the novel's complex of narratives. If we are to learn to see the 'something that has kept on' under the film, it is not by disentangling ourselves from the System with an alternative oppositional discourse, but via a 'progressive *knotting into*' it by means of the disruptive textual strategies that *Gravity's Rainbow* adopts to explore the origins of the present-day world.

Notes

1 Tanner, *Thomas Pynchon*, 75.
2 Norman Mailer, 'An Author's Identity: An Interview with Michael Lennon', in Mailer, *Pieces and Pontifications*, Boston: Little, Brown and Company, 1982, 157.
3 Pynchon, quoted in Tanner, *Thomas Pynchon*, 15. A transcript of Irwin Corey's acceptance speech is available on his website: www.irwincorey.org/routines.html.
4 Michael Wood, 'Rocketing to the Apocalypse', *The New York Review of Books* 20.4 (22 March 1973).
5 Tanner, *Thomas Pynchon*, 75.
6 Dugdale, *Thomas Pynchon*, 186. As we will try to show later, even the apparent respite from complexity offered in Dugdale's assertion of a 'single historical setting' is somewhat of an oversimplification of the novel's complex approach to history and time.
7 Hume, *Pynchon's Mythography*, xi.
8 Brian McHale, *Constructing Postmodernism*, London: Routledge, 1992, 10. The sense of a modernist 'discourse of critical interpretation' that McHale appeals to here is closely allied to what was introduced in the discussion of *V.* in the last chapter.
9 McHale, *Constructing Postmodernism*, 67.
10 McHale, *Constructing Postmodernism*, 80.
11 McHale, *Constructing Postmodernism*, 113.
12 In an important essay on paranoia in *Gravity's Rainbow* (to which we shall return in the next section of this chapter), Leo Bersani makes a similar point by comparing it with James Joyce's *Ulysses* and arguing that the 'puzzles of *Ulysses* are like Stations of the Cross; they are ritual agonies through which we must pass in order, finally, to be at one' whereas *Gravity's Rainbow*, instead of 'holding out the promise of postexegetical superiority to the world that it represents ... permanently infects us with the paranoid anxieties of its characters' (Bersani, 'Pynchon, Paranoia and Literature', 106–7).
13 Michael Bérubé, *Marginal Forces/Cultural Centres: Tolson, Pynchon, and the Politics of the Canon*, Ithaca: Cornell University Press, 1992, 209.
14 McHale, *Constructing Postmodernism*, 88.

15 A useful 'companion' to the novel has been published that sets out to begin to provide just such an encyclopaedic account of the text: see Weisenburger, *A 'Gravity's Rainbow' Companion*.

16 For an interesting and detailed discussion of the V2 and other key elements of the factual-historical background to the novel, see Khachig Toloyan, 'War as Background in Gravity's Rainbow', in Charles Clerc, ed., *Approaches to 'Gravity's Rainbow'*, Columbus: Ohio State University Press, 1983, 31–67.

17 A thorough and incisive reading of the complex narrative structure of the opening evacuation passage forms the central example of McHale's argument about the un-readability of *Gravity's Rainbow* discussed in the last section.

18 In a retrospective revision typical of the novel, we are later told '"There never was a Dr. Jamf," opines world-renowned analyst Mickey Wuxtry-Wuxtry – "Jamf was only a fiction, to help him explain what he [Slothrop] felt so terribly, so immediately in his genitals for those rockets each time exploding in the sky ... to help him deny what he could not possibly admit: that he might be in love, in sexual love, with his, and his own race's, death"' (*GR* 738). Of course, it is not just the absurd name of the 'renowned analyst' that forces us to question whether this version of events is any more true or real than Slothrop's paranoia-inducing earlier discovery: Wuxtry-Wuxtry's imposition of a psychoanalytic interpretation on the events cannot but appear reminiscent of the sorts of controlling interpretative violence displayed by other characters aligned to the 'They' of the text, whose categories have already been demonstrated to be crassly reductive.

19 James W. Earl, 'Freedom and Knowledge in the Zone', in Clerc, ed., *Approaches to 'Gravity's Rainbow'*, 229.

20 Shawn Smith takes this and the immediately following passages that make up the apparently proleptic interview with the Vietnam veteran as the moment at which the 'anachronistic narrator's metahistorical consciousness' emerges with a direct address to the reader (Shawn Smith, *Pynchon and History: Metahistorical Rhetoric and Postmodern Narrative Form in the Novels of Thomas Pynchon*, London: Routledge, 2005, 59). Although this assertion allows an interesting and informative discussion of *Gravity's Rainbow*'s engagement with history to develop, which we shall return to in the last section, the privileging of one particular voice threatens to close down the proliferation of meanings and possibilities which, as we have tried to show in relation to McHale's sense of unreadability, is unleashed by the narrative complexity of the text and essential to the experience of reading it.

21 Slade, *Thomas Pynchon*, 185.

22 In his essay 'The Quest for Pynchon', Matthew Winston makes a very

interesting case for the allusion here to Pynchon's own seventeenth-century ancestor William Pynchon, whose Puritan book was burned for its perceived sacrilege. See Winston, 'The Quest for Pynchon', 278–87.

23 Bérubé, *Marginal Forces/Cultural Centres*, 235, 224. Bérubé's argument here draws on the deconstructive reading developed by Alec McHoul and David Wills in *Writing Pynchon*, which suggests that the opposition between elect and preterite is simply one more binary to be broken down (3), a suggestion which McHoul and Wills themselves never follow up in detail.

24 Louis MacKey, 'Paranoia, Pynchon, and Preterition', *SubStance* 1.1, Issue 30 (1981): 17.

25 It might be objected that a character such as the Pavlovian behaviourist Pointsman is on the side of the elect as he manipulates and seeks to control those such as Slothrop or Brigadier Pudding, but it is important to recognise both his own continual paranoid self-doubt about his place (see, for example, *GR* 143–4) and his eventual fall from the possibility of grace as the novel progresses so that by the time of his final appearance in the text we learn that 'at odd moments, he could detect a reflex he'd never allowed himself to dream of: the tolerance of men in power for one who never Made His Move, or made it wrong' (*GR* 752). Serving the elect does not necessarily allow one to join their number, and that possibility is ruled out entirely for the characters in *Gravity's Rainbow*. The most likely candidate for membership of the elect in the novel is probably Laszlo Jamf, but he remains an indistinct and shadowy figure at best, and is finally written off (albeit possibly ironically) as never having existed at all – see note 18, above.

26 Bersani, 'Pynchon, Paranoia, and Literature', 102.

27 Hume, *Pynchon's Mythography*, xi.

28 Eric Meyer, 'Oppositional Discourses, Unnatural Practices: Gravity's History and the 60's', *Pynchon Notes* 24–5 (1989): 81–104 (81). This sense of an engagement with Vietnam-era politics and social anxiety is also presented in Shawn Smith's discussion in *Pynchon and History*, which discusses the way the novel deploys a 'cruel parody of Richard Nixon, "Richard Zhlubb, night manager of the Orpheus Theatre on Melrose" [*GR* 754]' in a manner that 'savagely portrays the political divisions in America over the Vietnam war ... as Zhlubb's "crackdown" on the harmonica playing dissidents' in the queues outside his theatre (65–6).

29 Jeffrey S. Baker, 'Amerikka Über Alles: German Nationalism, American Imperialism, and the 1960s Antiwar Movement in *Gravity's Rainbow*', *Critique* 40.4 (Summer, 1999): 323–41 (324–5).

30 David Cowart, 'Pynchon and the Sixties', *Critique* 41.1 (Fall, 1999): 3–12 (6).

31 Stefan Mattessich is quite correct to claim that 'the Counterforce produces no coherent program for undoing the structures of death that menace civilization in the novel' and, in these terms at least, to describe *Gravity's Rainbow* as an 'unforgiving parody of political action' (Mattessich, *Lines of Flight*, 72).

32 Paul Crosthwaite, *Trauma, Postmodernism and the Aftermath of World War II*, Basingstoke: Palgrave, 2009, 67.

33 Steven Best and Douglas Kellner, *The Postmodern Adventure: Science, Technology and Cultural Studies at the Third Millennium*, New York and London: Guilford Press, 2001, 10. A key contrast in Best and Kellner's argument is between *Gravity's Rainbow* and Michael Herr's account of Vietnam in *Dispatches* from 1977: they locate both on the border between modernism and the postmodern, but insist that the thorough-going critique of capitalist economics and technological transformation in Pynchon makes *Gravity's Rainbow* the much more radically postmodern text because its presentations of conflict, although explicitly located in the Second World War and Vietnam, always gesture beyond these to a fractured present of continual international struggle and violence.

34 Shell, for example, is presented as 'an outfit ... with no real country, no side in any war, no specific face or heritage: tapping instead out of that global stratum, most deeply laid, from which all appearances of corporate ownership really spring' (*GR* 243).

35 Smith, *Pynchon and History*, 95.

5

Cultural nostalgia and political possibility in *Vineland*

In the aftermath of the 11 September 2001 attacks, and the subsequent prosecution of a War on Terror by the Bush administration, Thomas Pynchon's 1990 novel *Vineland* has accrued a renewed sense of significance. The book is concerned to uncover the ways in which widespread paranoia serves as a strategy for forging political consensus. *Vineland* describes how the paranoid sensibility is encouraged and maintained by structures of power that require the identification and persecution of an enemy who is variously defined across the political history of the United States. Paranoia, as we have seen in previous chapters, has been a thematic preoccupation for Pynchon during the course of his career: Tyrone Slothrop in *Gravity's Rainbow*, for instance, is adept at projecting imaginary plots which might, or might not, allow him to make sense of his increasingly unreadable experiences ('For a minute here, Slothrop ... is alone with the paraphernalia of an order whose presence among the ordinary debris of waking he has only lately begin to suspect' [*GR* 202]); and Oedipa Maas, in *The Crying of Lot 49*, finds herself on a quest for meaning that is either being kept from her or does not exist ('Behind the hieroglyphic streets there would either be a transcendent meaning, or only the earth' [*CL* 125]). *Vineland*, of all Pynchon's works, is most explicitly concerned with twentieth-century US history, specifically the transition from the left-wing political radicalism of the 1960s to the repressions of the Reaganite 1980s, dual moments in which the production of paranoia in friend and foe alike works to support an authoritarian body politic. Patrick O'Donnell succinctly answers the question, 'Who is paranoia for?': 'It is for us, as national, corporate, historical subjects in a time when these formations are beset by questions about their cohesion and continuance.'[1] Building on our discussion of its presence in *Gravity's Rainbow*, this chapter explores how paranoia becomes a symptom of a late capitalist culture attempting to maintain its coherence in the face of perceived threats – real or imagined – to its integrity.

Any discussion of political paranoia needs to acknowledge Richard Hofstadter's classic enumeration of the 'paranoid style', which, he proposes, assumes 'the existence of a vast insidious, preternaturally effective international conspiratorial network designed to perpetrate acts of the most fiendish character'.[2] Such a mentality, Hofstadter goes on to suggest, operates at a level of apocalyptic intensity and regards history as being determined and driven by hidden forces of immense power. Its exponents

> regard a 'vast' or 'gigantic' conspiracy as *the motive force* in historical events. History *is* a conspiracy, set in motion by demonic forces of almost transcendent power ... The paranoid spokesman ... traffics in the birth and death of whole worlds, whole political orders, whole systems of human values. (29)

As Scott Sanders has commented of Pynchon's earlier work, 'God is the original conspiracy theory ... paranoia is the last retreat of the Puritan imagination'.[3] As already discussed, Pynchon's Puritan ancestry is well known: William Pynchon was a magistrate and trader during the New England witchcraft trials of the mid-seventeenth century, whose 1650 theological tome *The Meritorious Price of Our Redemption* was burned for its controversial views. Thomas Pynchon draws on his unorthodox Calvinist forebear in the depiction of William Slothrop, the first American ancestor of Tyrone Slothrop, whose opposition to 'the Winthrop machine' (John Winthrop being the first governor of the Massachusetts Bay Colony) identifies him as one of Pynchon's earliest members of the preterite, 'the "second Sheep" without whom there'd be no elect' (*GR* 555). The need to see patterns, to discern a plan (divinely inspired or demonically conceived), structures the Puritan imagination, as Susan Manning has observed:

> The puritan universe is anxious and insecure because of the distance which the Fall has interposed between man and God, which prevents man from perceiving God directly in Nature. God is mysterious and inscrutable; His universe is full of evidence about His nature, but man's corrupt vision is unable to read it reliably. The result is an obsessive search for significance, a relentless interpretation of 'clues'.[4]

Pursuing legibility, as we have seen, is a task undertaken by many of Pynchon's central characters, for the reassurances of a readable world, even a post-Puritan world in which the rewards of divine grace are no longer apparent, continue to exert a strong pull. Our reading of *Slow Learner* noted that Henry Adams was an early influence on Pynchon, and Adams's preoccupation with mapping the pathways of history represents an early twentieth-century incarnation of the paranoid sensibility. As Adams wrote about himself: '[H]e insisted on a relation of sequence, and if he could not reach it by one method, he would try as many methods as science knew'; '[T]he historian's business was to follow the track of the energy; to find where it came from and where it went to'.[5] The quest for these signs of epistemological certainty is continually undermined in Adams's autobiography, for contingency insists upon a more complex narrative than the clear and uncrossed lines so fervently sought. If plots cannot be discerned, as Tony Tanner noted, the compulsion to see patterns can 'easily turn into a tendency to suspect plots'.[6] While for Hofstadter the paranoid sensibility was 'the preferred style only of minority movements',[7] *Vineland* establishes a political terrain in which the fostering and manipulation of paranoia is a central tool of control within mainstream society – indeed, it is the very incarnation of an American body politic that is regarded with suspicion and loathing by the countercultural voices of the novel. Pynchon charts the new politics of the 1960s, with its sense that official ideologies of national identity, reinforced by political, military and commercial interests, impose a coercive stranglehold on the kinds of American citizenship that are possible;[8] within the 1980s of the narrative's present, such coercions are totalising. (The novel opens in the year 1984, after all.) Peter Knight has mapped a transition in the workings of political conspiracy in American culture, pointing to the shift from McCarthy-era paranoia in which subversive minorities pose a threat to an American way of life to a post-1960s reversal where danger now lies in mainstream America's threat to its marginalised elements.[9] Here we explore the contours of this historical terrain, and consider the extent to which Pynchon's novel is invested in possibilities of redemption from its persecutory force. Within a text that is split between two tumultuous decades of American history, Pynchon is able to establish a complex series of contrasts and continuations that work to disabuse the reader of any sense that the book is trading in the easy comforts of nostalgia for an earlier, more authentic moment.

Immanuel Kant established the temporal dimension of nostalgia as central in his lectures on anthropology, in which he discusses the complex conjoining of space and time in the construction of home-sickness, 'a longing that is aroused by the recollection of a carefree life and neighborly company'. We are faced with a remembered location that is structured temporally, a place that can be revisited but a time that can never be regained.[10] The impulse to return nostalgically to a place and time that we remember – or think we remember – becomes invested with affective imperatives, for, as Edward Casey notes, the past is required to assume a significance and potential that has been lost in the present moment. The 'particularity' of the past simultaneously 'bears up a lost world and exhibits it to our poignantly needful apprehension in the present'.[11] Nostalgia's 'lost world', under these conditions, inevitably becomes detached from time so as to be enshrined in a static, often idealised, past, a past which has outlived itself. Unfavourable critical responses to *Vineland* upon its publication often focused on this question of nostalgic return. Frank Kermode pronounced it a 'disappointing book', offering a reading that was also aware of its potential inadequacy: 'There is no disparagement, though there may be a false estimation of Pynchon's ambivalences, in saying that underneath the webbed and glittering surface there is a fairly simple nostalgia, or rather a rage for the lost innocence of America.' Similarly Alec McHoul faulted it for displaying a hazy '60s nostalgic quietism', and Ellen Friedman, in the same vein, dismissed its depiction of sexual politics where 'even the most radical expressions of rebellion and discontent ... are suffused with nostalgia for a past order, for older texts, for the familiar sustaining myths'.[12] Kermode's feeling for Pynchon's ambivalencies, however, is precisely the point, and, if *Vineland* does toy with nostalgia as a powerful cultural affect, the novel attempts to recuperate it from some of its standard, more retrograde definitions. Nostalgia's 'search for a simple and stable past as a refuge from the turbulent and chaotic present', in David Lowenthal's words, proves to be an overly reductive template for Pynchon's more politically nuanced text.[13] The danger of nostalgic narratives might be characterised in terms of their offer of the illusion of utopian idealism without providing knowledge of legitimate, albeit maybe embryonic, alternatives to our present circumstances. Nostalgia thus prevents knowledge by its insistence on looking back to a depoliticised and dehistoricised space of harmony. *Vineland*, by contrast, suggests that the more

progressive possibilities of our own time are only possible through
nostalgic (and often traumatic) evocations of lost communities. It is
tempting to overstate the redemptive trajectory of the novel, and, as
we point out, *Vineland*'s ending is carefully balanced between possibilities of healthy renewal and dangerous repetition. Yet Salman
Rushdie, in his review, was correct in pointing to the raised, and
more explicit, political stakes in its pages. 'What is new here', he
writes, 'is the willingness with which Pynchon addresses, directly,
the political development of the United States, and the slow (*but not
total*) steamrollering of a radical tradition many generations and
decades older than flower power'.[14] Rushdie's parenthetical gesture
here towards the possibility of alternative Americas alerts us to
what is perhaps the central dialectical tension in Pynchon's work,
that between containment and escape, or, to put it in slightly different terms, between immanence and transcendence. If Pynchon's
historical moment is one in which the instrumentalist ambitions of
a totally capitalised system seem to have been achieved, his writing
also reveals the limits of capitalism's reach by exposing those
spectral traces of an alternative identity that attempt to resist the
rationalising logic of modernity.

At the centre of Pynchon's novel is an idea of the family, a collective unit that is both attenuated and reconstructed during the
course of the narrative, and also differently configured according to
biological or political criteria. Zoyd Wheeler is a former hippie, living
in Vineland, California with his daughter Prairie. Zoyd's income is
subsidised by disability cheques from the government, payment
of which is dependent upon him performing an annual, televised
display of his mental instability by crashing through the window of
the Log Jam bar in Del Norte. This bizarre stunt represents the first
major set-piece of the novel, and is indicative of Pynchon's interest
in the gradual co-opting of the counterculture by the government
and media alike. Prairie's mother, of whom she has no recollection, is Frenesi Gates, the text's central character, who embodies
the slide from an apparently idealistic 1960s sensibility (Frenesi
was a member of an underground film collective) to one of political
betrayal and protected identity. The fractured biological family is
replaced by an alternative system of loyalty that comes to seem to
Frenesi as inevitable, a coming home to political and social realism.
'[T]he Nixonian Reaction continued to penetrate and compromise
further what may only in some fading memories ever have been a

people's miracle, an army of loving friends', the narrator writes, for 'betrayal became routine, government procedures for it so simple and greased that no one, Frenesi was finding out, no matter how honorable their lives so far, could be considered safely above it, wherever "above" was supposed to be ... These people had known their children after all, perfectly' (*VL* 239). The loyalty demanded of the government stooge is engendered by the co-opting of the language and affect of family, the replacement of blood ties with those of financial and – as Brock Vond, Frenesi's nemesis in the novel and a high-level government agent, understands – emotional need. Vond's ability to see 'in the activities of the sixties left not threats to order but unacknowledged desire for it' proposes a perverse craving for structure within the counterculture, a longing for discipline that is deliberately provoked by its dissident actions. Instead of hippie protests, Vond discerns 'the deep – if he's allowed himself to feel it, the sometimes touching – need only to stay children forever, safe inside some extended national Family' (*VL* 269). Like children returning to some institutional parental fold, Vond's analysis of the apparent ease with which one-time revolutionary activists become subsumed within the structures of government plays with the affective continuities of group membership. The securities offered by turning informant become a more powerful variant on those provided through biological kinship.[15]

Perhaps the most explicit recent articulation within critical theory of the problem of capitalist incorporation is found in the work of Alain Badiou, and specifically his 1997 book on St Paul (published in English in 2003 as *Saint Paul: The Foundation of Universalism*). Badiou argues that, because of our inevitable immersion in the powerful flows of capital in the market, the available definitions for any oppositional group identity are restricted to those which have already been approved by the global economy and its culture. 'The semblance of a non-equivalence', as Badiou calls oppositional identities, is necessary so that the machine of homogenisation can exert itself and thereby profit. Badiou's analysis is worth quoting at some length:

> There is nothing more captive, so far as commercial investment is concerned, nothing more *amenable* to the invention of new figures of monetary homogeneity, than a community and its territory or territories. The semblance of a non-equivalence is required so that equivalence itself can constitute a process. What inexhaustible potential for

mercantile investments in this upsurge – taking the form of communities demanding recognition and so-called cultural singularities – of women, homosexuals, the disabled, Arabs! ... Each time a social image authorizes new products, specialized magazines, improved shopping malls, 'free' radio stations, targeted advertising networks, and finally, heady 'public debates' at peak viewing times. Deleuze put it perfectly: capitalist deterritorialization requires a constant reterritorialization. Capital demands a permanent creation of subjective and territorial identities in order for its principle of movement to homogenize its space of action.[16]

Badiou's thesis, albeit articulated in an at times rhetorically inflated form, is a sobering one, for it proposes that our current global economy is the *only* horizon available to us, the default position for all thought and one which views stances of dissent or difference as opportunities for financial gain. What Adorno and Horkheimer, in the *Dialectic of Enlightenment*, had labelled as 'pseudo individuality' is here extended to the fabrication of group identities that are allowed to prosper so long as they accept their incorporation within capitalism's economic order.[17] For Badiou, our entanglement in these controlling imperatives ensures that no authentic revolutionary social formation can appear. However, in the figure of St Paul, Badiou locates the possibility of a truly antinomian figure: 'the poet-thinker of the event' who embodies values that stand opposed to, and outside of, existing narratives of law and morality.[18] He is 'a subject without an identity, a law without support' (5), for the truths he articulates are 'evental', erupting singularly rather than emerging as part of a discursive chain:

> [S]ince truth is evental, or of the order of what occurs, it is singular. It is neither structural, nor axiomatic, nor legal. No available generality can account for it, nor [can it] structure the subject who claims to follow in its wake. Consequently there cannot be a law of truth. Second, truth being inscribed on the basis of a declaration that is in essence subjective, no pre-constituted subset can support it; nothing communitarian or historically established can lend its substance to the process of truth ... [Truth] is offered to all, or addressed to everyone, without a condition of belonging being able to limit this offer or this address. (14)

What Badiou describes here is a theory of absolute singularity, in which an event demonstrates a truth value which is true to itself *only in the moment* of its realisation. As a response to incorporation, in which every form of relationship constitutes an encroachment, the unaffiliated instance is attractive indeed. 'Evental grace', as Badiou describes this moment, 'governs a multiplicity in excess of itself, one that is indescribable, superabundant relative to itself as well as with respect to the fixed distributions of the law' (78). Such an image of proliferation reaching beyond the codifying standards of language and law might serve as an apt description of the kinds of excess that characterise Pynchon's fiction. Indeed, as we discuss in Chapter Seven, the encyclopaedic copiousness of a text like *Against the Day* strives to push against normative structures of meaning, offering the chance of a politically liberating disruption to the capitalist default position. (That the novel ends with a journey towards 'grace' is also surely significant.) However, the antinomian impulse of Badiou's visionary – whose antecedents, in the context of nineteenth-century America, might include Ralph Waldo Emerson, Henry David Thoreau and John Brown – is untouched by the distinct ambivalence that Pynchon's writing evinces towards gestures of absolute transcendence, where independence of thought – whether that manifests itself in political action or countercultural lifestyle choices – is both admired and viewed with scepticism. Pynchon's texts illustrate the perceptiveness of Badiou's political diagnosis yet remain unconvinced by his remedy, as characters struggle to mount forms of resistance whose effectiveness is often tentative at best.

Visual expression and repression

In a later introduction to his now classic 1969 account of America's countercultural movement, Theodore Roszak identified the rise of consumer culture as being the catalyst for those voices of dissent and resistance ranged against the nation's normative goals and expectations. Protest 'was grounded paradoxically not in the failure, but in the success of a high industrial economy', as encounters with the 'delusionary consumer's paradise' triggered radical opposition to the mythology of American plenty.[19] As Erik Dussere has pointed out, Roszak's historical circumscription (1942–72) artificially narrows the ways in which we can trace America's dissenting tradition, for since at least the end of the nineteenth century affluence has been offered to the nation's citizens through 'the shared experience and activity of buying' a key component of America's exceptionalist self-image.[20] Pynchon's novel *Against the Day* will present the reader

with this longer historical perspective, in which capitalist consolidation at the turn of the twentieth century generates powerful – and
often violent – counter-impulses of resistance. But *Vineland* is also
concerned to map the trajectory of political awareness across a
number of decades, for in detailing Frenesi's own family history the
novel explores both her countercultural credentials and, following
the logic of Vond's theory, her prime susceptibility to their incorporation into the enforced ideological coherence of mainstream
society. The rebellions of the 1960s are thus placed in the context
of American radicalism that stretches back to communist sympathisers persecuted under McCarthyism (Frenesi's mother, Sasha,
experiences the effects of Hollywood blacklisting in the 1950s) and
beyond that to the Wobblies (the Industrial Workers of the World) of
the 1920s and 1930s, a global union whose membership peaked in
the early 1920s and whose members were frequently and violently
targeted by the enforcers of capitalism and big business. We read
how Jess Traverse, Frenesi's grandfather, attempts to unionise the
logging industry in Vineland, but is rewarded for his efforts by being
'accidentally' crippled during a baseball game by a falling redwood
tree 'driving half of him into the earth' (*VL* 75). The vision of history
described here is not one of linear progression, an Enlightenment
model of advance over time (something which, as we will see, preoc-
cupies Pynchon in *Mason & Dixon*); instead we are presented with
something akin to Walter Benjamin's depiction of history as 'one
single catastrophe, which keeps piling wreckage upon wreckage',
a cycle of oppression that can only be disrupted by the revolutionary able to 'blast a specific era out of the homogeneous course of
history'.[21] Through this genealogy of variously reincarnated social
oppression Frenesi inherits an acute knowledge of the histories of
political radicalism in the United States, and in her own historical
moment of the 1960s she joins a guerilla film collective – 24fps
– whose mission is to record US government oppression and to
dream of 'a mysterious people's oneness, drawing together toward
the best chances of light, ... timeless bursts, all paths, human and
projectile, true, the people in a single presence' (*VL* 117). For the
members of 24fps, film's political force represents a clear opposition to the despotic and repressive state (which is described by one
character as embodying 'the True Faith ... closed ideological minds
passing on the Christian Capitalist Faith intact' [*VL* 232]); cinematic
representation holds out the possibility of a political counterweight

to the authoritarian and militaristic regime of national government, as 24fps understands it.[22] Frenesi believes that the focus thrown on reality by the camera brings about 'learning how to pay attention' that, because of its apparent honesty, has the potential to 'reveal and devastate' (*VL* 195) the powers of social repression.

Watching the film reels shot by her mother, now haphazardly archived in a workshop on Ventura Boulevard, Prairie, from the narrative present of 1984, acknowledges for the first time the revolutionary idealism of Frenesi's 1960s moment:

> Up on the platform several people were screaming politics all at the same time, with constant input from the floor. Some wanted to declare war on the Nixon Regime, others to approach it, like any other municipality, on the topic of revenue sharing. Even through the crude old color and distorted sound, Prairie could feel the liberation in the place that night, the faith that anything was possible, that nothing could stand in the way of joyous certainty. She'd never seen anything like it before. (*VL* 210)

The cacophony of political debate, with its antimonies of absolutism and engagement, offers the watching Prairie – and by extension the reader – an affective vision of things mattering, of politics in action. The mediation of film allows her access to a 1960s sense of *unmediated* possibility, 'joyous certainty' that, from the perspective of the eighties, generates the strange sensation of radicalism's traces being carried into the era of Reaganite conservatism where the imperative is to 'dismantle the New Deal, reverse the effects of World War Two, [and] restore fascism at home and around the world' (*VL* 265).[23] The nostalgia of the backward glance works here as an attempt to prolong the currency of idealism in an almost uniformly materialistic culture; the affect provoked in Prairie by the old film images keeps alive the potential for a progressive politics. But this is a nostalgia that is also acutely aware of its constructed and occluding forms, for the 'joyous certainty' that is felt is conveyed through a medium that has become degraded over time, the sound 'distorted' and the images now 'crude'. Slavoj Žižek, in *In Defense of Lost Causes*, argues for the maintenance of a belief in the past's potentiality, its radical promise resurrected, perhaps in a transformed incarnation, in the present instance. 'The past is not simply "what there was"', he writes. Instead 'it contains hidden, non-realized potentials, and the authentic future is the repetition/retrieval of *this* past, not of the past as it was, but of those elements in the past which the past itself, in its reality, betrayed, stifled, failed to realize'.[24] *Vineland* depicts a more guarded iteration of this belief in the past as a site of present, and perhaps future, possibility; it is 'guarded' in the sense that Pynchon remains wary of subscribing to an uncompromised radicalism, one that can emerge uninfected by its historical betrayals or hesitancies. For instance, the novel is decidedly ambiguous about filmmaking as an act of radical collective identity, demonstrated most explicitly perhaps when Frenesi first meets her friend Darryl Louise (DL) Chastain. DL finds Frenesi 'filming a skirmish line of paramilitary coming up the street in riot gear, carrying small and [DL] hoped only rubber-bullet-firing rifles ... When the film roll ended and she [Frenesi] came up out of the safety of her viewfinder, Frenesi was alone, halfway between the people and the police, with no side street handy to go dodging down' (*VL* 116). What is significant about this moment is its placement of Frenesi midway between the protestors and the agents of law enforcement, apparently protected from unmediated engagement behind the lens of her camera. Instead of promoting revolutionary change, as the members of 24fps intend, the camera acts as a buffer between Frenesi and the crowd, undermining its potential to foster a collective identity. She is located exactly midway between opposing political sides, and the tableau anticipates the position she will inhabit later in the novel as a snitch for Brock Vond, 'halfway between the people and the police' aligned with neither. Recognising her isolation, Frenesi prays for rescue ('Oh, I need a Superman ... Tarzan on that vine' [*VL* 116]), and DL swoops into the scene to rescue her from immediate danger in a manner charged with cinematic cliché. As Shawn Smith astutely notes, it is a 'cinematically allusive' act 'that subverts the historical realism of the protest', as political space is translated into forms of cultural simulation.[25]

Moments such as this one demonstrate how film becomes a tool that is susceptible to conservative appropriation in its ability to repress political activism. Frenesi finds herself drawn further and further into Vond's manipulations on behalf of a system that finds its own uses for cameras and lenses, 'a 16mm Arri "M" on a Tyler Mini-Mount' being the equipment of choice for overhead surveillance. The film collective's naïve belief in the unmediated authenticity of the close-up image ('When power corrupts it keeps a log of its progress, written into that most sensitive memory device, the human face'

[*VL* 195]) is shown to be a delusion, for Brock's own appearance on film, as shot by Frenesi, suggests the artificially constructed nature of his self-image. He was 'more photogenic than cute, with his buffed high forehead, modish octagonal eyeglass frames, Bobby Kennedy haircut, softly outdoor skin' (*VL*, 200). These details constitute a complex series of empty signifiers: 'photogenic' and 'buffed' describe manipulation rather than authenticity; the kooky glasses hint at a countercultural avant-garde with which Vond has no sympathy; and the reference to Kennedy carries with it resonances of a liberal politics which, similarly, Vond refutes. Brock is a dangerous example of how the composition and performance of an image is able to undermine the progressive political investment made in representation. The rationalisations that Frenesi makes (to herself) about her involvement with Vond expose the naivety of 24fps's vision for the unmediated and progressive nature of film, as gradually cinematic autonomy is replaced by government-sponsored direction:

> When he [Vond] took copies of the footage she shot, he paid no more than lab costs. She told herself she was making movies for everybody, to be shown free anywhere there might be a reflective enough surface ... it wasn't secret footage, Brock had as much right as anybody. ... But then after a while he was not only seeing the outtakes, but also making suggestions about what to shoot to begin with, and the deeper she got into that, the deeper Brock came into her life. (*VL* 209)

Pynchon exposes the mistaken belief that film's democratic availability can defuse Vond's coercive manipulation, the ellipses in the passage indicative of Frenesi's own wavering certainty in this regard. Even if the 'surface' that Vond represents is reflective, the kind of image projected back from it disrupts and distorts the collective's progressive intentions, to the extent that the images shown have already been determined by his political agenda. Film's revolutionary force is thus translated, with apparent ease, into a medium for governmental surveillance. Vond makes clear to her that the camera is just an alternative phallic variation on the gun – another tool for 'Sticking It In' (*VL* 241), and one which reinforces our sense that Vond and Frenesi's relationship is determined by a complex interconnection of sexual, political and visual power.

The belief in the camera as a tool for progressive change is irrevocably betrayed by the murder of Weed Atman, Frenesi's lover, by Rex Snuvvle, an event that is choreographed by Frenesi and in which

the question of 'what to shoot to begin with' takes on a more alarming form. Rex uses the gun that Frenesi brings into the collective,
and the entire scene is filmed by two other of its members, Howie
and Ditzah. Viewed by Prairie in 1984, as she continues her quest
to find her mother, the footage reveals how the technology of film
determines the manner in which this event can be represented to the
reader. Weed's killing can only be re-enacted as a series of disjointed
images and sounds that finally cohere into a vision of horror:

> Ditzah took the close-ups while Howie kept further back, framing the
> three of them … Howie got his new roll in and on his way out offered to
> switch places with Frenesi, who may have hesitated – her camera, her
> shot – but must have waved him on, because it was Howie, innocent
> and slow-moving, who emerged into the darkness and, while trying
> to find the ring to open the aperture, missed the actual moment,
> although shapes may have moved somewhere in the frame, black
> on black, like ghosts trying to return to earthly form, but Sledge was
> right there on them, and the sound of the shot captured by Krishna's
> tape. Prairie, listening, could hear in its aftermath the slack whisper
> of the surf against the coast – and when Howie finally got there and
> Frenesi aimed the light, Weed was on his face with his blood all on the
> cement, the shirt cloth still burning around the blackly erupted exit,
> pale flames guttering out, and Rex was staring into the camera, posing,
> pretending to blow smoke away from the muzzle of the .38. He would
> not after all be lucky enough to sit under that oak on that dreamed hill-
> side someday with a miraculously saved Weed Atman, in some 1980s
> world of the future. The camera moved in on his face. 'Howie found the
> zoom,' Ditzah commented. 'We realised we were all there in an alley
> face-to-face with an insane person with a loaded gun.' (*VL* 246)

In this sequence it is the *failure* of film to record the key event that
constitutes the strongest refutation of 24fps's political ambitions.
The dislocations of sound and vision, and the mysterious traces of
ghostly figures apparently caught between life and death, disori-
ent the scene of violence, a moment surreally followed by its own
west-coast soundtrack, the 'slack whisper' of Californian calm. Once
the camera focuses on Weed's dead body, its framing is cinematically precise, aesthetically striking in its attentive detail; moreover,
the degree to which the images of visual culture have managed to
inhabit character and action is rendered explicit in Rex's clichéd
posturing. The possibility of a proleptic scene of pastoral reunion, in
which Weed survives and is able to reminisce about revolutionary

times with his attempted assassin, is nostalgically suggested (and, indeed, played out earlier in the novel [*VL* 232–3]), but it is proposed only to be denied as a narrative possibility, a fantasy of unrealised plotting. The murder, framed first as oblique visual detail and then as popular-culture stereotype, only subsequently registers as traumatic, as the close-up of Howie's face, Ditzah tells us from the narrative present of 1984, revealed the reality of the situation. Once more, though, it is the grammar of film that enables this revelation; affect can only be realised through the technology of cinema, so saturated are Pynchon's characters in its organising rubrics.

If film is the medium through which *Vineland* explores the corruptions of 24fps's political idealism, by the 1980s of the novel it is television which dominates the popular-cultural landscape. Many American writers in the second half of the twentieth century addressed television's hegemonic status, and these responses were often motivated by a Cold-War anxiety about the medium's pernicious effects on passive American minds. Unsurprisingly the countercultural Beats were explicit in their condemnation: in Jack Kerouac's novel *The Dharma Bums* (1958), for instance, the narrator Ray Smith, modelled on the author, laments the kind of conformity that television brings about, 'with everybody looking at the same thing and thinking the same thing at the same time'.[26] Paul Giles, in his examination of American literature's engagement with television and radio, has noted that 'the familiar figure of the jeremiad, warning of the weakened sense of neighborhood and fragmentation of urban centers' has tended to constitute the perspective of writers such as Philip Roth: Roth's fiction, Giles suggests, 'internalizes the rhetoric of a voice of America to structure national narratives in a way that is entirely commensurate ideologically with the evolution of network broadcasting in the middle part of the twentieth century, where the country found itself bound synchronically into a common language'. The dangers that television might pose to such an autonomously constituted national imaginary become apparent in later, more explicitly postmodern writing (such as Pynchon's or Don DeLillo's or Robert Coover's), in which the technology of television is internalised as part of a narrative cognisant of its global circuits 'whose perimeters can never again be entirely self-regulating'.[27] *Vineland* participates in this expansion of popular culture, in the deterritorialisation of media images via a globalised economy of brand names, advertisements, and satellite channels – a '24-hour cornucopia of video' (*VL* 171). References to actual television shows of all kinds – serious and ephemeral – pepper Pynchon's narrative, as well as to made-up ones, including a Japanese sitcom called *Babies of Wackiness* (*VL* 159). The blurring of the boundary between television and the 'real' world is frequently made explicit: we learn that Frenesi as a child, watching *Gilligan's Island*, 'wanted to climb inside the television set' (*VL* 368), and read of 'the primal Tubefreek miracle' (*VL* 84) that apparently brings to her door the same US marshals she has been fantasising about while watching a popular police drama. As Brian McHale suggests, television's function in the novel is to 'complicate, diversify, and destabilize the ontological structure of the fictional world', a world which is radically pluralised through the incursion into it of televisual structures of thought and feeling.[28]

One of the novel's most explicit incarnations of character determined by television is Hector Zuniga, an agent for the Drug Enforcement Agency, whose own form of addiction is to the small screen and for which he receives treatment from NEVER (the National Endowment for Video Education and Rehabilitation), an organisation established to 'study and treat Tubal abuse and other video-related disorders' (*VL* 33). Hector's ambition is to translate his career battling the drugs trade into a film starring Frenesi Gates, to 'bring her up out of her mysterious years of underground existence, to make a Film about all those long-ago political wars, the drugs, the sex, the rock an' roll, which th' ultimate message will be that the real threat to America, then and now, is from th' illegal abuse of narcotics' (*VL* 51). Towards the end of the novel, Frenesi reflects with dismay upon the degree to which Hector's televisual idea of law enforcement has brought about very real perversions of the US legal system. Zuniga 'depended upon these Tubal fantasies about his profession, relentlessly pushing their propaganda message of cops-are-only-human-got-to-do-their-job turning agents of government repression into sympathetic heroes'. The comforting aestheticisation of a fascist system, through its incarnation as television spectacle, not only elides serious discussion of law enforcement, it also, Frenesi laments, helps to perpetuate in 'the vernacular of American expectations' those 'routine violations of constitutional rights these characters performed week after week' (*VL* 345). The interchangeability of politics and entertainment has the unwelcome effect of normalising forms of social repression that, on screen, are packaged as acts of heroism.

McHale argues that while film is tied to the countercultural aspirations of the 1960s, television's dominance of representation in the narrative present of the 1980s serves as 'a kind of synecdoche, simultaneously symbol and example, of the betrayal and collapse of the revolutionary ethos'.[29] Television's impact is much discussed in the novel, and its ability, through visual excess, to hinder tangible political change is explicitly acknowledged by one of the characters, Mucho Maas, a local disc-jockey in *The Crying of Lot 49* who returns in *Vineland* as 'a music-business biggie' (*VL* 307). From within the comforts of corporate America, Mucho is still perceptive enough to realise that the commercialised products of mass representation that he peddles suffocate genuine thinking. They offer the consumer 'too much to process, fill up every minute, keep us distracted, it's what the Tube is for, and though it kills me to say it, it's what rock and roll is becoming – just another way to claim our attention, so that beautiful certainty we had starts to fade' (*VL* 314) – the 'beautiful certainty' here echoing Prairie's sense of 'joyous certainty' felt while watching the 1960s film footage shot by her mother. It is, of course, the unravelling of different forms of certainty that Pynchon's book explores, where the question of nostalgia and the viability of its preservative force becomes an acute one. As we have seen, even film as a medium of political emancipation cannot escape the corrupting processes of politicised representation, and McHale's own somewhat nostalgic reading of its status in the novel needs to be supplemented by these distinct ambivalences. Moreover, the historical division between film and television that he proposes is one that the novel itself wants to complicate when Isaiah 2:4, Prairie's boyfriend, admonishes her father's generation for its subservience to the small screen. The 'problem 'th you folks', he tells Zoyd, 'is you believed in your Revolution, put your lives right out there for it – but you sure didn't understand much about the Tube'. Once television 'got hold of you folks that was it', and the 'whole alternative America' represented by the counterculture was quickly bought by corporate America for 'too cheap' a price, 'even in 1970 dollars' (*VL* 373). Rather than embodying a generational falling away from the political progressiveness of film to the anodyne entertainments of television, Isaiah 2:4 indicts Zoyd for his generation's willingness to commercialise its politics, to see itself represented, in a cheapened form, on the small screen. Mark Miller, in the introduction to his series of acute readings of famous televisual images, has noted how the countercultural politics of the 1950s and 1960s was complicit in its own media representation, to the extent that the relationship between television and this particular demographic became one of mutually reinforcing identity construction. Miller writes that 'the "counterculture" was dependent on the mass media – contrary to the Luddite and/or pastoral mythology of the era', with the 'symbols and catchphrases of the young' given wider exposure at the same time as 'television left its traces on the high ground of countercultural ideology'. The 'psychedelic fantasy' of a collectively attuned culture, of 'universal, instantaneous communication', also happened to be the 'metaphysical projection of the national TV audience – everyone watching Ed Sullivan at once'.[30]

Pynchon's novel is all too aware of the entanglement of mass media in the lives of its characters. While *Vineland* complicates a reading that views television merely as a post-1960s phenomenon – a medium unable to display any progressive political credentials, so imbricated is it with the consumerism of an advanced capitalist culture – it is also attentive to the ways in which mass-media images provide the aesthetic and narrative structures that underwrite interpersonal exchange. Deborah Madsen suggests that the novel 'imitates the form of a television programme', constructed through 'short, discrete episodes, related through flashback and connected by shifts of angle, fading in and out of different scenes of action'.[31] If the historical sweep of the novel charts how 'revolution went blending into commerce' (*VL* 308), commerce is not only the thematics of the book, but also provides possibilities of communication that might not otherwise take place. Zoyd Wheeler characterises his life as 'like being on "Wheel of Fortune"', except there is 'no tanned and beautiful Vanna White at the corner of his vision to cheer on the Wheel, to wish him well' (*VL* 12–13); his imaginary out-of-body encounters with his wife, Frenesi, are 'like Mr. Sulu laying in coordinates, only different' (*VL* 40); and he tells her how he 'Feel[s] like Mildred Pierce's husband, Bert' (*VL* 57). The narrative does not sneer at these pop-culture references. The book is far too aware of its own implication in them to risk taking a lofty position of disdain; rather, these moments of film and television referencing provide an affective shorthand. They are structures of sensibility that can be conveyed in a postmodern space where possibilities of autonomous, authentic feeling are continually under threat of erasure. It is worth pointing out too how television also has the potential to disrupt settled ways of thinking or being; as much as it inevitably renders banal the cultural and political landscape, at other moments it can also provoke a jarring eruption of uncertainty, as when Brock Vond catches himself laughing at something on the screen and is unable to stop: 'Instead of reaching a peak and then tapering off, the laughter got more intense each time he breathed, diverging towards some brain state he couldn't imagine, filling and flooding him, his head taken and propelled by a supernatural lightness, on some course unaccounted for by the usual three dimensions' (*VL* 278). Television propels Vond out of his government-sponsored world and towards the threshold of an alternate set of spatial co-ordinates, 'territories of the spirit' (*VL* 317) that threaten his obsessively controlled and controlling environment. While Vond regains his composure on this occasion, this is a telling episode, not only for its reflection on television's disruptive potential, but also because it reminds the reader of Pynchon's abiding interest in resistant geographies, realms of potential that, although often precarious, mark the location of what Brian Jarvis calls 'a counter-hegemonic cartography located between the interstices of the Repression'.[32] As we explore in more detail in the next chapter, Pynchon's novel *Mason & Dixon* is explicitly concerned with the clash of instrumental mapping and these more unregulated temporal and spatial conceptions. In *Vineland*, in the wake of the failure of 1960s radicalism, the consolations of recuperative political possibility might be found in different configurations of space and time. Pynchon considers the viability of the nation's counter-cultural past and wonders what traces of it remain unreconciled in the present, acting as reminders to a repressive system of non-conformist voices that have not been silenced.

Nostalgic returns

Vineland explores how, at each historical moment with which the novel engages, a necessary 'enemy' is identified that allows the nation to divert attention from recurring structural tensions of inequality, whether that enemy is trade unionists in the 1930s, communist sympathisers in the 1950s, student radicals and anti-Vietnam protestors in the 1960s, or pot smokers in the 1980s. Each of these dissenting moments allows for the cultivation and maintenance of paranoia by the surveilling State, thereby forging a normalising consensus that seeks to elide alternative political or cultural perspectives. If, as

Walter Benjamin argues, history needs to reckon with the 'tradition of the oppressed', the class which is itself 'the depository of historical knowledge',[33] then *Vineland* offers its complex temporality of the past's repetitive and lingering presence as a form of politically aware nostalgia, a bearing witness to the struggles and self-incriminations of history as, in Terry Eagleton's words, they come into 'violent constellation with the political present'.[34] As we have already suggested, such a nuanced iteration of nostalgia does not generate its affective force through a desired return to pastoral wholeness. Any progressive redesigning of social relations that the novel considers is always already contending with the literary and cultural habitat of postmodern irony in which Pynchon operates, as well as with the overwhelming power of the capitalist machine upon which that habitat draws its inspiration. Pynchon's depiction of the 1960s generation is clear-sighted enough to recognise the entanglement of the counterculture in capitalism's structures. Ellen Meiksins Wood, in a study of capital's economic imperialism, notes that

> Capitalism is, by nature, an anarchic system, in which the 'laws' of the market constantly threaten to disrupt the social order. Yet probably more than any other social form, capitalism needs predictability and stability in its social arrangements. The nation state has provided that stability and predictability by supplying an elaborate legal and institutional framework, backed up by coercive force, to sustain the property relations of capitalism, its complex contractual apparatus and its intricate financial transactions.[35]

Wood's analysis recognises the structural coercions that are necessary both to contain the unpredictabilities of capitalism itself and to enforce those living under its economic imperative to subscribe to its reined-in protocols. While her reliance on the nation state as the final arbiter of economic stability deliberately flies in the face of much recent work on increasingly globalised cultures (a globalisation, as we discuss in the next chapter, with which Pynchon's texts contend), Wood's understanding that capitalist societies establish more and more intricate networks of policing and repression to maintain a hold in all cultural corners is acute. In *Vineland* Zoyd's 1960s generation imagines that it is possible to opt out of capitalism's clutches by rejecting its dominant values in favour of alternative communities of authenticity. The move northwards to Vineland County, away from the corporate centre of Los Angeles, represents a flight to an imagined space of pre-capitalist simplicity, one that Zoyd conjures up while remembering his wedding to Frenesi: 'everything in nature, every living being on the hillside that day ... was gentle, at peace – the visible world was a sunlit sheep farm' (*VL* 38), a description whose secure investment in the 'visible world' will prove to be complicated by the novel's interest in both darker and less transparent forms of reality. 'Vineland' evokes pastoral lushness, a landscape of fecundity that synechdocally signifies America as untainted land, an impression reenforced by echoes of 'Vinland', the word given by the Norse explorer Leif Eriksson to the newly discovered American continent some five hundred years before Christopher Columbus's accidental encounter with it. As Dussere notes, 'Vineland is offered as a version of the original America, although at the same time it recalls the first moment of European contact with and claiming of the American land – a paradise already lost at the moment of origin'.[36]

This process of encroachment, in which the myth of a fertile landscape is faced with its obvious diminishment, is apparent early on in the novel, with ancient redwood trees under threat from commercial logging and marijuana crops uprooted by agents of the DEA (Drug Enforcement Administration). The militarisation of Los Angeles, as noted by Mike Davis in his exploration of that city's spatial configurations and enforcements, has drifted northwards into the pastoral enclaves of Vineland County, now a key battleground for Ronald Reagan's war on drugs. What Davis describes as the relocation of Vietnam's military strategies to southern California, Pynchon echoes in his depiction of the incursion of battlefield tactics into the redwood coastal communities of his novel: 'CAMP [Campaign Against Marijuana Production] helicopters gathered in the sky and North California, like other U.S. pot-growing areas, once again rejoined, operationally speaking, the third world' (*VL* 49).[37] This pattern of declension – the falling away from an imagined, idealised state into one of militarised containment – is invoked early on in the narrative, when we read how, as a character surveys the Californian landscape, 'the fog now began to lift to reveal not the borderlands of the eternal after all, but only quotidian California again, looking no different than it had when he left' (*VL* 94): a dream of transcendence is quickly overcome by the homogeneity of the earthbound. Wood's vision of a pervasive culture of capitalist incursion is clearly at work in Pynchon's text, for even those hoping to opt out

of social conformity through a countercultural lifestyle find themselves located as elements of the market economy. Moving north
into Vineland County, 'former artists or spiritual pilgrims [were]
now becoming choker setters, waiters and waitresses, baggers and
checkout clerks, tree workers, truck drivers, and framers, or taking
temporary swamping jobs like this, all in the service of others, the
ones who did the building, selling, buying and speculating.' 'Former
tripping partners and old flames' now conduct business 'across
desktops or through computer terminals, as if chosen in secret and
sorted into opposing teams' (*VL* 321). The encroachment of technology reduces the chances of meaningful human contact to a series of
cyber encounters, and the capitalist economy insists upon competition as its model, rather than the collectivism that many of these now
incorporated hippies might have preferred. The divisiveness of such
a system re-enacts the familiar schism in Pynchon between the elect
and the preterite, those safely operating within the protocols of the
governing elite and those located on its dissident margins. What is
fascinating about this apparent divide is the way in which Pynchon
insists on rendering it permeable, so that even the most apparently
reclusive of communities finds itself engaging with (or chooses to
embrace) the mainstream market. Elect and preterite are often on
close speaking/trading terms.

A clear instance of this is the Sisterhood of Kunoichi Attentives,
who preach and market Karmic Adjustment as an alternative to the
brutalities of the capitalist regime, and to whom both DL and Prairie
turn for help and sanctuary. The Attentives are an order of female
Ninjas who have found their home in an old Catholic convent whose
original inhabitants, after 'a series of bad investments', were 'forced
to put it up for rent and disperse to cheaper housing'. Capital's power
over spiritual culture is further evidenced in Pynchon's depiction of
the Ninja nuns, who peddle New Age lifestyles to the gullible and
needy by offering 'fantasy marathons for devotees of the Orient,
group rates on Kiddie Ninja Weekends, help for rejected disciples of
Zen' (*VL* 107). The business culture of the Attentives ensures, as DL
recognises, that while 'Back then they let anybody who showed up
crash here for free', now 'it's group insurance, pension plans, financial consultant name of Vicki down in L.A. who moves it all around
for us' (*VL* 128). Terry Caesar and Takashi Aso have suggested
that Pynchon's deployment of aspects of Japanese spirituality in a
novel so saturated with the products and processes of commercial-

ism accomplishes two things. Firstly, *Vineland* 'exhibits itself as a text intricately aware of ... the moment of naïve idealism in a '60s version of Orientalism, whereby the Spirit of the East is posited as an alternative to what the novel characterizes as so many "karmic imbalances"'. Secondly, DL's training in Ninja techniques and practices results in her becoming 'a hybrid figure, at once American and Japanese. A corrupted ninjutsu tradition opens up the opportunity for an American to take possession of it.'[38] This dialectic between commercial contamination and expansive encounter is key to the novel, for while Pynchon expresses deep concern in *Vineland* for the ways in which capitalism has indeed reached into the most resistant spaces of dissent, what Fredric Jameson calls its capacity to colonise 'those very precapitalist enclaves (Nature and the Unconscious) which offered extraterritorial and Archimedian footholds for critical effectivity',[39] the kind of nostalgia for forms of alternative spirituality is nevertheless not simply parodic, stripped of its political potential. As Caesar and Aso make clear, the transnational identity of DL, through her engagement with an inevitably diminished series of non-western cultural forms, produces a model of identity that is not reducible simply to the political and economic contours determined by an oppressive United States regime. The Attentives, for all their compliance with the capitalist nexus, instruct DL in an alternative set of values for surviving in a postmodern world in which the option of escape into pure being is closed off. If Žižek is correct in his claim that an earlier radical politics can cross over and be reinvented in and for the present moment, then the presence of eastern traditions, in however reduced an incarnation, enables DL to acquire strategies of resistance to the imperatives of her consumer culture. Although, as we will see, Ralph Waldo Emerson is invoked late on in the novel, the kind of transcendence that, at his most romantic, Emerson celebrated (most famously through his image of the 'transparent eyeball' in which 'I am nothing; I see all'),[40] is an ideal that DL must learn to reject. The leader of the Attentives, Sister Rochelle, explains to her that 'the first of many kunoichi disillusionments ... is finding that the knowledge won't come down all at once in any big transcendent moment'. Instead, those techniques which prevent DL from being overwhelmed by the nation's capitalist drive are acquired in a more gradual and oblique fashion, 'out at the margins, using the millimeters and little tenths of a second ... scuffling and scraping for everything we get' (*VL* 112). Capitalism's expectations of immediate and total gratification – a kind of materialist transcendence – are refuted by a mode of living, born out of the conflation of countercultural and eastern philosophies, that prioritises patience and incremental progress. That an ideal of ninjitsu has been corrupted within Pynchon's eschatological vision of a fallen world is fully acknowledged by its practitioners, 'the original purity of ninja intent' now 'made cruel and more worldly, bled of spirit' (*VL* 126–7). Where 'once greater patterns' could be discerned, there were 'now only a string of encounters, single and multiple, none with any meaning beyond itself' (*VL* 127), an echo of and also a resolution to Oedipa's inability in *The Crying of Lot 49* to decide between 'transcendent meaning, or only the earth' (*CL* 125).

Vineland explores the difficulty of maintaining radical politics in the face of an increasingly commercialised and repressive social space. Voices from a more progressive past – ghosts that constitute what Hanjo Berressem calls the 'presence of an absence'[41] – can, nevertheless, be heard in the present, as if the injustices which they suffered demand continued recognition, thereby marking both the political distance between past and present and offering an albeit tentative model for the future. Walt Whitman, in a poem from the 1860 edition of *Leaves of Grass* called 'Proto-Leaf', captures this complex entanglement of past traces, present lives and future ambition. Surveying the United States, he declares:

> Still the Present I raise aloft – Still the Future of
> The States I harbinger, glad and sublime,
> And for the Past I pronounce what the air holds of
> the red aborigines.
> The red aborigines!
> Leaving natural breaths, sounds of rain and winds,
> calls as of birds and animals in the woods,
> syllabled to us for names,
> Okonee, Koosa, Ottawa, Monongahela, Sauk, Natchez,
> Chattahoochee, Kaqueta, Oronoco.
> Wabash, Miami, Saginaw, Chippewa, Oshkosh, Walla-
> Walla,
> Leaving such to The States, they melt, they depart,
> Charging the water and the land with names.

Amidst the promise of an American future, in all its expansive optimism, the poem pauses to catalogue, and account for, those indigenous societies that have been forced to disappear to make way for the United States. The strangeness of the words, as he lists the lost tribes, seems to collude with the process of nation building, as if these names are out of place in the new republic. Yet their beauty, as the eye and ear pause to read them, also accentuates the sense that their presence lingers, for 'what the air holds' are resonances of a continuing existence in the geography of a country which seeks to erase them. Indeed, the word 'Charging' in the final line is carefully ambiguous, simultaneously infusing the landscape and accusing it. Although the poem goes on to hymn 'A new race, dominating previous ones, and grander far',[42] in a mood of exceptionalism characteristic of Whitman's writing, the deletion of the past is nevertheless not quite achieved.

In *Vineland* the Yuroks, an indigenous tribe whose home was in northern California, embody the spectrality of this absent presence. Their legacy is to be found in what they called '*woge*, creatures like humans but smaller, who had been living here when the first humans came' but who have now, like Whitman's native peoples, withdrawn 'into the features of the landscape, remaining conscious, remembering better times' and resting 'in the nuances of wind and light as well as the earthquakes and eclipses and the massive winter storms that roared in, one after another, from the Gulf of Alaska' (*VL* 186). Hauntings of this kind, in which the expectation that the records of the past have been erased is refuted, insist on the legibility of ghost-writing in the face of, and against, imperial narratives. Frenesi's computer records, for instance, read by Prairie as she tries to track her mother down, are described as 'a haunted mansion' in which is detectable 'the peripheral whiteness, the earnest whisper, of her mother's ghost' (*VL* 114). Moreover these ghostly presences move across historical time periods, something which, figuratively at least, Jess and Eula Traverse accomplish (their surname gives this away). Their presence in the novel, from the 1930s through to the 1980s, takes the form of a genealogy of radical politics, a spectral family inheritance that is passed down through the four generations of the family – to Sasha, then on to Frenesi, and finally to Prairie. The transmission of a dissenting tradition in American political culture suggests the possibility of a useable past to counter the different, but politically linked, threats of the McCarthy's witchhunts, Nixon's militarism and social conservatism, and Reagan's economic and cultural moralism. Yet as we move closer to the narrative present of the novel, the repressions of the political culture would appear to suffocate any possibility of Jess and Eula's influence being felt. If Pynchon's novel trades in nostalgic attitudes, it is not at all clear if such tinted glances are able to achieve any kind of purchase in the brutal glare of mass-mediated, postmodern America.

Notes

1 Patrick O'Donnell, *Latent Destinies: Cultural Paranoia and Contemporary U.S. Narrative*, Durham: Duke University Press, 2000, 16.
2 Richard Hofstadter, *The Paranoid Style in American Politics and Other Essays*, New York: Knopf, 1965, 14.
3 Scott Sanders, 'Pynchon's Paranoid History', *Twentieth-Century Literature* 21.1 (1975): 177–92 (177).
4 Susan Manning, *The Puritan-Provincial Vision: Scottish and American Writing in the Nineteenth Century*, Cambridge: Cambridge University Press, 1990, 9.
5 Adams, *The Education of Henry Adams*, 363, 369.
6 Tanner, *City of Words*, 153.
7 Hofstadter, *The Paranoid Style*, 7.
8 Fredric Jameson's celebrated essay on the 1960s draws attention to the decade's consolidation of capitalist, commercial imperatives: it is, he judges, 'a period in which capital is in full dynamic and innovative expansion, equipped with a whole armature of fresh production techniques and new "means of production"' ('Periodizing the 60s', *Social Text* 9–10 [1984]: 178–209 [186]). Contra Jameson, *Vineland*'s sense of the capitalist continuities between the 1960s and the 1980s points to Pynchon's profound scepticism about the likely renewal of a structural progressive politics.
9 See Peter Knight, *Conspiracy Culture: From Kennedy to the X-Files*, London: Routledge, 2000, 34.
10 Immanuel Kant, *Anthropology from a Pragmatic Point of View*, trans. Victor Lyle Dowdell, Carbondale: Southern Illinois University Press, 1978, 69.
11 Edward Casey, 'The World of Nostalgia', *Man and World* 20 (1987): 361–84 (364).
12 Frank Kermode, 'That Was Another Planet', *The London Review of Books*, 8 February 1990: 3–4 (3, 4); Alec McHoul, 'TEENAGE MUTANT NINJA FICTION (Or, St. Ruggles' Struggles, Chapter 4)', *Pynchon Notes* 26–7 (1990): 97–106 (98); Ellen G. Friedman, 'Where are the Missing Contents? (Post)Modernism, Gender, and the Canon', *PMLA* 108 (1993): 240–52 (250). For a succinct survey of the novel's critical reception, see Douglas Keesey, '*Vineland* in the Mainstream Press: A Reception Study', *Pynchon Notes* 26–7 (1990): 107–13.

13 David Lowenthal, 'Nostalgia Tells it Like it Wasn't', *The Imagined Past: History and Nostalgia*, ed. Malcolm Chase and Christopher Shaw, Manchester: Manchester University Press, 1989, 21. See also Susan Stewart's *On Longing: Narratives of the Miniature, the Gigantic, the Souvenir, the Collection*, which characterises nostalgia as a 'social disease' (Durham: Duke University Press, 1993, ix); and Janice Doane and Devon Hodge's *Nostalgia and Sexual Difference: The Resistance to Contemporary Feminism*, which argues that nostalgia represents 'a retreat to the past in the face of what a number of writers – most of them male – perceive to be the degeneracy of American culture brought about by the rise of feminist authority' (New York: Methuen, 1987, xiii).

14 Salman Rushdie, *Imaginary Homelands: Essays and Criticism 1981–1991*, London: Granta, 1991, 356. Rushdie's praise of Pynchon's engagement with political history historical counters David Cowart's view that Vineland lacks the cultural and historical sense of *V.* and *Gravity's Rainbow*. See his 'Attenuated Postmodernism: Pynchon's *Vineland*', in *The Vineland Papers: Critical Takes on Pynchon's Novel*, ed. Geoffrey Green, Donald J. Greiner and Larry McCaffery, Normal, IL: Dalkey Archive Press, 1994, 3–13.

15 For more on the novel's alternative kinship systems, see N. Katherine Hayles, '"Who Was Saved?" Families, Snitches, and Recuperation in Pynchon's *Vineland*', *Critique* 32.2 (1990): 77–91.

16 Alain Badiou, *Saint Paul: The Foundation of Universalism*, trans. Ray Brassier, Stanford: Stanford University Press, 2003, 10–11.

17 Theodor W. Adorno and Max Horkheimer, *Dialectic of Enlightenment*, London: Verso, 1997, 154.

18 Badiou, *Saint Paul*, 2.

19 Theodore Roszak, *The Making of a Counterculture: Reflections on a Technocratic Society and Its Youthful Opposition*, Berkeley: University of California Press, 1995, xii, xix.

20 Erik Dussere, 'Flirters, Deserters, Wimps, and Pimps: Thomas Pynchon's Two Americas', *Contemporary Literature* 51.3 (2010): 565–95 (574).

21 Walter Benjamin, 'On the Concept of History', in Benjamin, *Selected Writings*, 392, 396.

22 See Stephen do Carmo, 'History, Refusal, and the Strategic-Essentialist Politics of Pynchon's *Vineland*', *Pynchon Notes* 44–5 (1999): 173–94, who points out that the state exercises power in the novel in forms that are always and inevitably reactionary. Progressive politics is to be found in other kinds of collective groupings.

23 Michael Rogin writes that Reagan's coercive politics was dependent upon a 'symbolic universe protected from the real-world obstacles that might threaten that toughness or expose its punitive character ... Reagan's dream of law and perfect order, deforming the world as it

is to preserve it as a wrinkle-free ideal, has punishing consequences for sensate human beings down below' (*Ronald Reagan, the Movie and Other Episodes in Political Demonology*, Berkeley: University of California Press, 1987, 36). Rogin's account of Reagan's presidency is a useful companion text to *Vineland*, a novel which explores the figurative dimensions of 1980s ideology to show how political language both protects and exposes.

24 Slavoj Žižek, *In Defense of Lost Causes*, London: Verso, 2008, 141.

25 Smith, *Pynchon and History*, 113.

26 Jack Kerouac, *The Dharma Bums*, London: André Deutsch, 1959, 39.

27 Paul Giles, *The Global Remapping of American Literature*, Princeton: Princeton University Press, 2011, 150, 180.

28 McHale, *Constructing Postmodernism*, 135. Chapter Five of McHale's book is the most detailed account of the impact and presence of television on the form and politics of *Vineland*.

29 McHale, *Constructing Postmodernism*, 122.

30 Mark Crispin Miller, *Boxed In: The Culture of TV*, Evanston: Northwestern University Press, 1988, 9.

31 Deborah L. Madsen, *The Postmodernist Allegories of Thomas Pynchon*, New York: St Martin's Press, 1991, 132.

32 Brian Jarvis, *Postmodern Cartographies: The Geographical Imagination in Contemporary American Culture*, London: Pluto Press, 1998, 72.

33 Benjamin, 'Theses on the Philosophy of History', 251.

34 Terry Eagleton, *Against the Grain: Essays 1975–1985*, New York: Verso, 1986, 136.

35 Ellen Meiksins Wood, *Empire of Capital*, London: Verso, 2005, 16–17.

36 Dussere, 'Flirters, Deserters, Wimps, and Pimps', 581.

37 Mike Davis writes that 'The official rhetoric of the contemporary war against the urban underclasses resounds with comparisons to the War in Vietnam a generation ago. The LAPD's community blockades evoke the infamous policy of quarantining suspect populations in "strategic hamlets". But an even more ominous emulation is the reconstruction of Los Angeles's public housing projects as "defensible spaces". Deep in the Mekong Delta of the Watts-Willowbrook ghetto, for example, the Imperial Courts Housing Project been fortified with chain-link fencing, RESTRICTED ENTRY signs, obligatory identity passes – and a substation of the LAPD. Visitors are stopped and frisked, the police routinely order residents back into their apartments at night, and domestic life is subjected to constant police scrutiny. For public-housing tenants and inhabitants of narcotic-enforcement zones, the loss of freedom is the price of "security"' ('Fortress Los Angeles: The Militarization of Urban Space', in Michael Sorkin, ed., *Variations on a Theme Park: The New American City and the End of Public Space*, New York: Hill & Wang, 1992,

166–7). For an extended discussion on how Pynchon's novel engages with a long tradition of US political and legal writing on civil liberties and their destruction, see David Thoreen, 'The President's Emergency War Powers and the Erosion of Civil Liberties in Pynchon's *Vineland*', *Oklahoma City University Law Review* 24.3 (1999): 761–98.

38 Terry Caesar and Takashi Aso, 'Japan, Creative Masochism, and Transnationality in *Vineland*', *Critique* 44.4 (2003): 371–87 (375).

39 Fredric Jameson, *Postmodernism, or, The Cultural Logic of Late Capitalism*, London: Verso, 1991, 49.

40 Ralph Waldo Emerson, *Nature* (1836), *The Complete Works of Ralph Waldo Emerson*, Centenary Edition, 12 vols, Boston: Houghton Mifflin, 1903–04, 1:10.

41 Hanjo Berressem, *Pynchon's Poetics: Interfacing Theory and Text*, Urbana: University of Illinois Press, 1993, 209.

42 Walt Whitman, 'Proto-Leaf', *Leaves of Grass*, Boston: Thayer and Eldridge, 1860, 20.

6

Mason & Dixon and the transnational vortices of historical fiction

If, as we have suggested, *Vineland* depicts a depthless, quintessentially postmodern United States of the 1980s, caught in the seductive embrace of an all-encroaching media landscape which is contrasted with a 1960s counterculture of dissent and political activism to question the trajectory of the national narrative, *Mason & Dixon*, published in 1997, takes the reader back to the period of the country's founding and the historical densities of eighteenth-century colonial culture. The ostensible source of the novel is the journal that Charles Mason kept in America as he and Jeremiah Dixon were employed surveying 233 miles of the Pennsylvania–Maryland border to settle a protracted boundary dispute, one that in the 1730s had led to the violence of what became known as Cresap's War. The pair took almost five years (1763–67), and the resulting survey would inaugurate into American topography a dividing line between slave-owning and non-slave-owning states. Initially intended to divide Penns from Calverts, Protestants from Catholics, the line, as we will see, inaugurates a wider meditation on the centrality of divisions and demarcations in the American national narrative, their persecutory effects and their usefulness in establishing forms of instructive difference. Addressing the Historical Society of Pennsylvania in 1854, the pro-slavery historian John H. B. Latrobe noted the historical significance of the line as a marker of oppositions, a cartographical inscription establishing a whole series of binary terms. 'There is, perhaps, no line, real or imaginary, on the surface of the earth', he declared, 'whose name has been oftener in men's mouths during the last fifty years.' Latrobe explicitly acknowledged the line's expansion beyond the specific remit of its drawing, for its 'geographical, thus became lost in its political, significance; and men cared little, when they referred to it, where it ran, or what was its history – or whether it was limited to Pennsylvania, or extended, as has, perhaps, most generally been supposed, from the Atlantic to the Pacific'.[1] The ability of this specific cartographic inscription to amplify its significance, both in terms of its geographical reach and its metaphorical potential, is central to Thomas Pynchon's 1997 postmodern fictionalisation of its genesis. *Mason & Dixon* itself ranges beyond the geography of the original mission, and is divided into three parts: part 1, 'Latitudes and Departures', describes Mason's and Dixon's first meeting in 1760, their visit to Cape Town to measure the transit of Venus between the sun and the earth, Mason's additional trip to the island of St Helena to undertake further astronomical calculations, and the two men's return to London; part 2, 'America', tells of the commissioning and then execution of the topographical survey of the disputed American terrain; and part 3, 'Last Transit', narrates the two men's return to England, Dixon's death, and Mason's decision to return to America.[2] The novel is written as an elaborate ventriloquising of eighteenth-century prose style, with capitalised words, unfamiliar punctuation, and a digressive mode which, as this chapter will go on to suggest, is perfectly suited to the book's more conceptual meditations on spatial and temporal shaping that expand beyond the borders of continental America and the historical moment of the Line's creation. Pynchon's mammoth work is carefully attuned to the forces of Enlightenment and global capitalism that exert their own, often pernicious, pressures on the project of national inscription being undertaken by Charles Mason and Jeremiah Dixon.

The key action of *Mason & Dixon* is the inscription of a line across America that anticipates over two hundred years of conflict and schism within the body politic, a line which marks out distinct ideologies and accentuates the possibilities of conflict. As Captain Zhang, a Chinese Feng Shui expert in Pynchon's novel, predicts, 'all else will follow as if predestin'd, unto War and Devastation' (*MD* 615). One of the preoccupations of *Mason & Dixon* is to reflect upon the political mapping of the United States, as its founding precepts of Enlightenment rationality are traversed by disruptive forces of both repression and imagination. In its sheer narrative exuberance and diversity, the novel counters the impulse to codify, and, in its scepticism of a national mythology of exceptionalism, *Mason & Dixon* continues Pynchon's engagement with uncovering the submerged voices of the preterite. This chapter will explore the strategies by which Pynchon's apparent pastiche of the eighteenth-century novel asks the reader to consider the relationship between the processes of representation (in fiction and in mapping) and the politics of representation thereby enacted within particular cultures, including those of occluded or marginalised peoples. *Mason & Dixon* is an historical novel that self-consciously places the status of history – its deceptions and manipulations – at the heart of its concerns.

The metafictional credentials of Pynchon's text are explicitly rendered, often through its primary narrator, the Reverend Cherrycoke, who tells the story of Mason and Dixon from a later historical moment (1786) to a group of listeners and who fades in and out of the narrative, often returning to reflect on the tale he is telling. The novel makes it clear too that, at times, Cherrycoke is inventing his story for the benefit of his listeners, being present at events only 'in a representational sense, ghostly as an imperfect narrative to be told in futurity' (*MD* 195). Early in the story Cherrycoke denotes himself as 'an untrustworthy Remembrancer' (*MD* 8) who sets himself the task of reconstituting Mason's and Dixon's narrative from shards of memory; he is a novelist disguised as an oral historian. Indeed, the very status of narrative, of how one chooses to describe episodes from the past, is self-consciously addressed:

> History is not Chronology, for that is left to lawyers, – nor is it Remembrance, for Remembrance belongs to the People. History can as little pretend to the Veracity of the one, as claim the Power of the other, – her Practitioners, to survive, must soon learn the arts of the quidnunc, spy and Taproom Wit, – that there may ever continue more than one life-line back into a Past we risk, each day, losing our forebears in forever, – not a Chain of single Links, for one broken Link could lose us All, – rather, a great disorderly Tangle of Lines, long and short, weak and strong. (*MD* 350)

These lines are taken from Cherrycoke's work, *Christ and History*, and imagine history as something multivalent, constantly rewritten by contrasting and conflicting strands that are potentially overwhelming in their complexity. The claims made by lawyers to accuracy in relating the past, Cherrycoke judges, are equally as suspect as the distorting subjectivities of memory, for neither does justice to the inchoate nature of experience that, Pynchon suggests, *any* narrative rendition will inevitably simplify. In the tangle of lines that is *Mason & Dixon*, he imagines new, diverse geometries through which the experience of colonial America might be represented. Pynchon's novel explores how the imposition of a line upon the landscape is designed to create the illusion of spatial readability; it is an organising gesture that procures a co-ordinated geography, what Henri Lefebvre describes as an 'encrypted reality' transformed into something 'readily decipherable'.[3] However, this clarifying impulse, born out of Enlightenment imperatives to measure, standardise and colonise, exists in a dialectical tension with more subterranean spatialities and temporalities, moments in the novel when the assurances of empiricism, and the national project it supports, are clouded by more occult, enchanted realms. Fabienne Collignon usefully describes these as 'other worlds interred by the surface surroundings, universes whose fabric of laws might be different, whose indeterminate regions might unfold according to unknown principles of physics and bizarre lines of force'.[4] In the novel, William Emerson, Dixon's teacher and something of a mystic, advises his pupil to look beyond the mere horizon, where we 'are bound withal to time, and the amounts of it spent getting from one end of a journey to another'. From a different perspective, he assures Dixon, 'one can apprehend all at once the entire plexity of possible journeys' (*MD* 505). As we will argue with regard to *Against the Day*, Pynchon's writing is preoccupied with interrogating the impulse to imagine alternative possibilities of spatial and temporal existence, in opposition to those forces organising the social and political realm. Writing of colonial America on the eve of its reconstitution into the United States, *Mason & Dixon* presents a moment of transition in which the New World's exceptionalism is tested and, at times tragically, found wanting. Even within the space of possibility that America represents, dissenting environments emerge or are imagined that serve to highlight the imperial and capitalist operations of both the colony and its soon to be realised independent successor.

Transnational geometries

Late in the novel, Mason and Dixon are reunited after a gap of four years, meeting in Dixon's home town and sharing stories of their separate efforts to map the transit of Venus, in Ireland and Norway respectively. Dixon relates how, before setting sail back to England, he is led towards the North Pole, where 'the Earth's Surface ... began to curve sharply inward, leaving a great circum-polar Emptiness' (*MD* 739). Proceeding beneath the surface, and into an unmapped but densely populated space, Dixon visits the Fellows of this realm's

Academy of Sciences to learn more about the subterranean world and its 'Tellurick Forces' (*MD* 740). He warns Mason that once 'the size and weight and shape of the Earth are calculated inescapably at last' (*MD* 741), the landscape of this submerged *terra incognita* will vanish forever, extinguished by the force of empirical observation taking place above it. As Collignon has also noted, the precariousness of secret spaces in the face of our compulsion to measure and control echoes Adorno and Horkheimer's analysis in the *Dialectic of Enlightenment* (1944), where they argue that the recourse to science and rationality as a counter to religion and superstition brings with it its own oppressions: the dialectic of their title is, then, a continual oscillation between the energies of measurement and those forces which the Enlightenment impulse is designed to overcome. Dixon, we have already learned, decides to become a surveyor so that '[t] he open countryside', which produces in him 'all the terrors imaginable to a boy', can be contained. Surveying 'provided me with an incentive', he tells Mason, 'to enclose that which had hitherto been without Form, and hence haunted by anything and ev'rything' (*MD* 504). Dixon's reaction to the prognostications of the 'inner-surface Philosophers' (*MD* 740) is indicative of his growing scepticism about his employment and the motivations that may lie behind it.

This scepticism is realised in the resistance offered by America's geography to the codifying demands of Mason and Dixon's survey. Cherrycoke describes how 'somewhere the Arc, the Tangent, the Meridian, and the West Line should all come together at the same perfect Point – where, in fact, all is Failure. The Arc fails to meet the Forty-Degree North Parallel. The Tangent fails to be part of any Meridian. The West Line fails to begin from the Tangent Point, being five miles north of it.' The geometry fails to cohere into a satisfactory resolution, for the systematic programme of containment is eluded by what Cherrycoke calls a 'spirit of whimsy' (*MD* 337) that runs counter to Enlightenment seriousness. The most explicit articulation of this notion of a fantastic residuum holding out against empirical mapping is the account of the 'notorious Wedge' (*MD* 469), where measurements taken in an area of land in the northeastern corner of Delaware generate readings that are jumbled to such an extent that the existence of the terrain itself seems open to question. It is, we read, 'an Unseen World, beyond Resolution, of transactions never recorded', seemingly immune from the inscriptions of technological modernity, and now a 'small geographic Anomaly, a-bustle with

Appetites high and low' (*MD* 470).[5] This space of freedom, even if only precariously maintained, presents itself as an opportunity to stall the imposition of a fixed identity; and in a novel that is preoccupied with exposing the sordid tale of modernity's slaveholding economy, the confusion of categories that the 'Wedge' inaugurates takes on additional significance. *Mason & Dixon* presents a globalised system of slavery, one that does not differentiate between Old and New Worlds, but instead conjoins the imperial ambitions of both. As Laura Doyle has pointed out, nations exist 'as transnations or internations' that share what she calls a 'tilted' interdependency: 'Nations are invested in each other, in every sense of the word, and they are invested in and attuned to each other's investments'.[6] In a novel that, as we will see, is so attuned to the global flows of a developing capitalist system, Doyle's words are particularly helpful in conceptualising the geometries of circulation which *Mason & Dixon* explores.

Captain Zhang laments the mapping of the 'Visto' across the American landscape, pointing out that 'ev'rywhere else on earth, Boundaries follow Nature ... so honoring the Dragon or Shan within, from which the Landscape ever takes its form'. To impose a 'Line upon the Earth is to inflict upon the Dragon's flesh a sword slash, a long, perfect scar, impossible for any who live out here the year 'round to see as other than hateful Assault' (*MD* 542). Later in the novel he asserts that the drawing of such artificial boundaries upon America's geography results in the institutionalisation of 'Bad History', whereby a culture of repression and segregation can be enforced by those who control its narrative. The 'first stroke', he warns, is the construction of division through mapping (*MD* 615). 'Bad History' then might be thought of as the embodiment of the diverse political, economic and rhetorical strategies by which an ideology can assert itself, to the dismay of those wishing to confront its influence. The critic Sacvan Bercovitch, in a now classic essay, offers a useful definition of ideology that emphasises its representational range. It is, he suggests, a 'system of interlinked ideas, symbols and beliefs by which a culture – any culture – seeks to justify and perpetuate itself; the web of rhetoric, ritual, and assumption through which society coerces, persuades, and coheres'.[7]

As we have already noted, Pynchon's work is preoccupied with the effects of such a system, in terms of both the psychological states it can induce and the possibilities of resistance it can generate. *Gravity's Rainbow* had already established an opposition between two modes of thought in the contrasting views of Edward Pointsman, a 'graying Pavlovian' (*GR* 55), and Roger Mexico. Pointsman's adherence to a rationalist worldview embodies, in extreme form, the Enlightenment urge to measure and classify that *Mason & Dixon* explores. Of Pointsman we read:

> Like his master I. P. Pavlov before him, he imagines the cortex of the brain as a mosaic of tiny on/off elements. Some are always in bright excitation, others darkly inhibited. The contours, bright and dark, keep changing. But each point is allowed only the two states: waking or sleep. One or zero. 'Summation', 'transition', 'irradiation', 'concentration', 'reciprocal induction' – all Pavlovian brain mechanics – assumes the presence of these bi-stable points. (*GR* 55)

The rigid categorisation of behaviour that such a model represents is countered by Roger Mexico, to whom 'belongs the domain between zero and one – the middle Pointsman has excluded from his persuasion – the probabilities' (*GR* 55). Preferring to find value in solutions located outside of, or between, the brutal alternatives of Pointsman's system, Mexico represents the possibility of resistance to its fascistic imperatives; yet the failure of Mexico's rebellion (he is a 'failed Counterforce' [*GR* 713]) reminds us of Pynchon's affectionate scepticism of the possibilities of effective dissent in the face of modernity's rationalising drives. In *Mason & Dixon* possible alternatives to official narratives of history abound in a novel of encyclopaedic range and exuberant structure. Captain Zhang, one of many fantastical figures populating the novel, offers an important corrective to the assumptions of American exceptionalism, reminding us that 'slavery is very old upon these shores, – there is no Innocence upon the Practice anywhere, neither among the Indians nor the Spanish nor in the behavior of the rest of Christendom, if it come to that' (*MD* 616). Zhang refutes the existence of a morally superior, self-contained geographical entity, positing instead a globalised economy in which colonial America (and a soon to be declared United States) participates. We will come back to this notion of the novel's international, transnational perspective a little later, but for now it is enough to recognise that Pynchon presents the reader with a delicate balancing act, with the narrative caught between wonderment at the romantic potential of the New World and a scepticism about America's ability (or willingness) to uphold its founding ethical traditions. As Cyrus Patell has noted, '*Mason &*

Dixon is thus a revisionist narrative that uses the historical novel to expose the underside of European and American history'. The 'appeal of freedom', he suggests, all too often 'hides the existence of an unholy truce between liberty and various forms of oppression'.[8]

Mapping inculcates what Brian Jarvis calls the 'fundamental politicality of space'.[9] Space can be made to hide its ideological pressures, offering instead a performed neutrality that overlooks the tensions for representation and ownership that can become occluded in the mapping process. Henri Lefebvre succinctly encapsulates this phenomenon in his observation that

> If space has an air of neutrality and indifference with regard to its contents and thus seems to be purely 'formal', the epitome of rational abstraction, it is precisely because it has been occupied and used, and has already been the focus of past processes whose traces are not always evident on the landscape.[10]

Inscribed palimpsestically onto landscape, then, are imperatives that organise and represent space as ideologically notated. Behind and beneath the veneer of an innocent vista are inscribed patterns of power and exclusion that have become normalised through their apparent invisibility. One aspect of this invisibility is the powerful rhetorical and political claim for New World uniqueness. *Mason & Dixon* both articulates this position and works to refute, or at least to complicate, it. This is partly achieved through the explicitly transatlantic structure of the novel, ranging geographically from England, South Africa, St Helena, colonial America, and Ireland. As Paul Giles has argued, Pynchon 'invokes the circuits of transatlantic exchange to problematize the old teleologies of American exceptionalism'.[11] Indeed, across his writing career, Pynchon has engaged with questions of nationality from a decidedly cosmopolitan perspective, with America (and by extension an early United States) fully implicated in a variety of global networks. We have seen this at work in Pynchon before, of course. In *V.*, for example, the twin focus on espionage and tourism ('perhaps the most absolute communion we know on earth' [*V* 409]) establishes the idea of a national identity as comparative, always in contagious contact with, and read alongside, its others. Pynchon often invokes the idea of America as a kind of utopian space, one that is imbued with innocence: 'Some mornings they [Mason and Dixon] awake and can believe that they traverse an Eden, unbearably fair in the Dawn, squandering all its Beauty, day after day unseen, bearing them fruits, presenting them Game, bringing them a fugitive moment of Peace' (*MD* 477). Yet America is also the location of cultures in conflict, where the hubristic effects of exceptionalism can be traced, and where such reverberations against the authorised narrative bring to hearing the voices of the marginalised and dispossessed.

Ghostly mappings

Paul Ricoeur's judgement that within historical narratives there is an oscillation 'between servile conformity with respect to the narrative tradition and rebellion with respect to any paradigm received from that tradition' offers a useful gloss on the conceptual fluidity of Pynchon's text.[12] The novel considers the embryonic United States from a perspective of cosmopolitan detachment, 'playing off', as Giles puts it, 'the formation of American national identity against its parallax appearances in transoceanic cultural mirrors',[13] for the book's depiction of America is refracted through the lenses of England, India and South Africa. The reader frequently encounters instances of an English class system in comparison to which America has the potential to embody a site of difference: a rioting crowd 'small and frail from Hunger' (*MD* 737) is set alongside 'Gloucestershire Nabobs' (*MD* 185), a phrase that aligns these members of an aristocracy with Britain's colonial project in India. Charles Mason and Jeremiah Dixon both suffer under the slights and prejudices of class: Mason is overlooked for the top job of Astronomer Royal, the position going to Nevil Maskelyne, who possesses the social capital of being the brother-in-law of Clive of India; Dixon is raised in a Quaker family in County Durham, intellectually and geographically outside of the metropolitan elite.

The two men's increasing dissatisfaction with the political and social climate of their own country might lead us to imagine that *Mason & Dixon* articulates a version of American republican virtue as theorised by George Washington, Thomas Jefferson and Benjamin Franklin, all of whom feature in small roles in the novel. Liberation from the constrictions of English society is certainly desired by William Emerson, Dixon's teacher, whose 'passionate Resentment' against a moribund and corrupt class system might be said to underwrite a reflection of America as potentially liberating, in the mould of his later namesake Ralph Waldo Emerson, as Tony Tanner has suggested.[14] Of William we read that 'Flow is his passion ... The first book he publish'd was upon Fluxions' (*MD* 220). And here is Ralph: 'all symbols are fluxional; all language is vehicular and transitive' ('The Poet'), and 'Every solid in the universe is ready to become fluid on the approach of the mind' ('Fate').[15] The construction of the Mason and Dixon line occurs at a moment in American history when national, and therefore personal, identity is in a state of transition, when allegiances become unstable and the movements between undermine the stabilising impetus of mapping. The final paragraph of the 'America' section of the book describes an imaginary future ending for its two central characters, one that denies Cherrycoke's knowledge that they are both already dead at the time of his narration. Instead they are situated in retirement on an island in the middle of the Atlantic: 'Betwixt themselves, neither [Mason nor Dixon] feels British enough anymore, nor quite American, for either side of the Ocean. They are content to reside like Ferrymen or Bridge-keepers, ever in a Ubiquity of Flow, before a ceaseless Spectacle of Transition' (*MD* 713).[16] Far from solidifying identity, the construction of the Line effects a sensation of homelessness, of being exiled from the comforting satisfactions of either potential nationality.

In a recent reading of the emergence and dominance of the so-called 'transnational turn' in American studies, Winfried Fluck has pointed to the ways in which theories of transnationalism have privileged tropes of mobility and flow as enacting resistance to the interpellating pressures exerted by the nation state. At its most politically optimistic, Fluck notes, transnational movement 'allows migrant workers and other marginalized or subaltern groups to resist internalization at least partially and thereby to become political and social actors again'.[17] Such a vision of deterritorialised and repoliticised identities is undeniably attractive, yet Fluck is clear to point to the paradox of a cherished flexibility that, rather than being indicative of transformed political possibility freed from the claims of the nation, is merely an 'adaptation to a neoliberal logic in which movements of peoples and ideas are now the instruments of a new order of global capital'.[18] Pynchon's novel is carefully attuned to the ways in which an insistence on flux and movement, as we have seen via Emerson, remains axiomatic of a national (and increasingly imperial) selfhood that prides itself on its flexibility. In a celebrated passage from the novel, America is evaluated as the site of fantastic possibility, a 'subjunctive' terrain that grammatically enacts a resistance to the normative pressures of the imperial centre. It is worth quoting at length:

> Does Britannia, when she sleeps, dream? Is America her dream? – in which all that cannot pass in the metropolitan Wakefulness is allow'd Expression away in the restless Slumber of these Provinces, and on West-ward, wherever 'tis not yet mapp'd, nor written down, nor ever, by the majority of Mankind, seen, – serving as a very Rubbish-Tip for subjunctive Hopes, for all that *may yet be true*, ... safe till the next Territory to the West be seen and recorded, measur'd and tied in, back into the Net-Work of Points already known, that slowly triangulates its Way into the Continent, changing all from subjunctive to declarative, reducing Possibilities to Simplicities that serve the ends of Governments. (*MD* 345)

It is not entirely clear if this is an intervention offered by Cherrycoke or from a layer above the novel's fluctuating narrator. Yet the passage articulates in an efficiently compressed form what might be thought of as a central ontological concern in Pynchon's writing. What is the status of dream and fantasy in the construction of identity, and how are its manifestations controlled by the keepers of efficiency? Pynchon has consistently expressed ambivalence about the forward momentum of 'progress', sympathetically regarding those who attempt to exist outside of, underneath, or beyond its reach. In *Gravity's Rainbow*, the preterite signifies such a shadow of dissenting reality, and the sheer formal exuberance of that novel works to counter the reductive 'Simplicities' of civilisation's programmes of control. Likewise *Vineland*'s Zoyd Wheeler's annual act of resistance, and the various countercultural manifestations that populate the book, point to Pynchon's deep engagement with the possibilities – both aesthetic and political – of dissent. Imagined in both temporal and spatial terms as a narrative possibility that might have been, and might yet be, freedoms from restriction are suggested by the structural heterogeneity of Pynchon's art, by a focus on magic and the supernatural, and by the playfulness of language itself. However, in the passage quoted above, the 'subjunctive Hopes' of American potential exist in inevitable tension with the similarly powerful American impulse to colonise. As Tony Tanner notes, 'The new country, the United States of America, depended for its existence both as entity and concept on two things – appropriated, surveyed, legally apportioned land; and a sense of an unchartered, inexhaustibly bounteous west, a plenitude of possibilities.'[19] The imperial impulse is as much a part of the national character as is the imaginative one. Moreover, the reference to plural 'Governments' indicates a seamless continuation of the narrative of empire, with the New World's push into its westward territories mirroring the European colonial project. The 'Net-Work' specifically refers to Britain's far-reaching empire, but might also be said to predict the westering impulse of the new American phenomenon as it exerts its manifest destiny across the continent.[20]

'Net-Work', while characteristically Pynchonesque in its attention to the ways in which different geographies and temporalities might be linked through the imagination, also of course draws our attention to the novel's concern with systems of influence – the Jesuits and the East India Company are two specified in the book – that exert an imperialism on a truly global scale. The second of these, the East India Company, is the most powerful, being truly transnational in its reach and an example of successful corporate capitalism *avant la lettre*. It is, we read, located 'ev'rywhere, and [in] Ev'rything' (*MD* 69), and its individual outposts are primed to generate 'the Doings of Global Trade in miniature', as one of its employees proudly asserts (*MD* 159). Its success as an all-pervasive entity, unbounded by national constraints and entirely efficient in its practice, resonates with Michael Hardt and Antonio Negri's reading of the postmodern imperial system as the operation of a voracious global capitalism no longer tied to geographical location. 'In its ideal form', they write, 'there is no outside to the world market: the entire globe is its domain', such that 'it is both everywhere and nowhere'.[21] Empire under these conditions is 'a regime that effectively encompasses the spatial totality, or really that rules over the entire "civilized" world'.[22] The Company in Pynchon's novel is suspected of being the controlling force behind events – including the mapping of the line (Dixon tells Mason that it is 'the East India Company who keep *thee* ever in motion' [*MD* 73]) – and moreover the network of capitalism is recognised as the organising entity in world affairs: Mason comments that 'both Pennsylvania and Maryland [the colonies that the line is designed to separate] are Charter'd Companies as well, if it comes to that. Charter'd Companies may indeed be the form the World has now increasingly begun to take' (*MD* 252). As Stacey Olster has pointed out, the intrusions of global capital take an increasingly violent form, performing the functions of enforcement and discipline that hitherto in Pynchon have been the domain of government agencies. As she notes, Pynchon's appropriation of Adam Smith's 'Invisible Hand' (*MD* 411) supplants Christian omnipotence with that of capitalist economics.[23] While on St Helena, Nevil Maskelyne, a fellow astronomer, describes for Mason the global narrative in which both men find themselves, 'Subjects of the same Invisible Power':

> Something richer than many a Nation, yet with no Boundaries, – which, tho' never part of any Coalition, yet maintains its own great Army and Navy, – able to pay for the last War, as the next, with no more bother than finding the Key to a certain iron Box, – yet which allows the Brittannick Governance that gave it Charter, to sink beneath oceanick Waves of Ink incarnadine. (*MD* 140)

Located in a world of powerful forces that no longer take national shape, a landscape in which the coherence of borders has been supplanted by the unmediated flow of capital, Mason and Dixon are unable to feel confident in their ability to cartographically fix a terrain which is an early incarnation of our current globalised world – 'the great global multinational and decentred communicational network' of the twenty-first century, in Fredric Jameson's words.[24]

New World expansionism is, then, explored alongside other narratives of colonisation and control, and one of the strongest incarnations of a mapped line in the novel is the demarcation between freedom and slavery. This issue is raised, though, long before Mason and Dixon arrive on American soil. In the Dutch colony of Cape Town Pynchon writes of 'the Great Worm of Slavery' that lies 'coiled behind all' (*MD* 147), and Mason is encouraged to impregnate one his host's slaves to assist in the increase of light-skinned stock. South Africa is a space haunted by its slave culture, where the 'Wrongs committed Daily against the Slaves' go 'unrecorded, charm'd invisible to history' (*MD* 68). Back in London, the pair discusses their forthcoming surveying project and considers the emergence of an American identity that is constituted by the right to own slaves:

> 'Savages, Wilderness. No one even knows what's out there. And we have just, do you appreciate, contracted, to place a Line directly thro' it? Doesn't it strike you as a little unreasonable?'
>   'Not to mention the Americans ...?'
>   'Excuse me? They are at least all British there, – aren't they? The

Place is but a Patch of England, at a three-thousand-Mile Off-set. Isn't it?'

'Eeh! Eeh! Thoo can be so thoughtful, helping me cheer up wi' thy Joaks, Mason, – I'm fine, really, —'

'Dixon, hold, – are you telling me now, that Americans are not British? – You've heard this somewhere?'

'No more than the Cape Dutch are Dutch ...? 'Tis said these people keep Slaves, as did our late Hosts, – that they are likewise inclin'd to kill the People already living where they wish to settle, — '

'Another Slave-Colony ... so I've heard, as well. Christ.' (*MD* 248)

The machinery of slavery is not confined to the corruptions of European empire. Exactly what constitutes an 'American' identity remains to be contested – Mason doubts here that such a denomination even exists. Yet Dixon is clear that, however it is to be defined, slavery serves as a marker of differentiation *and* continuity. The exceptionalist potential of the New World is fatally undermined by its aping of Old World practices, causing Dixon to exclaim at one point: 'No matter where in it we go, shall we find all the World Tyrants and Slaves? America was the one place we should not have found them' (*MD* 693). Whether Cherrycoke reports Mason's and Dixon's visit to South Africa and St Helena, Great Britain, or America, the novel is preoccupied with forms and practices of enslavement that are transnational in their impact. Before arriving in Cape Town, Cherrycoke relates the travellers' experience of crossing the equator:

To change Hemispheres is no abstract turn, – our Attentions to the Royal Baby, and the rest of it, were Tolls exacted for passage thro' the Gate of the single shadowless Moment, and into the South, with a newly-constellated Sky, and all-unforeseen ways of living and dying. (*MD* 56)

Cherrycoke describes a transition into an unmapped space whose practices are unknown, a movement 'into the South' that proleptically evokes the America south soon to be encountered in the novel and the Mason and Dixon line that will be cartographically constructed. To cross a threshold into the south means to be released from the norms and customs of European culture, to recognise 'this haunted and other half of ev'rything known, where spirit powers run free among the green abysses and the sudden mountain crests' (*MD* 58).

If Cape Town represents this space of strange possibility, it is nevertheless also organised around a model of European (Dutch) imperialism that is founded on slavery's racial binaries. Cherrycoke, though, is an acute enough narrator to recognise – and describe for us – the dialectic at work between slavery's rationalising mechanisms and the uncanny realm of the non-empirical. While 'Men of Reason', he suggests, 'will define a Ghost as nothing more otherworldly than a wrong unrighted', in South Africa (and, by extension for the reader, in America) there is a 'Collective Ghost of more than household Scale, – the Wrongs committed Daily against the Slaves, petty and grave ones alike, going unrecorded, charm'd invisible to history, invisible yet possessing Mass, and Velocity, able not only to rattle Chains but to break them as well' (*MD* 68). The passage is highly aware of its own, inferred, chronological flexibility, for it describes a recollected historical moment (1761) that resonates with a present time of narration (1786) and an extra-textual future of racial repression and its alleviation that the reader is encouraged to bring to the page. Cherrycoke's summary of the state of national affairs in 1786 authorises such comparative time-travelling: 'with the War settl'd and the Nation bickering itself into Fragments, wounds bodily and ghostly, great and small, go aching on, not ev'ry one commemorated, – nor, too often, even recounted' (*MD* 6). At the start of the novel, then, Enlightenment aspirations for a rationalisable space have not come to fruition, and the new nation is already unable to maintain its coherence in the face of faction. (Faction, of course, was to be a major concern for James Madison in his *Federalist Paper* number 10, published the year after Pynchon's narrative present.) Confronted with this knowledge, the reader cannot but help trace historical lines that lead to the Civil War, Reconstruction, the Civil Rights Movement, and beyond, where the traces of ghostly wounds, invisible yet sharply felt, persist.[25]

Invisibility, as Samuel Thomas has noted in his important reading of the concept in Pynchon's writing, generates 'some kind of utopian function against the power cells of Enlightenment' by making us aware of 'actions and objects not ordinarily accessible to atrophied senses'.[26] The 'collective ghosts' of South Africa, colonial America and (by extension) the United States indict a coercive regime that insists on measurability and visibility as standards of civilising virtue. Yet although Pynchon embraces the transgressive possibilities of invisibility, his utopianism, as Thomas argues, is not one of romanticised escape but instead provides 'localized resistances' (55) alongside or within the pervasive political or economic situation. Indeed, the concept of invisibility, as Pynchon deploys it in *Mason & Dixon*, suggests both resistance to *and* persecution by forces of authority expanding their influence across the continent. Cherrycoke acknowledges that although the voices of slavery have gone unrecorded, unmapped by the engines of Enlightenment modernity, their traces are everywhere, despite the best attempts by history to efface them. The resisting presence of slavery leads Cyrus Patell to suggest that Pynchon's novel 'makes us realize that the official narrative masks some abiding problems that refuse to go away as well as some difficult choices that can be deferred for only so long'.[27] Patell's is a provocative reading of the novel, seeking to advocate its force as a remedy for the flaws in America's national narrative: Pynchon, he argues, 'imagine[s] a new cosmopolitanism able to promote the ideals of self-autonomy and to expose and defeat slavery and oppression wherever they exist ... [He] point[s] the way to a new way of conceiving individual and communal identity that will enable us to reject the Old, Bad History, and begin to write anew' (196). This is reassuring, but not entirely convincing, for while *Mason & Dixon* is clearly concerned to explore the underside of empiricism's claims for transparency, as Patell notes, its role in providing a template for the extirpation of prejudice affords the novel an ethical ambition that may be beyond its reach or design. *Mason & Dixon* is forensic in its attention to the history of European and colonial American attitudes towards indigenous peoples, but Pynchon characteristically holds back from the kind of explicit politicising that Patell's words seem to imply. If the novel advocates anything, it advises a more self-conscious reading of narrative procedures, an awareness of the strategies through which authorised histories attempt to overwrite rogue or dissenting ones, a procedure that we saw at work in Pynchon's story 'The Secret Integration'. One of the earliest commentators on the novel, Charles Clerc, argues that the drawing of the Mason & Dixon line makes tangible the benefits to be derived from modernity: 'Progress cannot be forestalled; the line brought civilization, which in itself hardly qualifies as bad or evil'. However, such a reading, with its complacent assumption that terms such as 'civilization' and 'progress' are politically neutral, fails spectacularly to take account of the vantage point from which these judgements are being made. While Pynchon writes from the perspective and through the

voices of his colonising explorers, Mason and Dixon themselves are
more acutely ambivalent about the benefits of their mission than
Clerc wants to acknowledge. He goes on to propose that 'perhaps life
is better off with divisioning, property demarcation, walls, a Mason
and Dixon line ... [T]he line brings order.'[28]

Clerc's analysis, while finding comfort in the idea of securely
mappable spaces, overlooks the extent to which *Mason & Dixon*
teems with the presence of spectres that serve as a reminder of the
violence that such mapping enacts. Behind 'the Arras' (another kind
of dividing line) of Mason's apparently idyllic English childhood,
he recognises that 'all manner of fools lay bleeding, and real rats
swarm'd, their tails undulating, waiting their moment'. That Mason's
childhood enemies label him and his friends 'Red Indians', and are in
turn called 'White People' (*MD* 313), indicates the degree to which
the binaries of racial identification structure, even at a geographical
distance, the terms of social engagement. The impact in America of
contact between colonisers and indigenous peoples is undisguised
in the novel. Mason is compelled to visit the town of Lancaster,
Pennsylvania, by reports of a massacre of Native Americans the year
before: 'What brought me here', he writes in his Field-Record, 'was
my curiosity to see the place where was perpetrated last Winter
the Horrid and inhuman murder of 26 Indians, Men, Women and
Children, leaving none alive to tell.' Lancaster, 'a Town notorious
for Atrocity' (*MD* 341), is not chosen by accident, for Pynchon is
surely aware of another Lancaster, in Massachusetts, the location
of an Indian attack in 1676 that resulted in the abduction of Mary
Rowlandson, whose subsequent 1682 captivity narrative is one of
colonial America's earliest textual responses to Native American
peoples. Pynchon, through this echoing, establishes a line of racial
continuity in which control over land is joined to questions of
the convertibility or otherwise of the savage other. The extent to
which Native Americans can be brought into, and contained by,
the codifying strategies of the Enlightenment is of baffling interest within the novel, and the ethnic rationalisation of continental
space that the Mason–Dixon Line inscribes is contested by an
indigenous population with an alternative geographical sensibility.
In this, Pynchon's surveyors both anticipate a later model of spatial
organisation, Thomas Jefferson's Land Ordinance of 1784–85, which
established a rectangular template for surveying the American continent. As a means of containing troubling diversity, the ordinance

act was designed to nullify, in Philip Fisher's words, 'the two great diversities – that of geography and that of population' by producing 'a homogeneous, cellular medium of life'.[29] The surveying process thus imposed a global model of standardisation on local spaces, transforming diverse geographical imaginations into the common uniformity of the grid.

Jefferson makes a brief appearance in *Mason & Dixon*, in which his subsequent iconic status as national patriarch is comically undermined. Drinking in Raleigh's Tavern in Virginia, Dixon proposes a toast: 'To the pursuit of Happiness.' An unnamed figure overhears him: '"Hey, Sir, – that is excellent!" exclaims a tall red-headed youth at the next table. "Ain't it oh so true. ... You don't mind if I use the Phrase sometime?"' Scribbling down the words for a possible future occasion (the sacred phrase thus coming into being by chance rather than by inspiration), the young man has his interest raised on learning Dixon's profession. The landlord of the tavern then jokes: 'Tom takes a *Relative* interest in West Lines ... his father having help'd run the one that forms our own southern border' (*MD* 395). The pun on 'relative' here points to a familial relationship (Jefferson's father, Peter, was a mapmaker and surveyor) and an imperial one (the generational transition from colonial expansion to, with Thomas, the settling of the continent by an independent United States). Both Jeffersons, though, embody the Enlightenment imperative to self-regulate, to overwrite the landscape with what Franco Moretti has described as 'the impersonal and automatic mechanisms of the market economy'.[30]

In *Mason & Dixon* this imperial geography is competing with an already crowded terrain, for the land is inscribed with earlier – and differently configured – markings that cannot easily be accommodated into the strict geometries of the surveyors' line. Towards the end of their expedition westwards, Mason and Dixon are joined by 'a Delegation of Indians ... most of them Mohawk fighters' who will inform the two men when they reach 'a certain Warrior Path' that 'this Path is as far West as the Party, the Visto, and the Line, may proceed'. Running north to south, this path, 'one of the major Highways of all inland America', stands 'as a boundary line' (*MD* 646), an alternative cultural geography whose invisibility offers resistance to the 'classificatory urge' of the Royal Society.[31] As William Emerson advises his pupil to look beyond or through the rational world, so did the character's real-life namesake, Ralph Waldo, and it is hard not to think that *this* Emerson's embrace of the irrational and the heretical is being registered and transplanted back in time here. Emerson regards rationality as only a temporary way of looking at the world, for it is always susceptible to the liberating incursions of the eccentric, the insane or the transgressive. Thinking, he proposes in a lecture in 1841, can only advance through these modes; can only become mobile and responsive once it is no longer tethered to reason:

> In the brain of a fanatic; in the wild hope of a mountain boy, called by city boys very ignorant, because they do not know what his hope has certainly apprized him shall be; in the love-glance of a girl; in the hair-splitting conscientiousness of some eccentric person who has found some new scruple to embarrass himself and his neighbors withal is to be found that which shall constitute the times to come, more than in the now organized and accredited oracles.[32]

The markers of Emerson's romanticism are neatly encapsulated in this passage, all militating against the kinds of territorialisation that mainstream society mandates. In Pynchon's novel, as the characters approach the Warrior Path, a space of irrationality, the tools of measurement prove to be ineffective, for Hugh Crawfford, the colonist accompanying the Mohawks, warns that 'Distance is not the same here, nor is Time' (*MD* 647). Indeed, the presence of the Warrior Path is felt rather observed, as the novel's narrator informs us:

> We all feel it Looming, even when we're awake, out there ahead some-place, the way you come to feel a River or Creek ahead, before any-thing else, – sound, sky, vegetation, – may have announced it. Perhaps 'tis the very deep sub-audible Hum of its Traffic that we feel with an equally undiscover'd part of the Sensorium, – does it lie but over the next Ridge? the one after that? We have Mileage Estimates from Rangers and Runners, yet for as its Distance from the Post Mark'd West remains unmeasur'd, nor is yet recorded as Fact, may it remain, a-shimmer, among the few final Pages of its Life as Fiction. (*MD* 647)

The subjunctive of fiction, a landscape of the senses and imagina-tion, is enjoined to hold out against the dominance of a scientific rationalism that is intent on elbowing aside its more precarious and vulnerable anti-type. As Adam Lifshey has argued, the American subjunctive 'comprises not one narrative or narratological element but many, an aggregate that is extraordinarily varied and irreducible', evidenced in the delight Pynchon takes in incorporating the surreal and the fantastic into his text (talking clocks and dogs, a time-travelling duck, and a runaway cheese, to cite just some instances).[33] The fate of fiction's 'final Pages' is indeed ominous, for Cherrycoke goes on to imagine the scenario of its conquest by 'Fact'. At the intersection of both, lines 'would have sprung into being ... a civic Entity' with 'wagon-smiths, stock auctioneers, gun-makers, feed and seed merchants, women who dance in uncommon attire' and much more (*MD* 650). Here paradoxically the subjunctive mood imagines into being the conditions of its own demise; and of course historically the incursion of commerce is exactly what did happen, and happens still, once Mason and Dixon completed their commission. The romanticism of Emerson finds it difficult to maintain a vantage point in a terrain overcome by business. As one of Dixon's drinking companions in The Rabbi of Prague tavern informs him, 'this Age sees a corruption and disabling of the ancient Magick. Projectors, Brokers of Capital, Insurancers, Peddlers upon the global Scale, Enterprisers and Quacks, – these are the last poor fallen and feckless inheritors of a Knowledge they can never use' (*MD* 487–8).

Temporal and spatial subjunctives

Paul Giles points to surrealism as a key influence on Pynchon's work, a desire 'to explore the idea of heterogeneity and dispersal' as aesthetic strategies for refusing the conformist patterns of an organised and policed 'reality'.[34] Such a strategy of deterritorialisation, following Deleuze and Guattari, works to uncover what Giles calls 'the blinkers of smug social hierarchies and assumptions'[35] embodied in Pynchon's description of 'a permanent power establishment of admirals, generals and corporate CEO's [*sic*], up against whom us average poor bastards are completely outclassed'.[36] *Mason & Dixon* exposes the rifts in authorised narratives of history and nation-building, drawing our attention to the contingencies of time that might enable alternative expressions of life to prosper, different lines of planetary inhabitation to be carved. After their American expedition, Mason and Dixon go their separate ways for further astronomical observations, Mason to Ireland and Dixon to the North Pole. Upon meeting once more, Dixon describes how, 'at the top of the World' (*MD* 739), he followed the curve of the earth inward to discover an alternative, subterranean civilisation whose inhabitants warn him

..ne dramatic effects that the Enlightenment cartographic project will have on their culture. 'Once the solar parallax is known,' Dixon is told, 'once the necessary Degrees are measur'd, and the size and weight and shape of the Earth are calculated inescapably at last, all this will vanish.' The failure of the Enlightenment project to foster civilisation is symbolically pointed out to Dixon as a matter of global positioning, for 'wherever you may stand, given the Convexity, each of you is slightly *pointed away* from everybody else, all the time'. Inside the earth, by contrast, 'everyone is pointed *at* everyone else' (*MD* 741). The novel asks us to consider the potential loss of this alternative geography, with its lines of contact and proximity. Even as we know that such a place cannot exist, its spectral fictional existence seems all the more precious because of its endangered status. Lifshey writes that although the 'imperial project is effectively an exorcism meant to conjure away this ghostly realm and the alternative local narrators and narratives that populate it', the landscape remains haunted by that which it attempts to write out of existence – 'haunting always signifies unbalanced accounts'.[37]

Pynchon's delight in the surrealism of space, where different geometries and geographies collide, is matched by his deployment of temporal disjunctions. We have already noted the telescopic chronology of the novel, looking back in and projecting forward over time. *Mason & Dixon* also includes talking clocks (*MD* 121–2), a perpetual-motion timepiece (*MD* 318), and reference to 'the cruel flow of Time'. Most troublingly for his characters, Pynchon includes an episode of temporal confusion that results in the loss of eleven days, when England decides to switch to the Gregorian calendar in September 1752 (2 September that year was followed by 14 September). If the drawing of the line represents the imposition of measurement onto a timeless – or at least differently timed – space, this act is contested by the novel's meditations on Pope Gregory's 1582 reforms so belatedly adopted by the English. What these bring about is the eruption once more of what Hanjo Berressem calls 'a timeless moment within human time',[38] for the missing eleven days generate much discussion as to what happens to blocks of time when chronology is rearranged in this way. The standardisation of time is linked to trade (it is 'the money of Science' [*MD* 192]), and also viewed with suspicion as a Jesuit-led plot to further papal interests: 'Roman Whore's Time', as one tavern drinker puts it, is dangerous for 'if the Popish gain advantage in Time's Reckoning, they may

easily carry the Day' (*MD* 190). Mason tries to conc⟨
relationship between the lost time and the new calend
geometric terms, telling Dixon of his belief 'In a slowly rotau..⟨
or if you like, Vortex, of eleven days, tangent to the Linear Path ⟨.
what we imagine as Ordinary Time, but excluded from it, and repeating itself, – without end' (*MD* 555). Any moment of linear time also
has the potential to have instances of cyclical temporality spinning
around inside it. This is 'Tempus Incognitus', a conjoining of spatial
and temporal discordance that, we learn, Mason has already inhabited, waking up on 3 September 1752 to find 'instead of Populations,
there now lay but the mute Effects of their lives'. The clocks are
frozen at midnight, except for those now inhabiting the new calendar, for whom 'they continued to tick onward' (*MD* 556). Within this
arrested world, Mason finds himself able to transgress the protocols
of the Enlightenment, for the removal of clock-time brings with it
'the Occupancy of all that Reason would deny' (*MD* 559), a thrilling,
dangerous space of non-temporality that liberates Mason – 'anything, inside this Vortex, was possible', he recalls (*MD* 560). Before
he can enter deeper into this realm, however, Mason is sprung
from the vortex and returns to standard time, back to linearity.
Against the risky pleasures of the timeless, the project of the line is
to transform such possibilities into precision and accountability. As
Cherrycoke points out, 'Conditions hitherto shapeless are swiftly
reduc'd to Certainty' (*MD* 636). It is the alternative reality of an 'out
There, the Timeless, ev'rything upon the Move, no pattern ever to
repeat itself' (*MD* 209) that represents an answer to the regime of
the straight line. The counter to authorised history and its power
may be the moment crossed by 'the tangle of purposes' (*MD* 79),
what Berressem calls 'the multiplex, differently "timeless" moment
in its sheer complexity and potentiality'.[39] This possibility, as we
will argue, is pursued further by Pynchon in his subsequent novel,
Against the Day.

Chronological permeability of this kind, in which the linear experience of reading is confronted with a radical interweaving of what
were hitherto imagined as discrete temporal moments, is clearly
exemplified in the way that Pynchon threads the *Ghastly Fop*, a por-
nographic fiction published serially and enthusiastically consumed
by his characters, through the narrative. (It is first mentioned in
Chapter Twelve [*MD* 117], then again in Chapters Seventeen [*MD*
178], Thirty-Four [*MD* 347] and Forty-Six [*MD* 457].) Its complex

status in the novel only becomes apparent in Chapter Fifty-Three, which opens by signalling itself as a clear division in the narrative, as Mason and Dixon take a winter hiatus from drawing the line and the Reverend Cherrycoke's tale-telling takes a break as well. Suddenly a new figure, unnamed, is central; she later is discovered to be called Eliza Fields. This chapter and the next represent Pynchon's version of Rowlandson's captivity narrative: Eliza is captured by Native Americans, escapes and subsequently travels to Quebec and the Jesuits, then later joins the camp of workers accompanying Mason and Dixon, impressing Mason for her striking likeness to his dead wife Rebekah: she is a 'Point-for-Point Representation' (*MD* 536). Eliza's abduction and escape appears initially as conventional narration, offering analeptic information on a character who will appear in Mason's and Dixon's story. However, as her narrative advances, we discover that it is not, in fact, part of either the written or oral version of Cherrycoke's history of Mason and Dixon. Instead it is an episode from the *Ghastly Fop* serial that is being read by Tenebrae and Ethelmer, two of Cherrycoke's narratees in the frame tale and to whom the Mason and Dixon story is being told in 1786. They 'become detour'd from the Revd's narrative Turnpike onto the pleasant Track of their own mutual Fascination' (*MD* 529). However, at some point in Chapter Fifty-Four, difficult to determine precisely, Eliza exits the 1786 frame narrative and appears, via Cherrycoke's narration, in the time of the survey, later to exit from it again without fuss. The intersection of these discrete and logically incompatible chronologies, vortices of time that collide with the linearity of our reading experience, is just one explicit instance of *Mason & Dixon*'s redrawing of historicity's shape, its acutely self-conscious desire to interrogate the territorialisation of the past by the standardising spatial and temporal imperatives of western civilisation.

Moreover, the novel's recourse to anachronism, creating what Michael Wood characterises as 'a world saturated with echoes and ready-made phrases, patchwork cultural material which runs backwards and forwards in time',[40] is a more localised, if pervasive, strategy for disrupting the seamless linearity of historical narrative, conjoining the preoccupations and vocabularies of the eighteenth and the twentieth century. Anachronism also works to resist the temptation we may have to read the past as obsolete, alien to our own moment. Instead, the temporal crossing-over of objects and phrases suggests a continuum between the eighteenth and late

twentieth centuries. As Mitchum Huehls has suggest'
difference, we find the Enlightenment and rampant
the two dominant prongs of Pynchon's eighteenth-centu₁ ,
– manifesting the same globalized urge to instantaneity that wᴜ
experience today'.[41] The name of the novel's narrator – Cherrycoke
– is only the most obvious example of this merging of registers;
similarly, 'The All-Nations Coffee-House' in Philadelphia, at which
one can purchase a 'Mount Kenya Double-A, with Java High-land'
(*MD* 298) both acknowledges the prevalence of coffee-house culture
in the eighteenth-century and riffs on our current globalised brand-
ing of the drink, with its specialised brews and hidden labour costs
of production. As a local Quaker remarks, in a way that continues to
resonate with our own anxieties about where and how our commodities are produced, the luxury of coffee is 'bought … with the lives of
African slaves, untallied black lives broken upon the greedy engines
of the Barbadoes' (*MD* 329). The collapse of historical differences
creates what Elizabeth Hinds has termed 'a counter-Enlightenment
movement in the novel' that serves 'to puncture expectations of
hermetically sealed conceptual subjects'.[42] In its eighteenth-century
incarnation of the World Wide Web, initially a paranoid projection of
'a great number of Jesuit Observatories, flung as a Web, all over the
World' (*MD* 223) that turns out to have a reality requiring 'an extensive Rigging … lines [that] must ever be shifted, individual Winches
[that] adjust constantly the tension in stays and backstays and pre-
venters' (*MD* 516). Despite its historically appropriate, cumbersome
technology, and its focus on very specific anti-Catholic anxieties,
this example of global communication cannot but help remind the
reader of our current digital and cyber age, of lines of connection and
interaction that overwrite linearity with different, more complex
geometries of exchange and interaction, what Arjun Appadurai usefully calls the simultaneous existence of 'multiple worlds that are
constituted by the historically situated imaginations of persons and
groups spread around the globe'.[43]

In his review of *Mason & Dixon* Michael Wood considers the status
of history within fictional narrative. 'Why should we care', he asks,
'about this amiably imagined old world, this motley and circumstan-
tial eighteenth century smuggled into the twentieth?'[44] Pynchon
has, of course, frequently sought to integrate historical events and
figures within his fictional worlds. The sixteenth-century postal
service established by the Thurn and Taxis family is referenced in

The Crying of Lot 49's own secret mail system, WASTE; the fate of the Herero people of southwest Africa, colonised by Germany at the end of the nineteenth century, is invoked in both *V.* and *Gravity's Rainbow*; *Vineland* is most explicit in its political and popular-cultural references, with Presidents Nixon and Reagan consorting with George Lucas and characters from *Star Trek*, amongst others. In *Mason & Dixon* Pynchon's deployment of eighteenth-century phenomena – cultural, economic, linguistic – has the effect of making readers conscious of the strategies of erasure that have structured, and continue to structure, our forms of social engagement. Our current moment loops back into the time of the novel, which in turn makes recognisable the continuities between then and now. Histories are not opposed to one another, but rather exist as a series of conversations or exchanges, '"dialogical" connections', as Dominick LaCapra puts it, 'between past and present through which historical understanding becomes linked to ethicopolitical concerns'.[45] *Mason & Dixon* maps out the contested ground of historical representation, pitting the machinery of authorised narratives against the fragile but persistent occlusions that are invisible to the rationalising project. As LaCapra goes on to observe, 'aspects of the past sedimented by intervening historical developments (including interpretations) emerge in more or less contestatory moments of "profane illumination"', where profanity operates as a register of eccentricity to reveal those outside of, or beyond, spaces of legibility.[46] Pynchon's is not, however, a utopian vision. Our consciousness of the continued failures of those moments of illumination to sustain themselves in the face of a national narrative that wishes to streamline and simplify registers their loss as both strongly felt and sadly inevitable.

Notes

1   John H. B. Latrobe, *The History of Mason and Dixon's Line; Contained in an Address*, Philadelphia: The Historical Society of Pennsylvania, 1855, 5, 7. For an analysis of Latrobe's (at times fictionalised) depiction of Mason and Dixon read alongside Pynchon's novel, see Pedro García-Caro, '"America was the only place ...": American Exceptionalism and the Geographic Politics of Pynchon's Mason & Dixon', in Elizabeth Jane Wall Hinds, ed., *The Multiple Worlds of Pynchon's Mason & Dixon: Eighteenth-Century Contexts, Postmodern Observations*, Rochester: Camden House, 2005, 101–24.

2 See Hugh Mason, ed., *The Journal of Charles Mason and Jeremiah Dixon*, Philadelphia: American Philosophical Society, 1969. Edwin Danson narrates the story of Mason's and Dixon's drawing of the line, as well as the that of the two Venus transits, in his *Drawing the Line: How Mason and Dixon Surveyed the Most Famous Border in America*, New York: Wiley, 2001.

3 Lefebvre, *The Production of Space*, 28.

4 Fabienne Collignon, 'A Glimpse of Light', *Textual Practice* 22.3 (2008): 547–62 (550).

5 David Cowart offers an astute reading of the novel that situates it within a tradition in Pynchon's writing concerned to expose the fallacies of scientific and technological rationalism. See David Cowart, 'The Luddite Vision: Mason & Dixon', *American Literature* 71.2 (1999): 341–63.

6 Laura Doyle, 'Towards a Philosophy of Transnationalism', *Journal of Transnational American Studies* 1.1 (2009): 1–29 (11).

7 Sacvan Bercovitch, 'The Problem of Ideology in American Literary History', *Critical Inquiry* 12 (1986): 631–53 (635).

8 Cyrus K. Patell, *Negative Liberties: Morrison, Pynchon, and the Problem of Liberal Ideology*, Durham: Duke University Press, 2001, 5, 32.

9 Jarvis, *Postmodern Cartographies*, 52.

10 Henri Lefebvre, 'Reflections on the Politics of Space', trans. M. Enders, *Antipode* 8 (1976): 30–7 (31).

11 Paul Giles, *Virtual Americas: Transnational Fictions and the Transatlantic Imaginary*, Durham: Duke University Press, 2002, 227.

12 Paul Ricoeur, *Time and Narrative*, Vol. 1, Chicago: University of Chicago Press, 1990, 208. For more on *Mason & Dixon*'s deconstruction of the myths of American romance, see Smith, *Pynchon and History*, 161–78.

13 Giles, *Virtual Americas*, 237.

14 See Tanner, *The American Mystery*, 236.

15 Emerson, *Complete Works*, 3:34, 6:43.

16 For an excellent account of the trope of 'transition' in American writing, see Jonathan Levin, *The Poetics of Transition: Emerson, Pragmatism & American Literary Modernism*, Durham: Duke University Press, 1999.

17 Winfried Fluck, 'A New Beginning? Transnationalisms', *New Literary History* 42 (2011): 365–84 (373).

18 Fluck, 'A New Beginning?', 379.

19 Tanner, *The American Mystery*, 225.

20 For more on the novel's cognisance of manifest destiny and the romance of the American west, see Smith, *Pynchon and History*, 140–8.

21 Michael Hardt and Antonio Negri, *Empire*, Cambridge, MA: Harvard University Press, 2000, 190.

22 Hardt and Negri, *Empire*, xiv.

23 Stacey Olster, 'A "Patch of England, at a Three-Thousand-Mile Off-Set"?

Representing America in *Mason & Dixon*', *Modern Fiction Studies* 50.2 (2004): 283–302 (292).

24 Jameson, *Postmodernism*, 44.

25 For more on the ghostly in Pynchon, see Daniel Punday, 'Pynchon's Ghosts', *Contemporary Literature* 44.2 (2003): 250–74.

26 Samuel Thomas, *Pynchon and the Political*, New York: Routledge, 2007, 50, 51.

27 Patell, *Negative Liberties*, 32.

28 Charles Clerc, *Mason & Dixon & Pynchon*, Lanham: University Press of America, 2000, 138.

29 Philip Fisher, *Still the New World: American Literature in a Culture of Creative Destruction*, Cambridge, MA: Harvard University Press, 1999, 38, 37. See also 42–7.

30 Franco Moretti, *Signs Taken for Wonders: The Sociology of Literary Forms*, London: Verso, 1983, 154.

31 The phrase 'classificatory urge' is from Elizabeth Jane Wall Hinds, 'Sari, Sorry, and the Vortex of History: Calendar Reform, Anachronism, and Language Change in *Mason & Dixon*', *American Literary History* 12.1/2 (2000): 187–215 (188).

32 Emerson, 'Lecture on the Times', *Complete Works*, 1:264.

33 Adam Lifshey, *Specters of Conquest: Indigenous Absence in Transatlantic Literatures*, New York: Fordham University Press, 2010, 127.

34 Giles, *Virtual Americas*, 230.

35 Giles, *Virtual Americas*, 231.

36 Thomas Pynchon, 'Is It O.K. to be a Luddite?', *New York Times Book Review* 28 October 1984: 40–1 (41). In *A Thousand Plateaus: Capitalism and Schizophrenia*, Gilles Deleuze and Felix Guattari write that 'Individual or group, we are traversed by lines, meridians, geodesics, tropics and zones marching to different beats and differing in nature ... [S]ome of these lines are imposed on us from outside, at least in part. Others sprout up somewhat by chance, from a trifle, why we will never know' (trans. Brian Massumi, London: Continuum, 2004), 223.

37 Lifshey, *Specters of Conquest*, 125, 129–30.

38 Hanjo Berressem, 'Pynchon Reads Serres', *Postmodern Culture* 11.3 (2001). http://muse.jhu.edu/journals/postmodern_culture/v011/11.3berressem.html.

39 Berressem, 'Pynchon Reads Serres'. For an account of the controversy surrounding Gregorian calendar reform, see Robert Poole, '"Give Us Our Eleven Days!": Calendar Reform in Eighteenth-Century England', *Past and Present: A Journal of Historical Studies* 149 (1995): 95–139.

40 Michael Wood, 'Pynchon's *Mason & Dixon*', *Raritan* 17.4 (1998): 120–30 (125).

41 Mitchum Huehls, *Qualified Hope: A Postmodern Politics of Time*,

Columbus: Ohio State University Press, 2009, 61. For an excellent discussion of anachronism's disruptive potential in literary texts, see Jeremy Tambling, *On Anachronism*, Manchester: Manchester University Press, 2010.

42 Hinds, 'Sari, Sorry, and the Vortex of History', 198.

43 Arjun Appadurai, 'Disjuncture and Difference in the Global Cultural Economy', in Peter Marcuse and Ronald van Kempen, eds, *Globalizing Cities: A New Spatial Order?*, Oxford: Blackwell, 2000, 325.

44 Wood, 'Pynchon's *Mason & Dixon*', 120.

45 Dominick LaCapra, *History, Politics, and the Novel*, Ithaca: Cornell University Press, 1987, 9–10.

46 LaCapra, *History, Politics, and the Novel*, 10.

7

'I believe in incursion from elsewhere': political and aesthetic disruption in *Against the Day*

Against the Day (2006) is an epic novel of global and other-worldly proportions that plays fast and loose with the geographical and temporal conventions of fiction writing in its desire to interrogate the effects and enforcements of modernity's capitalist project. The book's sheer length (over 1,000 pages) makes any attempt at plot exposition redundant, nor could such an account do justice to the effects of disorientation, displacement and possible disaffection that the reader may feel as he or she is immersed in its narrative world. To note that there are four main plot areas (the exploits of the youthful aeronauts the 'Chums of Chance'; the anarchist politics of the American west played out by the Traverse family; contemporary science wars about the nature of light and time involving, amongst others, Nikola Tesla; and an imperial espionage romp played out in European battlegrounds before, during and after the First World War) merely scratches the surface of a complex structure of entanglement that pushes the reader's ability to maintain interpretative control to the limit. Stefan Mattessich, writing of *V*, argues that Pynchon's text pushes 'its own referentiality to a point of breakdown', becoming a 'broken machine' that refuses 'its own stabilization in a single semantic identity'.[1] In *Against the Day* Pynchon similarly strives towards a fictional architecture that undermines at every opportunity the apparent stabilities of linearity, character singularity, genre and tonal consistency. This results in a radically unfamiliar reading experience, in which we have to take account of our own interpretative uncertainty at the same time as we strive to connect the multiple strands of Pynchon's story. Luc Sante, in his review of the novel, characterises it as 'wolfsbane nailed up against the possibility of reductive interpretation',[2] and more generally Henry Veggian notes that 'Pynchon's novels have often claimed to reconfigure the pathways – neural and otherwise – that readers travel'.[3] Conventions of genre are both lovingly maintained and critiqued, recreated with an attention to detail that is astonishing and yet also viewed with historical hindsight from the current perspective of Pynchon's reader. For instance, Webb Traverse's murder at the hands of two of the mine-owner Scarsdale Vibe's stooges sets in train a revenge narrative that places the reader knowingly within the parameters of the dime-novel western genre. Frank Traverse, Webb's son, feels himself to be in 'a dime novel of Old Mexico, featuring gringo evildoers in exile, sudden deaths, a government that had already fallen but did not yet know it, [and] a revolution that would never begin though thousands were already dying and suffering in its name' (*ATD* 374). In this highly over-determined environment, Frank succeeds in killing one of his father's murderers in a stylised sequence reminiscent of a Sam Peckinpah film, the victim 'blown over backward, one of the chair legs breaking under his already dead weight so that he was sent into half a spin, throwing a dark slash of blood that trailed in the air and feathered in a crescent slap' (*ATD* 395). As Brian McHale has noted in his discussion of the generic plurality of the novel, Pynchon is careful to identify modes of writing that have a currency during the period in which *Against the Day* is set, so the popularity of the western narrative is matched by other sections in the book which adopt the conventions of the juvenile adventure story (the 'Chums of Chance' are modelled on the 'Tom Swift' books created by Edward Stratemeyer in 1910) and the imperial romance (made famous by Erskine Childer's *Riddle of the Sands* [1903] and John Buchan's *Greenmantle* [1916]). Yet this 'synchronization', as McHale terms it, between popular genres and the era of the novel's story-world, is itself, appropriately, mirrored by Pynchon's awareness of '*our* historical position as latter-day readers of these early-twentieth-century popular genres, looking back from the distance of a century at the world on the eve of the Great War'.[4]

While it is straightforward to propose that *Against the Day* is a historical novel (indeed, other than *The Crying of Lot 49*, *all* of Pynchon's major fictions describe, to some extent, a past time), quite what constitutes historical fiction in the contemporary, postmodern moment is a more vexed question. Perry Anderson has recently mapped out a narrative of the form's development in Europe, the Middle East and the Americas. While his story sweeps along at a rapid pace (inevitably so, given its appearance as a *London Review of*

Books article), it is nevertheless instructive in helping us position the formal and ideological mutations that historical fiction has undergone. From its inception as 'a nation-building exercise', 'an affirmation of human progress, in and through the conflicts that divide societies and the individuals within them', Anderson describes its current incarnation as 'Not the emergence of the nation, but the ravages of empire; not progress as emancipation, but impending or consummated catastrophe'.[5] In its postmodern guise, the historical novel looks a thoroughly anarchic beast, intent on overturning the progressive teleologies of its ancestor:

> Since postmodernism was famously defined, by Jameson himself, as the aesthetic regime of an 'age that has forgotten how to think historically' [in *Postmodernism, or, the Cultural Logic of Late Capitalism*], the resurrection of the historical novel might seem paradoxical. But this is a second coming with a difference. Now, virtually every rule of the classical canon, as spelled out by Lukács, is flouted or reversed. Among other traits, the historical novel reinvented for postmoderns may freely mix times, combining or interweaving past and present; parade the author within the narrative; take leading historical figures as central rather than marginal characters; propose counterfactuals; strew anachronisms; multiply alternative endings; traffic with apocalyptics.[6]

Anderson's litany of historical fiction's updated form serves as a useful checklist for Pynchon's own literary experimentation. Moreover, the structural explosion into bricolage, fracture and anachronistic incursion makes very different demands on the reader. The kind of 'creative reading' that Derek Attridge has termed the process by which we attempt 'to respond to the otherness, inventiveness, and singularity of a work' is deliberately disruptive of our interpretative habits, leading us into narrative's potentially anarchic terrains.[7] This chapter explores the impact of anarchy as a strategy for disrupting the coherencies of ideology – those of politics and of reading. Within the novel, anarchist activity is rife, as several characters attempt to resist the inexorable march of capitalism, and anarchist violence is felt across the world. The phenomenon is first encountered in the bizarre context of Pugnax, a dog aboard the 'Chums of Chance' airship, reading *The Princess Cassamassima*, an 1886 novel by Henry James that pivots on the conflicting impulses of political revolution and aestheticism. As Noseworth, one of the Chums, remarks, James's subject 'is the inexorably rising tide of World Anarchism, to be found peculiarly rampant, in fact, at our current destination [Chicago] – a sinister affliction to which I pray we shall suffer no occasion for exposure more immediate than that to be experienced, as with Pugnax at this moment, safely within the fictional leaves of some book' (*ATD* 6). The metafictional joke here, in which it is hoped that anarchy will be confined to the pages of James's novel within the pages of Pynchon's novel, asks us to consider the viability of separating political and literary activity and reminds us that anarchism can also be a textual phenomenon. To read *Against the Day* is to encounter a vertiginous experience, whose *aesthetic* anarchy entices the unwary reader to exert control over a narrative which insists on disrupting its fictional conventions.[8]

But what might anarchism look like in the context of Pynchon's postmodernist textuality? Lewis Call suggests that anarchism, 'by its very nature sceptical of fixed structures', is flexible enough to have continuing political relevance.[9] While its classical nineteenth-century incarnations were wedded to the idea of an homogeneous activist subject (Marx's proletariat or Bakunin's worker-peasant) who is susceptible to scientific analysis, as well as to the protocols of what Call terms a 'rationalist semiotics' whereby the vocabulary of social science provided the language of self-expression, postmodern distrust of both instrumental reason and the claims for a unified self has brought about a revised anarchism more attuned to the contemporary moment.[10] The postmodern subject, as *Against the Day* demonstrates with dizzying intensity, is multiple and synchronous, no longer coherently singular: '[b]y constantly reradicalizing the subject, ... [the] anarchist evades the possibility that her subjectivity will recrystallize in a totalizing fashion'.[11] Likewise postmodern anarchism seeks to shed outdated discursive frameworks, sceptical of the language of authenticity and originality that, in a culture of simulation (as Jean Baudrillard has reminded us), no longer has political purchase. As Call points out, anarchism in this guise 'create[s] new vocabularies, new languages to replace the empty signifiers of political economy. ... [It] create[s] new cultures and new economic systems, and in doing so ... [it] provide[s] an answer to a charge which is commonly leveled against both anarchism and postmodernism, namely that these bodies of theory contain a great deal of critique, but little in the way of positive alternatives'.[12] This question of anarchism's ability to fashion constructive responses to capitalist oppression is an important aspect of *Against the Day*, where the imagining of post-capitalist worlds performs 'the art of leaving the futureless places where I was', as one character describes the present (*ATD* 975).

As we saw in *Mason & Dixon*, Pynchon is interested in exploring those spaces that exist outside of or alongside the terrains measured by the rationalising imperatives of the Enlightenment, and in *Against the Day* he returns to this theme on an even grander scale. The novel begins in 1893, at the Chicago World's Fair, and concludes in the early 1920s, after the cataclysm of the First World War with its brutalities of technological warfare. Corporate capitalism is represented in the novel by Scarsdale Vibe, a plutocrat of enormous power whose desire to control energy and its circulation is but one instance of the novel's concern to explore the harnessing of technology and money in the construction of a singular and often violent version of reality. The countering of such blunt instrumentality is enacted through encounters with strange geographical realms and with travels in time that work to disrupt the colonising coherence of modernity's rational world. If, as Samuel Thomas has noted in a recent study of Pynchon's political imagination, the 'real "price" of capitalism' lies in its 'unflinching and sophisticated engagement with violence',[13] *Against the Day* is attuned to complicities that such violence requires at the same time as it proposes that fiction is supremely placed to remind us of imaginative alternatives to capitalist force. Narrative's ability to reach beyond the empirical and the everyday, to construct imaginative worlds that liberate us from the constrictions of the three-dimensional time and space, signify for Pynchon a powerful riposte to modernity's desire to delimit the range of human experience and possibility. As our readings of *Vineland* and *Mason & Dixon* suggested, American history is conceived by Pynchon as a repeated narrative of aspiration giving way to disappointment, in which alternative, utopian possibilities are located, in Heinz Ickstadt's neat phrase, 'between parody and hope',[14] their progressive potential both entertained and undermined, so that our investment in political or spiritual transcendence is never allowed to take complacent hold. Too aware of the degradations of political processes to have a romantic faith in structural change, in *Against the Day* Pynchon nevertheless considers more small-scale incarnations of communal belonging – family, friendship – as modes of resistance to a standardising civilisation that seeks to colonise the spatial and temporal perspectives of human existence. As *Gravity's Rainbow* had already made clear, 'time is an artificial resource to begin with, of no value to anyone or anything but the System' (*GR* 412). This chapter explores what one character in *Mason & Dixon* calls the 'Provisions for Survival in a World less fantastic' (*MD* 22), where capital, imperialist ambition and technology have all conspired to produce a thoroughly rationalised system of persecutory, wealth-generating force. It is the extraordinary, in its various, often fragile, incarnations in the novel, that constitutes both the thematics and the form of *Against the Day*; Pynchon's text takes as its subject matter, and embodies in its narrative technique, provisions of multivalency that stand opposed to the unitary imperatives of so-called Enlightenment civilisation.

Pynchon writes of capitalism's dominance over history, to the extent that history's narratives of process, change and development have been overcome by the stasis of an achieved, immutable state. As the ghost of a character summoned from beyond the grave during a séance comments in *Gravity's Rainbow*, 'You think you'd rather hear about what you call "life" … But it's only another illusion. A very clever robot … All talk of cause and effect is secular history, and secular history is a diversionary tactic' (*GR* 167). The reality is 'a rational structure in which business [is] the true, the rightful authority' (*GR* 165), and where claims for human significance ('life') are swallowed up in the all-encompassing structure of the globalised machine. *Against the Day* calls this 'the end of the capitalistic experiment' (*ATD* 415), the culmination and termination of an historical process in which time and space are shaped solely for the accumulation of wealth. As this chapter goes on to discuss, the appearance of counterpoints to this state of affairs, in the novel's depiction of political anarchism, fourth-dimension mathematics, and a variety of religious experiences, establishes a tense dialectic in which the claims for countercultural resistance are always located in the shadow of modernity's achieved teleology. The plurality of life – in a world that, through the imagination, 'can be dissected and reassembled into any number of worlds' (*ATD* 1078) – is pitched against an instrumentally 'harsh nonfictional world' (*ATD* 36) of corporate capital and imperial force. We saw in Pynchon's previous novel, *Mason & Dixon*, how science is deployed to contain and commodify the landscape, to render readable the strangenesses of American space so that it can become fit for colonisation. *Against the Day* is similarly preoccupied with the way in which science and technology enforce a reductive perspective on reality, closing down possibilities of experience that

lie outside the controlled dimensions of capitalist culture as we insist
upon 'name-giving, dividing the Creation finer and finer, analysing,
setting namer more hopelessly apart from named' (*GR* 391). Science
in *Against the Day* shares the earlier novels' cartographic imagination, one which gets materialised into a blunt utilitarianism. The narrator at the start of the novel describes Chicago's instrumentalised
topography as 'unshaped freedom being rationalized into movement
only in straight lines and at right angles and a progressive reduction
of choices' (*ATD* 10). As a model for generating maximum income
it is brutally effective, and its predictable vectors enforce what the
Argentinian anarchist Squalidozzi in *Gravity's Rainbow* thinks of
as a 'closed white version of reality' (*GR* 264). This is a world of
complete bureaucratic order that seems to leave no room for the
resistances of metaphysics, as if '*capitalism* decided it didn't need
the old magic anymore' (*ATD* 79). Heinz Ickstadt, in describing the
affective architecture of Pynchon's most recent novels, notes how an
uneasy nostalgia finds itself overtaken by necessary historical forces
that consign those earlier evocations of rosy possibility to oblivion,
'forces powerful enough to define what we have come to accept as a
linear path from past to present'.[15] Against such power, as Pynchon
had noted in his piece on the 1965 Watts riots in Los Angeles, 'Far
from a sickness, violence may be an attempt to communicate or be
who you really are'.[16]

Doublethink and dissent

The absolutism of modernity's grip on time, and the kinds of narratives we are subsequently able to tell, is a dominant theme of
George Orwell's dystopian novel *Nineteen Eighty-Four*. (We have
already noted the dating of *Vineland*'s narrative present to this
year, as if Pynchon's novel self-consciously presents us with an
American west-coast incarnation of the seductive power of absolut-
ist government.) The centenary in 2003 of Orwell's birth saw the
publication of a new edition of his work, with an introduction by
Pynchon that offers some telling insights into his reading of both
Nineteenth Eighty-Four's imagined future and his own very real
political moment. Orwell's focus on the State's elimination of futurity, on the relationship between sexuality and resistance, and on
the contemporary political resonances of the book's composition
all receive due attention in Pynchon's account, yet the insistent

(although unnamed) context in which his reading operates is the long shadow cast by 9/11, the Patriot Act and the War on Terror. The resonances here are hard to ignore, where a state of emergency authorises the suspension of civil liberties and a creeping fascism becomes accepted as political responsibility. 'With the homeland in danger,' Pynchon writes, 'strong leadership and effective measures become of the essence, and if you want to call that fascism, very well, call it whatever you please, no one is likely to be listening.'[17] In the face of this, 'the good-humored anarchism'[18] of Orwell's heroine Julia is doomed to failure, her belief that she can retain an ontological independence and at the same time appear to conform to the demands of Big Brother is viewed by Pynchon as hopeless naivety:

> You want to grab her and shake her. Because that is just what they do – they get inside, they put the whole question of soul, of what we believe to be an inviolable inner core of the self, into harsh and terminal doubt. By the time they have left the Ministry of Love, Winston and Julia have entered permanently the condition of double-think, the anterooms of annihilation, no longer in love but able to hate and love Big Brother at the same time. It is as dark an ending as can be imagined.[19]

Double-thinking of this kind, so destructive of personal and political integrity, is countered by Pynchon with doubleness of an alternative kind, what we might characterise as an openness to options that resists the temptation to codify or finalise. 'For Walt Whitman', he states, 'it was being large and containing multitudes, for American aphorist Yogi Berra it was coming to a fork in the road and taking it, for Schrödinger's cat, it was the quantum paradox of being alive and dead at the same time.'[20] All of these examples resonate in *Against the Day*. One of the novel's characters, Cyprian Latewood, quotes approvingly Whitman's embrace of duality 'Do I contradict myself? Very well, I contradict myself' (*ATD* 491); the reference to the baseball player Yogi Berra's celebrated aphorism of reluctant choosing gets recycled in Pynchon's novel as 'Directions for journeying to Shambhala', a mythical realm of contentment (*ATD* 766); and Schrödinger's many-worlds theory, a key component of quantum physics that proposes that multiple worlds can co-exist as long as they are not observed, is endorsed by one of the leaders of TWIT (a mystical order opposing the materialist restrictions of three-dimensional physics), who declares that 'Lateral world-sets, other parts of the Creation, lie all around us, each with its crossover points or gates of transfer from one to another' (*ATD* 221).

Doubleness and multiplicity of this kind, rather than indicative of Orwell's dystopian paralysis, invite the reader to account for, and incorporate, what Brian McHale describes as the 'forking paths and excluded middles' of postmodern fiction.[21] Such a narrative strategy, for Pynchon, is designed to persuade us to embrace a similar mental discipline, to believe and to be sceptical at the same time by renouncing strict categorisations of the real and the fictional. As we will see, 'bilocation', the ability to exist simultaneously in two places, is *Against the Day*'s disruptive iteration of Orwell's repressive doublethink. Indeed, the novel is dominated by references to, and variations on, doubling and mirroring, as if characters and objects are unable to exist singly and singularly in Pynchon's fictional world. *Against the Day* sustains a radical recalibration of time in which doubles and counterforces proliferate. *Vineland*'s focus on the dissenting 1960s is matched here by an earlier countercultural moment, the anarchist movements at the end of the nineteenth century, and the prefix 'counter' (and its cognates) permeates the novel. From the character Chick Counterfly, to 'counterfactual' (*ATD* 9), 'counterpart[s]' (*ATD* 123), 'counter-Cit[ies]' (*ATD* 585), 'contra-Venezia' (*ATD* 587), 'counter-light' (*ATD* 581) and 'counter-time' (*ATD* 454), to cite just a small sample, *Against the Day* explores the possibility of multiple geographical and temporal realms, in which the apparent stabilities of national borders and linear history are disrupted via an often surreal mapping of time and space. If the anarchism of Julia in Orwell's novel can be dismissed as ineffective in the face of overwhelming institutional power, Pynchon seems to be proposing, through proliferating multiverses that both reflect and refute, a re-enchanted terrain that might resist, however tentatively, the entropic pull of technological capitalism. The final paragraph of his essay on Orwell locates this possibility of re-enchantment in human affect, a curious move, perhaps, given *Nineteen Eighty-Four*'s deep scepticism about this option, but one which, nevertheless, Pynchon finds in a photograph of Orwell with his adopted son:

> The little boy, who would have been around two at the time, is beaming with unguarded delight. Orwell is holding him gently with both hands, smiling too, pleased, but not smugly so – it is more complex than that, as if he has discovered something that might be

worth even more than anger ... He was impatient with predictions of the inevitable, he remained confident in the ability of ordinary people to change anything, if they would. It is the boy's smile, in any case, that we turn to, direct and radiant, proceeding out of an unhesitating faith that the world, at the end of the day, is good and that human decency, like parental love, can always be taken for granted – a faith so honorable that we can almost imagine Orwell, and perhaps even ourselves, for a moment anyway, swearing to do whatever must be done to keep it from ever being betrayed.[22]

The emotional endurance that Pynchon reads into this image is genuinely affecting, a moment of interaction between generations that holds out the promise of continued human significance. As Henry Veggian notes, the photograph is rescued 'from the fixed and monolithic designs of a Ministry of Truth' and made 'a dynamic entity, suffused with a genealogical care'.[23] Nevertheless, it is important to notice that these evocations of love are carefully couched in qualifying phrases that emphasise their fragility, their vulnerability to extinction at the hands of powerful forces. Indeed, Pynchon's reading of the photograph wants to claim an emotional authenticity that, he acknowledges, is not quite attributable to Orwell, for 'we can almost' (but not quite?) imagine him vowing to protect the genuineness of his bond with the child. The reader too is not spared this uncertainty, with the phrase 'perhaps even ourselves' simultaneously articulating the hope of emotional honesty and sceptical of its viability. *Against the Day*, with its focus on generational obligations amid the tensions and innovations of modernity as the twentieth century dawns, enacts on a large canvas the precariousness of human significance in a world seemingly locked into a narrative of impersonal and mechanised destruction. The search for 'human decency', perhaps to be found via anarchist politics, sexual non-conformity, or spiritual transcendence, is for Pynchon a kind of aversive thinking, following Stanley Cavell's influential reading of Ralph Waldo Emerson's politics of non-conformity.[24] Cavell is clear about what is at stake when one chooses to consent to, or to dissent from, a given society, and the absolutism of his position is marked:

You may or may not take an explicit side in some particular conflict, but unless you find some way to show that this society is not yours, it is; your being compromised by its actions expresses the necessity of your being implicated in them. That you nevertheless avoid express participation or express disavowal is what creates that ghost-state of conformity Emerson articulates endlessly, as our being inane, timid, ashamed, skulkers, leaners, apologetic, noncommittal; a gag, a masquerade, pinched in a corner, cowed, cowards, fleeing before a revolution.[25]

Cavell's claim for the necessity for making our position clear to ourselves and to others is marked here; quietism is equated with conformity, and clear statements of participation or resistance are preferable to such empty passivity.

Pynchon, as we have already seen, is also fully aware of our complicities in those structures that conspire to make transcendence an illusory or tarnished goal. Yet unlike Cavell he retains a more troubled sense of the possibilities of achieving this state of deliverance, unsure that that we might ever be able to make ourselves clearly understood, for strategies that might seem to promise a path to political or personal revival reveal themselves to be corruptible or, at best, precarious. The book's search for spaces of escape is unsettled by the constant interrogation of the possibility of dissent in the face of dissent's very own entanglements with authority. The reader encounters numerous revolutionaries and anarchists, activists and charlatans whose distance from the dominant currencies of power burnishes their countercultural potential, yet as Stefan Mattessich has argued (in a reading of *The Crying of Lot 49*) the Pynchon subject is never 'a figure against a ground grasped in perspective, seen from outside' but instead '[a]bsorbed in its implicated or implicate order'.[26] Even the 'Chums of Chance', Pynchon's boy's-own aeronautical adventurers we meet at the very start of *Against the Day*, who would seem to have the opportunity to attain most clearly the detached perspective of elevated vision, come to recognise their immanence in a system of coercion that they have never understood. Much later in the novel, Pynchon's suspicion that radical activity is fated to be co-opted by the dominant politics is encapsulated in the narrator's summary of a Mexican revolution: 'the Madero Revolution had moved on, specifically south to the Capital, where it lost no time in lapsing into some urban professionals' fantasy of liberal democracy' (*ATD* 982). Even so, Pynchon's preterite figures are characteristically resilient, ghostly spectres of a system that has exiled them but which cannot completely erase their traces. Describing ghosts who avail themselves of a train's hospitality as it travels through a tunnel in the Swiss Alps, Pynchon's narrator details certain spirits who once had chosen to surrender into the fierce intestinal darkness of the mountain would reappear among paying passengers, take empty seats, drink negligibly from the engraved glassware in the dining cars, assume themselves into the rising shapes of tobacco smoke, whisper a propaganda of memory and redemption to salesmen, tourists, the resolutely idle, the uncleansably rich, and other practitioners of forgetfulness, who could not sense the visitors with anything like the clarity of fugitives, exiles, mourners, and spies – all those, that is, who had reached agreement, even occasions of intimacy, with Time. (*ATD* 659)

Inhabiting a darkness that is, in one reading of the novel's title, firmly located against the day of European civilisation, these apparitions remain undetected by those who are either thriving in the daylight world of capitalist exchange or, in the case of the 'resolutely idle', deliberately untouched by its injustices. Only the marginalised and the disaffected are able to discern the incursion of these presences, those whose relationship with 'Time' has developed into something more complex and knowing than the template of linearity adopted so enthusiastically by industrial modernity and Enlightenment historiography. Temporality, as we discuss in more detail below, is thus linked to a politics of resistance, as Pynchon's characters go in search of realms that lie outside of the reach of capitalist codification. As one character remarks, 'Watches and clocks are fine, don't mistake my meaning, but they are a sort of acknowledgment of failure, they're there to glorify and celebrate one particular sort of time, the tickwise passage of time in one direction only and no going back' (*ATD* 456–7). Instead what are sought are '"invisible" lines and surfaces' that represent 'the architecture of dream, of all that escapes the net-work of ordinary latitude and longitude' (*ATD* 250). The novel's interest in imagining the political realm as both temporally *and* spatially configured complicates Fredric Jameson's neat division between modernism's focus on representing complex time (through techniques such as stream of consciousness and free indirect discourse) and postmodernism's experimentation in narrative space (through, for example, collage, simulacra, and juxtaposed worlds).[27] As Linda Hutcheon, among others, has noted, postmodernism's interest in time, as it manifests itself as history, is to convert or reduce temporality to spatiality: time is fragmented and history is flattened out of its historicity.[28] *Against the Day*, by contrast, combines an explicit attentiveness to spatial *and* temporal forms, investing in both categories as viable – and plural – politicised modes of experience.

The shapes of anarchism

That Pynchon is returning to the kind of family genealogy – that is to say, a very specific temporal and historical model – that structured his earlier novel *Vineland* is clear when we remember that one of *Against the Day*'s key plot strands involves the Traverse clan: Webb and his three sons (Frank, Reef and Kit) and one daughter (Lake). Jess(e) Traverse, the union activist and political patriarch of the family in *Vineland* is, in this book, the son of Reef and Stray (*ATD* 218), and grandson of Webb, who lives a double life in *Against the Day* as both a Colorado miner and an anarchist dynamiter ('the Kieselguhr Kid'). The genealogy and political history of the Traverse family are thus given an even greater chronological reach, as *Vineland*'s depiction of the 1930s, 1960s and 1980s is further contextualised by the later novel's immersion in turn-of-the-century national and transnational politics. Webb is a member of a loose cohort of anarchists who aim to destroy the structures of capitalist America; he takes his inspiration from Bill Haywood, the founder of the Industrial Workers of the World (also known as the Wobblies, and a key player in the Traverse political history described in *Vineland*), and whose slogan 'Labor produces all wealth; all wealth belongs to the producer thereof' Webb quotes with approval: 'Straight talk. No double-talking you like the plutes do, 'cause with them what you always have to be listening for is the opposite of what they say' (*ATD* 93). His twin career as Colorado miner and dynamiting anarchist is further encouraged by the Reverend Moss Gatlin, who preaches impromptu sermons of political radicalism: 'For dynamite is both the miner's curse, the outward and audible sign of his enslavement to mineral extraction, and the American working man's equalizer, his agent of deliverance, if he would only dare to use it.' Gatlin's anarchism is acutely attuned to the complicities of capitalist culture, in which, he insists, a position of political detachment, of uncorrupted identity, is impossible. Our involvement must be absolute, for 'If you are not devoting every breath of every day waking and sleeping to destroying those who slaughter the innocent as easy as signing a check, then how innocent are you willing to call yourself?' By throwing the language of finance back at capitalists who circulate money without regard for the material consequences of their actions, Gatlin refuses to countenance political innocence, and at the same time he yokes his radicalism to a Christian rhetoric of apocalypse and salvation: 'It would have been almost like being born again' (*ATD* 87), the narrator notes.

Anarchism is an international phenomenon in Pynchon's text, part of a global reaction to the globalised forms of capitalism that in the novel are unsettling the geographical coherence and political stability of nation states. In New Orleans (itself, of course, a thoroughly cosmopolitan city), Reef Traverse, who takes up the mantle of his father's radicalism most explicitly, meets up with a collection of 'desperados of one kind and another who were waiting, most of them, for ships to take them out of the country' (*ATD* 371). Amongst these are an Irish Land Leaguer, Wolfe Tone O'Rooney, and a Spanish anarchist, Flaco, a survivor of 'struggles in a number of places both sides of the Atlantic' whose definition of the State stretches to include 'the Church, the latifundios [commercial land estates], the banks and corporations' (*ATD* 372). In *Against the Day* the narrative of the exceptionalist nation state, as Sascha Pöhlmann notes, is a fraudulent one, ideologically loaded to support particular political acts (often of warfare), and Pynchon's anarchists counter it by 'when possible working across national boundaries' (*ATD* 933).[29] The novel then explores the transnational credentials of anarchism, in which the very cartoon Irishness of a figure like Wolfe Tone O'Rooney is as much a performance as the identity of Eusebio the Mexican that he assumes (by stamping his passport with a potato) to be able to leave the United States (*ATD* 373). The category of nationality comes under pressure both through the urge to escape its political limitations and through recognising the corruptibility of the language used to uphold it. The distant horizon of a utopian realm is constantly sought, as if

> there might exist a place of refuge, up in the fresh air, out over the sea, someplace all the Anarchists could escape to, now with the danger so overwhelming, a place readily found even on cheap maps of the World, some group of green volcanic islands, each with its own dialect, too far from the sea-lands to be of use as a coaling station ... and so left forever immune to the bad luck and worse judgment infesting the politics of the Continent – a place promised them, not by God, which'd be asking too much of the average Anarchist, but by certain hidden geometries of History, which must include, somewhere, at least at a

single point, a safe conjugate to all the spill of accursed meridians, passing daily, desolate, one upon the next. (*ATD* 372–3)

Removed from the reaches of capitalist trade, such a space is, simultaneously, clearly marked on the page for those who wish to see it and yet hidden from visible history. The quest to attain it, one no longer underwritten by the security of religious sanction, is typically couched in tentative phrasing, in which the hope for the 'safe conjugate' is far from assured. Geography's alliance with commerce, these lines suggest, can only be resisted by escape, 'up' or 'out' from ground level, as if conceding that political change within the material world is impossible. Yet such gestures towards retreat (and implied failure) exist alongside strands of anarchist thought that include Gatlin's absolutism and the more particular approach of Ewball Oust, who insists that targets must 'be gone after in a professional way, anything else is being just like them, slaughterin the innocent, when what we need is more slaughterin of the guilty' (*ATD* 922). The novel countenances the possibility that violent action is a legitimate form of self-expression, maybe the only form still available to the citizen in a corporatised, rationalised state.

In the novel it is Scarsdale Vibe who embodies the values and prejudices of a capitalist class that produces, as one of the 'Chums of Chance' concedes, only 'groundhog sweat, misery and early graves' (*ATD* 1033). Addressing the Las Animas-Huerfano Delegation of the Industrial Defense Alliance (LAHDIDA for short – and it's worth pronouncing the acronym), Vibe gives an unapologetic account of the exploitation that drives big business. '[W]e harness and sodomize them [the workers],' he declares, 'photograph their degradation, send them up onto the high iron and down into mines and sewers and killing floors, we set them beneath inhuman loads, we harvest from them their muscle and eyesight and health, leaving them in our kindness a few miserable years of broken gleanings' (*ATD* 1000).[30] 'Money speaks', and it is a currency that seduces, for, in a parody of Christ's disciples, capitalism's 'fishers of Americans' build a nation according to 'clean, industrious, Christian' values in which 'the jabbering Union scum ... have gone forever unrecorded', written out of the sanctioned national narrative.[31] Vibe presents a vision of eugenicist survival, in which the masters of capital, and those willing to work under them, thrive. Anarchism 'will degenerate into silence', the choice of verb surely a nod by Pynchon in the direction of Max

Nordau's influential 1893 book *Degeneration*, published in transla-
tion in the United States in 1895 (and so contemporaneous with
Against the Day's broad chronology).[32] Ideas of degeneration carry
with them, of course, an antonym of racial and ethnic purity, and
behind Vibe's words lies a *fin-de-siècle* anxiety about the increasingly diverse complexion of the United States. The capitalist ideal,
in both its political and racial incarnations, stands opposed to a
working (under)class all too ready to foment rebellion. President
Woodrow Wilson, giving his State of the Union Address in 1915,
warned of 'citizens of the United States, I blush to admit, born under
other flags, but welcomed under our generous naturalization laws
to the full freedom and opportunity of America, who have poured
the poison of disloyalty into the very arteries of our national life;
... I am urging you to do nothing less than save the honor and self-
respect of the nation ... disloyalty, and anarchy must be crushed out.
... I need not suggest the terms in which they may be dealt with.'[33]
Wilson's attorney general, Alexander Mitchell Palmer, would go on
to authorise widespread raids against political leftists (mentioned in
Pynchon's novel as one of several instances of government oppression [*ATD* 1058]). Vibe's avoidance of the American Civil War accentuates the zeal with which he fights what increasingly sounds like a
religious conflict against an anarchism driven by foreign elements
(the resonances for Pynchon's readers and their current political
moment are clear):

> These communards speak a garble of foreign tongues, their armies are
> the damnable labor syndicates, their artillery is dynamite, they assas-
> sinate our great men and bomb our cities, and their aim is to despoil
> us of our hard-won goods, to pull us down, our lives, all we love, until
> they become as demeaned and soiled as their own. O Christ, Who has
> told us to love them, what test of the spirit is this, what darkness hath
> been cast over our understanding, that we can no longer recognize the
> hand of the Evil One? (*ATD* 333)

Vibe fuses eschatological and economic language in a vision of
politics that shifts with apparent ease between class and racial/
ethnic targets; indeed, the transformation of political dissent into
racial otherness is an astute strategy for making visible the kinds of
Americans who are not welcome in Vibe's capitalist nation. The idea
of community that he advocates is bogus, with 'good lowland towns-
folk' living in 'their little vacation bungalows' while the capitalist
barons 'dwell in top-dollar palazzos befitting our station, which their

mortgage money will be paying for us'. In the novel money is seen as a corrosive force, negating forms of plural identity through its deterministic presence. Vibe exults in the fact that the language of organicism now applies to capital, for 'money will beget money, grow like the bluebells in the meadow, spread and brighten and gather force, and bring low all about it. It is simple. It is inevitable. It has begun' (*ATD* 1001). Such a supremely rationalising system intrudes into all aspects of society, including the ontological status of individuals themselves, an effect seen most clearly in Vibe's transformation from businessman to impersonal incorporation of transnational capitalism. Foley Walker, Scarsdale Vibe's 'double' in the novel and his substitute during the Civil War (in itself, an act on Vibe's part of acquisition), reflects on his own position in the light of his mentor's increasing one-dimensionality: 'You suffered through the Wilderness and at last, at Cold Harbor [the site in Virginia of a Civil War battle], lay between the lines three days, between the worlds, and this what you were saved for? this mean, nervous, scheming servitude to an enfeebled conscience' (*ATD* 335). It is Foley who ends up killing Vibe, freeing himself from a twin who has lost his singular identity: 'what had been Scarsdale Vibe settled facedown into the dirtied snow and ice of the street, into the smell of horses and horse droppings, to rest' (*ATD* 1006).

However this apparent victory against the forces of capital has already been placed in the novel within the context of an imminent First World War, a conflict which, one character predicts, will see the rebirth of nationalism and the destruction of the kinds of international, progressive politics that anarchism might help foster. With fighting in the Balkans already brewing (Samuel Thomas writes persuasively of Pynchon's interest in this 'region's rich but deadly history of resistance, rivalry and outlawism'),[34] the British spy Ratty McHugh reflects on the likelihood of war bringing about a resurgence of the nation state, underwritten by a capitalism reaping the benefits:

> Industrial corporations, armies, navies, governments, all would go on as before, if not more powerful. But in a general war among nations, every small victory Anarchism has struggled to win so far would simply turn to dust. Today even the dimmest of capitalists can see that the centralized nation-state, so promising an idea a generation ago, has lost all credibility with the population. ... If a nation wants to preserve itself, what other steps can it take, but mobilize and go to war?

Central governments were never designed for peace. Their structure is line and staff, the same as an army. The *national idea* depends on war. (*ATD* 938)

War generates the kinds of international antagonisms that undermine alternative social and political forms (a lesson that, of course, Orwell's *Nineteen Eighty-Four* also teaches), and for the western powers the splintering of the Ottoman empire can only be resisted by fostering the kinds of national (and, in this region, often ethnic) confrontation that create simplified narratives of belonging and adherence. Ratty is looking at a map that ostensibly depicts the Belgian Congo, but which is actually a cartographic code for the Balkans and the plans that the European powers have in the region. Geography here, then, is doubled, 'bilocated' so that two separate places can be represented simultaneously, 'like reading ancient Tibetan or something'. Reef Traverse, also present, suggests that the map looks like 'South Texas' (*ATD* 935), thereby adding a further continental space to what seems to be becoming a list of transhistorical sites of imperial aggression. (South Texas is perhaps a reference to the incorporation of large swathes of Mexico within the United States following the 1848 signing of the Treaty of Guadalupe Hidalgo that ended the US–Mexico war.) Written 'in very small italic print' on the map is an instruction as to how its multiple geographical incarnations should be read: 'Having failed to learn the lessons of that now mythical time – that pleasures would have to be paid for in later years again and again, by confronting situations like the present one, by negotiating in damaged coin bearing imperial faces too worn to be expressive of any fineness of emotion – thus has the Belgian Congo descended into its destiny' (*ATD* 937). The map embodies a synchronous political analysis that holds in view multiple instances of territorial aggression, the repetition of depressingly familiar patterns of national self-definition.

Appearing after 9/11, *Against the Day*'s apparent advocacy – or at least tolerance – of political violence is inevitably cast in the shadow of that day's terrorist attacks. This poses a challenge to readers asked to adjudicate for themselves between discussion in the novel on the morality of political action: when, how or if principled violence slips over into acts of terrorism. (The ease with which political anarchism might become corrupted and co-opted by the forces of reaction is made clear when Kit Traverse, having discovered the

thrill of dive-bombing, participates in an attack on some Bolshevik
strikers in Torino: 'For a while he allowed himself to be seduced
into the Futurist nosedive, with its aesthetics of blood and explosion'
[*ATD* 1073].) More widely, the difficulty for writers trying to grapple
with the implications for representation that the 9/11 attacks pose
has been the subject of a number of recent works.[35] In *The Spirit of
Terrorism* (2002), Jean Baudrillard suggested that the acts of terrorism were the inevitable result of state hegemony, 'when there is
such a formidable condensation of all functions in the technocratic
machinery, and when no alternative form of thinking is allowed'.[36]
While not in any way setting out to diminish the horror of that day,
Baudrillard views the attacks as the result of American globalised
capitalism, a terrifying response to a political and economic system
which is itself violent and coercive. The uncertainty of our vocabulary, and by extension the conceptual apparatus that it articulates,
means that 9/11 'defies not just morality, but any form of interpretation'.[37] While Baudrillard's reading is, typically, polemical, it is
nevertheless instructive in reminding us to consider how writing
which voices anti-establishment and anti-government views might
be affected by the political realities of the so-called War on Terror.
We have already noted Pynchon's coded allusions to the political
aftermath of 9/11 in his essay on *Nineteen Eighty-Four*, where he
writes of the euphemistic language of 'the homeland', 'strong leadership' and 'effective measures'; as Graham Benton has pointed out,
those such as Pynchon whose politics might be expressed through
their aversion to the ideological centre (however difficult it might
be to maintain such a position), 'find themselves pinned by rhetoric and subsequent legislation in the name of "antiterrorism" that
further erode civil liberties'.[38] In the face of this, rather than directly
confronting 9/11 as subject in his writing, Pynchon's strategy in
Against the Day is to comment obliquely on its impulses and effects
through genre twisting, refracting the political concerns of terrorism
and its triggers through recourse to the kind of monster invasion
narrative previewed in the giant reptile footprint left behind after
the mysterious destruction of a large conglomerate in *Vineland*
(*VL* 142). In *Against the Day* the Vormance expedition to the Arctic
brings back to the United States what appears to be a meteorite, but
on its arrival in New York this object transforms into a being with 'an
ancient purpose' (*ATD* 149), devastating the city with an apocalyptic
power:

From these turret windows, one might view some good-sized wedges of the city, here and there all the way to the horizon – charred trees still quietly smoking, flanged steelwork fallen or leaning perilously, streets near the bridges and ferry slips jammed with the entangled carriages, wagons, and streetcars which the population had a first tried to flee in, then abandoned, and which even now lay unclaimed, overturned, damaged by collision and fire, hitched to animals months dead and yet unremoved. (*ATD* 150)

The impetus for such destruction, the novel suggests, is the emergence of a dehumanised, capitalist self (of the kind that Scarsdale Vibe becomes), the next step on an evolutionary process that results in what one character calls a '*compound organism*, the American corporation, ... in which even the Supreme Court has recognized legal personhood – a new living species, one that can out-perform most anything an individual can do by himself'. Scarsdale's son, Fleetwood Vibe, whose journal we are reading at this point in the narrative, begs to differ, imagining the intervention of undefined but disruptive forces come to shake civilisation out of its capitalist complacency:

I believe in incursion from elsewhere. They've swept upon us along a broad front, we don't know 'when' they first came, Time itself was disrupted, a thoroughgoing and merciless forswearing of Time as we had known it, as it had gone safely ticking for us moment into moment, with an innocence they knew how to circumvent. (*ATD* 148)

New York becomes 'the material expression of a particular loss of innocence' (*ATD* 153), though we are encouraged to believe that it is innocence cultivated to hide an acknowledged complicity in a system whose violent demise surprises no one: 'Down the years of boom and corruption, they'd been warned, repeatedly, about just such a possibility. ... Who outside the city would have imagined them as victims taken by surprise – who, for that matter, inside it?' (*ATD* 151) New York's destruction, then, is a form of purging; the city's embrace of a monstrous capitalism brings about a conflagration for which it is itself culpable. This recalls Baudrillard's reflections on the cause of 9/11 (i.e. a reaction against a political and economic system that is perceived to be overwhelming), and, by couching his episode of urban terror through a revengeful monster, the 'incursion from elsewhere', Pynchon is able to refract his concerns about current events into a hybrid of capitalist critique and pop-culture, B-movie plotting.

Time and transcendence

Fleetwood Vibe's reference to a revenging 'They' who have arrived at a time that is not locatable on any linear axis, as well as recalling the preterite paranoia of the focalisation of *Gravity's Rainbow*, brings to our attention the relationship that *Against the Day* explores between action and temporality. What forms of temporality are best suited, or designed, for particular activities – economic, political, or cultural? Does the reassuring template of clock-time allow for the range and plurality of perspectives that, Pynchon suggests, are necessary if capitalism's dominance is to be confronted? The novel's obsessive interest in forms of temporal disruption and doubling indicates the extent to which *structural* anarchism of this kind might also provide the ground for political dissent. Time became commodified at the end of the nineteenth century with its deployment as a marker of productivity within the burgeoning industrialisation of the United States. In her account of the impact of technology on the social fabric of the nation, Ruth Schwartz Cowan writes of how the development of a transcontinental railroad system brought along with it the creation of four uniform time zones across the country, 'although Congress did not actually confirm the arrangement by legislation for another thirty-five years' – a powerful instance of capital's impulse to standardise in the interests of maximising profits.[39] Moreover, the establishment of cable – and later wireless – telegraphy and telephone systems allowed for almost instantaneous communication around the world, with the result that the experience of time was radically altered. As Stephen Kern notes, the idea of the present was 'expanded spatially to create the vast, shared experience of simultaneity', such that 'The present was no longer limited to one event in one place, sandwiched tightly between past and future and limited to local surroundings. In an age of intrusive electronic communication "now" became an extended interval of time that could, indeed must, include events around the world.'[40]

Pynchon's interest in technology's ability to refashion time into something conducive to the profit motive informs his discussion of 'sloth' in a piece written for the *New York Times Book Review* in 1993, part of a series on the seven deadly sins. 'Nearer, My Couch, to Thee' considers what, for Pynchon, is the lamentable secularisation of this particular sin, whose 'offspring ... are not always evil'. Sloth can generate 'episodes of mental traveling' in which 'writers are known to do good work, sometimes even their best, solving formal problems, getting advice from Beyond'. Citing Herman Melville's Bartleby (and his mantra of resistance 'I would prefer not to'), Pynchon asserts that 'Idle dreaming is often the essence of what we do'. The demonisation of sloth is tied to what Pynchon describes as America's consolidation of itself as 'a Christian capitalist state', and his representative of the efficiency of this transition is Benjamin Franklin, whose productive vision of time earns him scorn for its brutal utilitarianism. With Philadelphia no longer William Penn's Quaker haven but instead a 'high-output machine' working with 'rectified, orthogonal' energy, time becomes a precious commodity from which any iteration of the non-productive must be expunged. Sloth becomes a sin 'against a particular sort of time, uniform, one-way, in general not reversible'. The 'continual evasion' of sloth, with its alternative rationales and patterns, its 'ungovernable warp of dreams', is resisted by a regime of strict timetabling in Franklin's *Autobiography* and aphoristic reminders in his *Poor Richard's Almanac*: for example, 'Lost time is never found again', 'prodigality of *Time*, produces Poverty of Mind as well as of Estate'.[41] Franklin becomes the most visible exponent, for Pynchon, of the repression of those alternatives to linearity's collusion with capitalism, and *Against the Day*'s obsessive interest in forms of the miraculous, the unexplained, and the sublime is deployed as a counterweight to the insistently scheduled day. Writing *Against the Day* in this sense is an assertion of political dissent as potentially radical as anything Pynchon's anarchist bombers are able to express. It validates the writing of fiction by valorising the author as a prime exponent of slothful resistance. Television, too, offers the opportunity to step outside of, or away from, the straitjacket of linearity. This might be thought of as surprising, given Pynchon's reflections on the malign influence of the medium elsewhere in his work; but 'the timely invention' of the remote control and the video cassette recorder (this is 1993, remember) now allows the viewer to perform some basic manipulations of time, rapidly jumping between different images or spooling backwards and forwards at different speeds: 'Video time can be reshaped at will. What may have seemed under the old dispensation like time wasted and unrecoverable is now perhaps not quite as simply structured. ... [W]e may for now at least have found the illusion, the effect, of controlling, reversing, slowing, speeding and repeating time.'[42] The technology of capitalism, then, those inventions which are driven by an economy's insatiable need to create and market, can also bring about transgressions in its fundamental laws. *Against the Day*, with its self-conscious awareness of science-fiction conventions and time-travelling possibilities, offers up a challenge to linearity's dominance, formally and thematically exposing the lengths to which our perceptions of time are controlled and exploited in the service of corporate and state interests.[43] Narrative digressions, pronounced shifts backwards and forwards in time and across space, and transitions into dream-worlds ensure a reading experience that is bereft of the reassurances of linear progression: even for readers attuned to the structural flexibilities of cinema, *Against the Day*, with its teeming life, is hermeneutically challenging.

In the novel Ganesh Rao, a celebrated quaternion 'seeking a gateway to the Ulterior, as he liked to phrase it' (*ATD* 130), argues for a temporal geometry of 'eternal return', for 'mappings in which a linear axis becomes curvilinear … [to] suggest the possibility of linear time becoming circular' (*ATD* 132). Rao's own bodily form is similarly mutable – we read later in the narrative that he had 'today metamorphosed into an American Negro' (*ATD* 557) – and his resistance to somatic confinement is matched by a theoretical commitment to temporal escape. 'Time', he explains, 'is the Further term, … the dark visitor from the Exterior, the destroyer, the fulfiller of the Trinity. It is the merciless clock-beat we all seek to escape, into the pulselessness of salvation' (*ATD* 558). Death – actual pulselessness – is one way out of time's imposition, and this is, of course, the option that Melville's Bartleby chooses for himself. As we have already seen, the ghosts who appear on the train as it passes through a tunnel in the Swiss Alps are the spectral embodiment of this release from metronomic time. Indeed, certain locations, like the tunnel, seem to function as focal points in which temporal disruption can occur. When the 'Chums of Chance' attend a conference on time travel at Candlebrow University, we learn that some of its participants return to it from the future (of which more shortly), and that the real-life quantum physicist Niels Bohr was present at the conference of 1895 when, in chronological time, he would only have been ten years old (*ATD* 412). That year is also significant, of course, for being the date of publication for H. G. Wells's novel *The Time Machine*, as if a fictional text has 'invented' (*ATD* 407) the possibility of the conference's theoretical speculations. As Inger Dalsgaard points out in her astute reading of the varieties of temporality in the novel, the

Candlebrow conference is itself 'an example of a narrative strand that, while present in the plot, might not, in strictly orthogonal terms, logically exist yet'.[44] It has all the trappings of an eternal event at which different temporalities collide and overlap.

It is at the conference that the 'Chums of Chance' meet Mr Ace, a trespasser from a future time who, along with many others, lives undetected in the present until he chooses to reveal himself. Pynchon's incorporation of time travellers from a moment still to come allows him to introduce into the text the benefit of historical hindsight that we, as readers, already possess. Mr Ace comes from a world where the capitalist hegemony that Scarsdale Vibe represents has all but collapsed, leaving those in power desperate to maintain their authority in the face of dissent. The conditions Mr Ace describes are recognisable features of our contemporary moment, and refute the complacencies of modernity's bright, assured future – a future which, in the novel's present, the imminent First World War will start to tarnish:[45]

> We are here among you as seekers of refuge from our present – your future – a time of worldwide famine, exhausted fuel supplies, terminal poverty – the end of the capitalistic experiment. Once we came to understand the simple thermodynamic truth that Earth's resources were limited, in fact soon to run out, the whole capitalist illusion fell to pieces. Those of us who spoke this truth aloud were denounced as heretics, as enemies of the prevailing economic faith.

Likened to America's pilgrim fathers escaping religious persecution in Europe, the 'Trespassers' (as they are called) are time-travelling dissenters, exiled from their present and 'set forth upon that dark fourth-dimensional Atlantic known as Time' (*ATD* 415). As Dalsgaard reminds us, the presence of the Trespassers within Pynchon's text offer (at least) two possible relationships to temporal movement: one is either tied to a single orthogonal line, moving endlessly backwards and forwards on it (in the case of Ryder Thorn); or one is able, like Mr Ace, to 'change tracks toward a future in which the destructive end of the "capitalistic experiment" is somehow avoided',[46] travelling a path that is 'ninety degrees from a moving timeline' (*ATD* 752). These options also represent incentives for us, the readers. Are we able to accept the anarchy that time travel represents and imagine the expansions to our knowledge that other ages and spaces might offer? Is our entrapment within a linear reading experience indicative of an inability to take imaginative flight in which '[h]undreds, by now thousands, of narratives ... [are] all equally valid' (*ATD* 682)?

One of the functions of the 'Chums of Chance' in Pynchon's novel is as surrogate readers. The aeronauts' adherence to the demands of their mysterious and anonymous masters comes under pressure as they are exposed to the effects of the new physics and its political implications; like us, they are required to adjust their conventional interpretative habits to take account of the transformed parameters of time and space. Initially depicted as jovial instruments in the maintenance of social order within an authorised American national narrative, they move away from loyalty to the nation state to what Sascha Pöhlmann has astutely described as a more 'postnational' configuration.[47] If, as we have been suggesting, Pynchon is interested in how technology and temporality are put to work in the service of the capitalist nation state, by the end of the novel the Chums have uncoupled themselves from government control, prepared at last to read their status in terms of a more complex, expanded set of co-ordinates. This had always been their aim, for we learn early in the novel about the balloonists from whom the Chums take their inspiration: the 'Garçons de '71', who had recognised 'how much the modern State depended for its survival on maintaining a condition of *permanent siege* – through the systematic encirclement of populations, the starvation of bodies and spirits'. Faced with such a political reality, the 'Garçons' 'chose to fly on, free now of the political delusions that reigned more than ever on the ground, pledged solemnly only to one another, proceeding as if under a world-wide, never-ending state of siege' (*ATD* 19). Abandoning national loyalty for a self-determined exile in the skies, this early incarnation of the 'Chums' points the way towards a politics of transcendence that opts out of the tarnished realities of earthbound affairs in favour of a postnational alternative. The Chums themselves, faced with the disappearance of both their orders and their funding, come to the point of abandoning their allegiance to an 'American Republic whose welfare they believed they were sworn to advance' but which had 'passed so irrevocably into the control of the evil and moronic' (*ATD* 1021). In its place, the Chums construct an airborne community with their female counterparts, 'the Sodality of Aetheronauts' (*ATD* 1030), expanding the shape of this collective so that it appears to observers 'as large as a small city. There are neighborhoods, there are parks. There are slum conditions. It is so big that when people on the ground see it in the sky, they are struck with selective hysterical blindness and end up not seeing it at all' (*ATD* 1084). Substantial yet ultimately invisible to those still trapped at ground level, the novel appears to conclude on a vision of transcendent living, a mode of social organisation no longer fettered to the corrupting demands of a national agenda. Indeed, David Porush, in a reading of *Vineland*, has suggested that this is a strategy that Pynchon relies on to convey a sense of political emancipation. Such a 'macrocosmic posture', Porush contends, is characterised by the recognition that 'the only hope for redemption from pedestrian, but ubiquitous, evil is to allow epistemological and ontological commitments to collapse into the transcendental'.[48] The final sentence of *Against the Day* – 'They fly toward grace' (*ATD* 1085) – would seem to support such a reading. Yet, as our discussions of *The Crying of Lot 49* and *Vineland* sought to show, one needs to qualify any apparent embrace of the transcendent in Pynchon with a recognition that his writing itself often throws cautionary glances at such an impulse. Two pages before those concluding words, Lindsay Noseworth, Master at Arms of the Chums, tempers the romanticism of one of his fellow flyers who speaks of being able to 'transcend the old political space'. Noseworth responds: 'There is, unfortunately ... another school of thought which views the third dimension not as an avenue of transcendence but as a means for delivering explosives' (*ATD* 1083). Both a site of imminent grace and a space for conducting violence, the sky that the Chums and their burgeoning society inhabit is simultaneously transcendent and material, such that Seán Molloy's assertion that 'The grace they fly toward is essentially to escape the finite and the determined, to avoid wreckage against infinity and to finally ascend toward the sun' overstates the degree to which Pynchon's novel securely countenances such a future.[49] As we have argued in relation to *Lot 49*, *Gravity's Rainbow* and *Vineland*, the possibilities for utopian escape in Pynchon tend, at the very least, to be precarious or vulnerable to state coercion. Our belief that the Chums, with their own developing 'slum conditions', will remain immune from the forces of political tension can only be a tentative one. But it is a hope that is nevertheless reinforced by a novel that, through its structural extravagance as well as its political thematics, has the capacity to open readers' eyes to the potential for alternative ways of seeing.

Notes

1 Mattessich, *Lines of Flight*, 13.
2 Luc Sante, 'Inside the Time Machine', *The New York Review of Books* 54.1 (11 January 2007): 8–10, 12 (8).
3 Henry Veggian, 'Thomas Pynchon Against the Day', *boundary 2* 35.1 (2008): 197–215 (212).
4 Brian McHale, 'Genre as History: Pynchon's Genre-Poaching', in Jeffrey Severs and Christopher Leise, eds, *Pynchon's 'Against the Day': A Corrupted Pilgrim's Guide*, Newark: University of Delaware Press, 2011, 15–28 (21, 25).
5 Perry Anderson, 'From Progress to Catastophe', *London Review of Books* 33.15 (28 July 2011): 24–8 (24, 28).
6 Anderson, 'From Progress to Catastophe', 27–8.
7 Derek Attridge, *The Singularity of Literature*, London: Routledge, 2004, 79. Attridge writes that 'creative reading' is characterised by 'a readiness to have one's purposes reshaped by the work to which one is responding' (80).
8 Mattessich's characterisation of Pynchon's 'oscillating text-world that is dazzlingly complex, mixed and unlocatable, nonlinear and differential' captures succinctly the anarchist aesthetics this chapter goes on to explore (*Lines of Flight*, 93).
9 Lewis Call, *Postmodern Anarchism*, Lanham: Lexington Books, 2002, 11.
10 Call, *Postmodern Anarchism*, 16.
11 Call, *Postmodern Anarchism*, 22.
12 Call, *Postmodern Anarchism*, 24. Call turns to the 'cyberpunk' writing of William Gibson and Bruce Sterling as his central literary exponents of the philosophical terrain his book maps out (117–42). In an article in *Spin* magazine, Timothy Leary names *Gravity's Rainbow* as the 'Old Testament' of cyberpunk ('Cyberpunks', *Spin* [April 1987]: 88–93 [91]). Brian McHale is less convinced of the case for cyberpunk's specific indebtedness to Pynchon: 'identifying Pynchon's presence ... in cyberpunk texts is less a question of "source-hunting" (a dubious and ultimately uninteresting exercise anyway) than of tracking the circulation of motifs, models and materials through an intertextual network that includes Pynchon and the cyberpunks, and in which Pynchon's texts are not so much "sources" as reservoirs or catchment basins' (*Constructing Postmodernism*, 233).
13 Thomas, *Pynchon and the Political*, 156.
14 Heinz Ickstadt, 'Setting Sail Against the Day: The Narrative World of Thomas Pynchon', in Sascha Pöhlmann, ed., *Against the Grain: Reading Pynchon's Counternarratives*, Amsterdam: Rodopi, 2010, 45.

15 Ickstadt, 'Setting Sail Against the Day', 45.
16 Pynchon, 'A Journey Into the Mind of Watts', 84.
17 Thomas Pynchon, Foreword to George Orwell, *Nineteen Eighty-Four* (London: Penguin Books, 2003), v–xxv (viii).
18 Pynchon, Foreword to *Nineteen Eighty-Four*, xxii.
19 Pynchon, Foreword to *Nineteen Eighty-Four*, xxii.
20 Pynchon, Foreword to *Nineteen Eighty-Four*, x.
21 McHale, *Postmodernist Fiction*, 107. Oedipa Mass, in *The Crying of Lot 49*, conditioned to think in binaries, worries about the 'excluded middles; they were bad shit, to be avoided' (*CL* 125).
22 Pynchon, Foreword to Orwell, *Nineteen Eighty-Four*, xxiv–xxv.
23 Veggian, 'Thomas Pynchon Against the Day', 200.
24 See, for example, Stanley Cavell, *Conditions Handsome and Unhandsome: The Constitution of Emersonian Perfectionism*, Chicago: University of Chicago Press, 1990, where he writes that 'the worst thing we could do is rely on ourselves as we stand – this is simply to be the slaves of our slavishness: it is what makes us spawn'. He continues, 'We must become averse to this conformity, which means convert from it, which means transform our conformity, as if we are to be born (again)' (47).
25 Stanley Cavell, 'What is the Emersonian Event: A Comment on Kateb's Emerson', in Stanley Cavell, *Emerson's Transcendental Etudes* (Stanford: Stanford University Press, 2003), 190.
26 Mattessich, *Lines of Flight*, 69.
27 See Jameson, *Postmodernism*, 1–54, esp. 16.
28 See Hutcheon, *A Poetics of Postmodernism*, esp. 105–23.
29 See Sascha Pöhlmann, 'The Complex Text', in Pöhlmann, ed., *Against the Grain*, 16–33. Ratty McHugh gives the clearest account in the novel of how nationality and anarchism are opposed to one another; see *ATD* 938.
30 Vibe's vision of an enslaved working class matches Jeffory Clymer's analysis of the status of labour at the end of the nineteenth century. See Jeffory A. Clymer, *America's Culture of Terrorism: Violence, Capitalism, and the Written Word*, Chapel Hill: The University of North Carolina Press, 2003, 22–4.
31 This recalls Rex Snuvve's observation in *Vineland* that the counterculture is up against 'closed ideological minds passing on the Christian Capitalist Faith intact' (*VL* 232). In such descriptions we encounter the routinisation of religion explored most influentially in Max Weber's 1930 book *The Protestant Ethic and the Spirit of Capitalism* (London: Routledge, 1992). See Ralph Schroeder, 'Weber, Pynchon and the American Prospect', *Max Weber Studies* 1.2 (2001): 161–77. Significantly, Weber uses Benjamin Franklin as an example of the American capitalist imperative to accumulate wealth (48–51). Franklin,

as we discuss below, is a central figure in Pynchon's conceptualisation of the relationship between capitalism and temporality.

32 The dedicatee of Nordau's book is Cesare Lombroso, the Italian criminologist who believed that criminality was inherited and could be detected from certain physical attributes. Lombroso appears most prominently in *Vineland*, where we learn that Brock Vond is an advocate of his theories (*VL* 272–3); he is also highly regarded by Inspector Aychrome in *Against the Day* (*ATD* 606).

33 Arthur S. Link et al., eds, *The Papers of Woodrow Wilson*, vol. 35 (1 October 1915–27 January 1916), Princeton: Princeton University Press, 1980, 306.

34 Samuel Thomas, 'Metković to Mostar: Pynchon and the Balkans', *Textual Practice* 24.2 (2010): 353–77 (356).

35 See, for instance, Martin Randall, *9/11 and the Literature of Terror*, Edinburgh: Edinburgh University Press, 2011; Ann Keniston and Jeanne Follansbee Quinn, eds, *Literature After 9/11*, London: Routledge, 2010; Richard Gray, *After the Fall: American Literature Since 9/11*, Oxford: John Wiley & Sons, 2011; and Kristiaan Versluys, *Out of the Blue: September 11 and the Novel*, New York: Columbia University Press, 2009.

36 Jean Baudrillard, *The Spirit of Terrorism*, London: Verso, 2002, 8.

37 Baudrillard, *The Spirit of Terrorism*, 13.

38 Graham Benton, 'Daydreams and Dynamite: Anarchist Strategies of Resistance and Paths for Transformation in *Against the Day*', in Severs and Leise, eds, *Pynchon's 'Against the Day'*, 191–213 (208).

39 Ruth Schwartz Cowan, *A Social History of American Technology*, Oxford: Oxford University Press, 1997, 156. See also 189–90.

40 Stephen Kern, *The Culture of Time and Space, 1880–1918*, Cambridge, MA: Harvard University Press, 1983, 314.

41 Benjamin Franklin, *Writings*, New York: Library of America, 1987, 1245, 1303.

42 Thomas Pynchon, 'Nearer, My Couch, to Thee', *New York Times Book Review*, 6 June 1993. www.nytimes.com/books/97/05/18/reviews/pynchon-sloth.html. The typist narrator of Nicholson Baker's time-travel novel *The Fermata* similarly proposes a link between communications technology (in this case cassettes into which dictation is recorded) and temporal disruption: 'The daily regimen of microcassettes has kept me unusually sensitive, perhaps, to the editability of the temporal continuum – to the fact that an apparently seamless vocalization may actually elide, glide over, hide whole self-contained vugs of hidden activity or distraction – sneezes, expletives, spilled coffee, sexual adventures – within' (London: Vintage Books, 1994, 38–9).

43 In his 1984 essay 'Is It O.K. to Be a Luddite?', Pynchon takes pains to rescue science fiction writing from its detractors who regard it as

'escapist fare'. In fact, he suggests, the genre offers 'those of a Luddite persuasion' (40) a forum in which to critique the diminution of human possibility through technology's advance.

44 Inger H. Dalsgaard, 'Readers and Trespassers: Time Travel, Orthogonal Time, and Alternative Figurations of Time in *Against the Day*', in Severs and Leise, eds, *Pynchon's 'Against the Day'*, 115–37 (119). See also Toon Sates, '"Quaternionist Talk": Luddite Yearning and the Colonization of Time in Thomas Pynchon's *Against the Day*', *English Studies* 91.5 (2010): 531–47.

45 Another trespasser, Ryder Thorn, points out the fields of Flanders, 'the mass grave of History', with the following warning: 'You have no idea what you're heading into. This world you take to be "the" world will die, and descend into Hell, and all history after that will belong properly to the history of Hell' (*ATD* 554).

46 Dalsgaard, 'Readers and Trespassers', 132.

47 Pöhlmann, 'The Complex Text', 23.

48 David Porush, '"Purring into Transcendence": Pynchon's Puncutron Machine', in Green, Greiner and McCaffery, eds, *The Vineland Papers*, 32.

49 Seán Molloy, 'Escaping the Politics of the Irredeemable Earth: Anarchy and Transcendence in the Novels of Thomas Pynchon', *Theory & Event* 13.3 (2010), http://muse.jhu.edu/journals/theory_and_event/v013/13.3.molloy.html. See also Kathryn Hume's 'The Religious and Political Vision of Pynchon's *Against the Day*', *Philological Quarterly* 86.1/2 (2007): 163–87 (182), which suggests that the novel sees Pynchon turning 'to a Catholic perspective'. In contrast, Robert E. Kohn has pointed out that Pynchon's use of the word 'grace' generates a number of possible interpretations, not all of them conducive to the kind of spiritual transcendence that Molloy and Hume favour. See 'Pynchon's Transition from Ethos-Based Postmodernism to Late-Postmodern Stylistics', *Style* 43.2 (2009): 194–214 (210).

Conclusion: *Inherent Vice* as Pynchon Lite?

Thomas Pynchon's most recent novel, *Inherent Vice*, was published in August 2009. At just over 350 pages, it is his shortest book since *The Crying of Lot 49*. The novel's comparative brevity, its having what appears at first sight to be a relatively straightforward narrative structure, and the recognisable generic form of private-eye fiction were among the first things that critics and reviewers noticed, and discussion of them formed the centre-points of almost all of the early responses to the novel. In a review for the *New York Times*, Michiko Kakutani argued that, in comparison to *Gravity's Rainbow*, *V.* and *Mason & Dixon*, 'this novel is Pynchon Lite', a phrase that immediately caught reviewers' imaginations and has subsequently been repeated frequently in accounts of the book.[1] This label of 'Pynchon Lite' identifies the widespread sense among commentators that *Inherent Vice* is a more accessible and less complex novel than its predecessors, and that, although it contains many recognisably Pynchonesque elements, it marks a retreat from the sheer ambition, difficulty and range of his earlier work. There is certainly at least an element of truth in this impression, but that ought not to suggest that the novel is entirely simple, straightforward or unchallenging (to call something 'less complex than *Gravity's Rainbow*' is, after all, nothing like claiming it is easy to follow), or that it doesn't present many similar ideas, themes and challenges to those discussed so far in this book.

Some of the consequences of the idea of 'Pynchon Lite' are expressed with admirable clarity by Christopher Taylor in a review for *The Guardian* that explores Pynchon's place as what it calls 'America's senior postmodernist writer':

> You could argue, of course, that Pynchon can deploy as many talking animals and Star Trek jokes as he wishes without putting a dent in

his super-highbrow status. I'd have to agree, but I'd also have to point to his latest novel, *Inherent Vice*, which shows, if nothing else, that his brow is less rigid than is commonly assumed. Arriving as it does on the heels of *Against the Day* (2006) – 1,085 pages pastiching half-forgotten pulp genres while inviting the reader to contemplate such topics as pre-Einsteinian theories of light – the new book delivers at least two big surprises. The first is that it starts out as a pastiche of a well-known genre, the big-city private eye tale, though with a psychedelic twist: Pynchon's private eye is a permanently stoned hippie based in southern California, 'circa 1970'. The second is that it more or less stays that way, with no sustained excursions into mathematical logic or mind-bending shifts of narrative direction.[2]

In terms of both style and subject matter, then, Taylor finds *Inherent Vice* considerably more accessible than the author's previous works. Pynchon's earlier challenges to readers stemmed partly from the practice of 'flamboyantly mixing "high" and "low" culture' to create styles of postmodern pastiche that are now considerably more familiar to readers than they might have been in the 1960s and 1970s, and that while *Against the Day*'s attempts to push this to an extreme of complexity were (for Taylor at least) largely unsatisfactory, the more straightforward playfulness of *Inherent Vice* is a welcome return to form.[3] If nothing else, Taylor claims that Pynchon's normal comedy is even more pronounced and successful as 'it's difficult not to warm to the barrage of jokes'.

While Kakutani's and Taylor's comments indicate a widely shared critical surprise at the novel's accessibility and light-touch humour, the conclusions that emerge from the novel's disruptions of their expectations about Pynchon differ quite significantly. While Taylor takes the comedy pretty much at face value, and sees the novel as finally offering an elegiac view of 1960s America with its 'simple sadness about lost possibilities and the things that America chooses to do to itself', Kakutani is less impressed:

> Though *Inherent Vice* is a much more cohesive performance than the author's last novel, the bloated and pretentious *Against the Day*, it feels more like a Classic Comics version of a Pynchon novel than like the thing itself. It reduces the byzantine complexities of *Gravity's Rainbow* and *V.* – and their juxtapositions of nihilism and conspiracy-mongering, Dionysian chaos and Apollonian reason, anarchic freedom and the machinery of power – to a cartoonish face-off between an

amiable pothead, whose 'general policy was to try and be groovy about most everything', and a bent law-enforcement system.

This sense of being let down by the apparent simplicity of the novel, shared by many of the early American reviewers (though significantly less so by British reviewers, who more often seemed relieved to find a narrative they were able to follow and enjoy) consistently emerges from extended comparisons with Pynchon's other work, which the reviews spend more time evoking than one might generally expect in this sort of assessment of a new publication. The monuments to postmodern complexity and intellectual challenge that *V.* and *Gravity's Rainbow* have become and, for some critics in different ways, the continuing radical experimentation of *Mason & Dixon* and *Against the Day* frame almost all of the responses to *Inherent Vice* and shape its meanings and reception. The novel seems always to have been approached as evidence for either Pynchon's continuing or failing powers as a writer, and the comparison and contrast with his previous work has been used by reviewers to attempt to sum up the meaning of 'Pynchon' as one of America's most important literary figures.

Taking the key ideas in these reviews as a starting point, and focusing on the novel as a sort of response to some of the issues introduced in earlier chapters of this book that will allow for their 'summing up', the aim of this conclusion is to begin to explore *Inherent Vice* in terms of the ideas, imagery, styles and themes of Pynchon's work that we have discussed so far. In other words, we shall take the idea of 'Pynchon Lite' as a starting point, and assess the extent to which such an idea (and such an overall evaluation of his writing) might help us approach Pynchon's work as a whole. After a brief introduction to the novel itself, the conclusion will comprise three short sections that compare it with the his early works (*V.* and *Gravity's Rainbow*) with which it has generally been unfavourably contrasted by reviewers, with the other two Californian novels (*The Crying of Lot 49* and *Vineland*) that share a number of thematic and historical concerns, and with his more recent novels (*Mason & Dixon* and *Against the Day*), which some reviewers seem to find wilfully obscure in comparison to his last work.

The plot of *Inherent Vice* is, as the critics cited above suggest, comparatively straightforward for a Pynchon novel. Larry 'Doc' Sportello, a hippie detective and spiritual descendant of *Against the Day*'s Lew Basnight, receives a plea from an ex-girlfriend to track down her current lover, a billionaire land developer who has disappeared in mysterious circumstances. Doc's search through the southern California of the very end of the psychedelic 1960s leads him to encounters with a gallery of colourful characters ranging from corrupt policemen and shady government agents to recovering drug addicts, surf band members, hoodlums, lawyers, insurance underwriters, property developers and even a sinister organisation of dentists. The meaning of the novel's title is explained towards the end when Doc receives an envelope of photographs depicting a murder that took place earlier in the book:

> There were close-ups of the gunman who'd nailed Glen, but none were readable. ... Doc got out his lens and gazed into each image till one by one they began to float apart into little blobs of colour. It was like finding a gateway to the past unguarded, unforbidden because it didn't have to be. Built into the act of return finally was the glittering mosaic of doubt. Something like what Sauncho's colleagues in marine insurance liked to call inherent vice.
>
> 'Is that like original sin?' Doc wondered.
>
> 'It's what you can't avoid,' Sauncho said, 'stuff marine policies don't like to cover. Usually applies to cargo – like eggs break – but sometimes it's also the vessel carrying it.' (*IV* 351)

An inherent vice is, in other words, an intrinsic fault or flaw, one that is 'built into' an object or system and thus unavoidable, which makes it, from the perspective of insurance, not liable to be covered for damages. In Pynchon's hands, this inescapable but fatal flaw is rapidly expanded from being just an insurance matter into a structure that appears intrinsic to the novel's world: the hippie-inspired surfer society of southern California at the end of the 1960s, which is rapidly imploding upon itself. Doc suggests the example of the 'San Andreas Fault' as a key instance of this problem, and Sauncho agrees that 'if you wrote a marine policy on L.A., considering it, for some closely defined reason, to be a boat' (*IV* 351), then the Fault would be its inherent vice. According to several stories told by various of the book's characters, the Fault makes California what it is in the novel (its population includes descendants of the escapees from the mythical sunken island of 'Lemuria', which was brought to grief by a previous earthquake) and is the source of the mystical 'great wave' that underlies the quasi-theological belief systems of its surfing culture (see 99–102). Yet the inevitability of further quakes shapes that nature in another way by making its demise inevitable. In Pynchon's narrative, southern Californian culture's defining feature is simultaneously its fatal flaw. This sense of inevitable impending demise and the destruction of the 1960s culture that the novel celebrates resonates like a 'glittering mosaic of doubt' throughout the plot of *Inherent Vice*.

'That's because you think everything is connected': Pynchon's paranoid narratives

One of the main points of focus in the preceding chapters has been Pynchon's uniquely complex and experimental narrative style, and the aim of this section is to recap some of the conclusions reached about this style by contrasting *Inherent Vice* with *V.* and *Gravity's Rainbow* to explore briefly the continuities and differences between their narrative techniques and see what conclusions might be drawn about the modes of storytelling he employs.

Our discussions of *V.* and *Gravity's Rainbow* focused quite extensively on the complexity of the narrative forms of the two novels, and explored the ways in which Pynchon's early work extends modernist experimentation as it challenges critical interpretation by continually shifting narrative register between reality and fantasy, rational cognition, dream, delusion, madness and deliberate disinformation on the part of some perceived 'other' (the various incarnations of V. in *V.* and the menacing 'They' of *Gravity's Rainbow*), in a manner that constantly undermines the traditional sense-making processes of modern literary criticism. We argued that this continual change of register generated a sense of overarching paranoia, either the obsessively paranoid discovery of V. in every aspect of experience in Stencil's narratives or the more generally induced interpretive paranoia produced by constant disruption of expectations in the ontological uncertainties of *Gravity's Rainbow*'s shifts of fictional worlds, each of which we suggested defined the experience of reading those texts. In subsequent chapters, we discovered similarly challenging and disorientating experiments with narrative form, from the questioning of historical ordering in *Mason & Dixon* to the complex games with parody, pastiche and intertextuality played in the narratives of *Against the Day*.

As the reviewers we cited earlier all seem to agree, reading *Inherent Vice* produces quite a different set of experiences. To take one example as an illustration of the stakes of this difference, the bananas which so disturbed Norman Mailer in *Gravity's Rainbow* that he claimed to be unable to read more than the opening section of that novel return in *Inherent Vice*, but in a quite dissimilar form as the 'frozen-banana shop near the Gordita Beach pier', 'Kozmik Banana', is introduced:

> Kevin the owner, instead of throwing away the banana peels, was cashing in on a hippie belief of the moment by converting them to a smoking product he called Yellow Haze. ... Some who smoked it reported psychedelic journeys to other places and times. Others came down with horrible nose, throat and lung symptoms that lasted for weeks. The belief in psychedelic bananas went on, however, gleefully promoted by underground papers which ran learned articles comparing diagrams of banana molecules to those of LSD and including alleged excerpts from Indonesian professional journals about native cults of the banana and so forth, and Kevin was raking in thousands. (*IV* 140)

Despite sharing the broad comic tone of the description of the banana breakfast in *Gravity's Rainbow* (*GR* 7–10), the focalisation, the voice and the referential structures and contexts of this passage are all quite different. Here, Doc is being told about the banana-drug business by Bigfoot Bjornsen, the 'hippie-hating mad dog' LA cop (*IV* 9), who weaves in and out of the narrative as, variously, a friend, foe, ally and nemesis of the private eye. The focalisation is his and the tone ironically deflationary: a 'hippie belief' is being cashed in upon, the magical properties are 'reported', the 'symptoms' verified and thus apparently more real, and the language of the passage implies quite clearly that the theories propounded by the 'underground papers' ought to be treated sceptically as, in the end, the reality of the product is its capacity to work as a commodity making 'thousands'. The attitude of the narration and the relation between textual world and reader is clear and, despite the continual evocation of possible or potential alternate realities as *Inherent Vice* progresses, this remains the case throughout the novel: fantasies, dreams, visions and so on are explained and located as effects of intoxication, drugs or other products and practices of late 1960s hippie culture – although not necessarily condemned as they are here, they are continually defined and located in relation to a sober reality. In contrast, the *Gravity's Rainbow* passage is part of a rapidly shifting series of incongruous moments (the doomed evacuation that becomes a dream, the comic-book heroics of the saving of Teddy Bloat as he falls from a balcony, the breakfast itself that coincides with the appearance of a V2 rocket on the horizon, and the sudden further shift to an apparently fantastical vignette about the invasion of London by a giant adenoid) that are focalised predominantly through the extended consciousness of Pirate Prentice. This character's 'strange talent for – well, for getting inside the fantasies of others' (*GR* 12) seems to motivate (although without explaining) the kaleidoscopic range and tonal variety of the series, and makes any one of its episodes all but impossible to identify as a sort of base reality in distinction to the unreality of dream, fantasy and delusion of each of the others. The transition into and out of the banana breakfast is thus exemplary of what Brian McHale identifies as the 'irreducibly ambiguous, or, better, multiguous features', 'recurrent concretization–deconcretization structure' and 'all but unmanageable analogical patterning' of that novel.[4] Focalised, as we argued, from the preterite position of those unable to distinguish chance from the malicious projects of an elect that just might be pulling the strings behind their backs, these inexplicable transitions generate an overarching sense of paranoia. In terms of these particular passages as well as the novels more generally, then, it seems clear that the paranoia-inducing ontological uncertainty of *Gravity's Rainbow* gives place to the more readily identifiable and explicable fantasy/ reality oppositions of *Inherent Vice*, in which it seems always possible to be certain (even if only in retrospect) about the truth or illusion of any particular passage.

Although the paranoia that structures the narrative tone of *Gravity's Rainbow* (and to different extents all of Pynchon's work) is still central to *Inherent Vice*, its modality has also shifted somewhat: rather than encompassing the fictional worlds to emphasise the continual disruptions of their reality and truth, and thereby challenging the reader's sense-making abilities, paranoid feelings in *Inherent Vice* tend to be explained and thus held at a distance from the reader – it is the paranoia of a stoned hippie rather than an out-of-control universe. The connections made between events and characters are demonstrably real or unreal (again, sometimes only retrospectively) rather than either all-encompassing and world-creating as they are for Stencil or simply the random and unmotivated coincidences they become in Profane's meanderings in *V*.

Equally, as Kakutani and Taylor note in their reviews, the sheer scope and range of intertextual cross-reference that we explored in our discussions of *V.* and *Gravity's Rainbow* are much less evident in *Inherent Vice*. In *V.*, for example, the continual refraction and refocusing of events through the lenses of a constantly transforming literary style, ranging from the avant-garde and modernist modes of Stencil's 'forcible dislocations of personality' to the popular comic tones taken on in the present-day narratives that follow Profane, explicitly evoke questions of narrative reference, knowledge and truth. On this basis, we argued that *V.* (and, again, to different extents all of Pynchon's works) playfully parodies and critiques established forms of literary writing in a manner that challenges critical analysis and disturbs readerly expectations. There are elements of this in *Inherent Vice*, and the complex twists of the detective plot with its myriad characters and connections can be far from easy to follow, but the sheer variety and incongruity of intertextual wandering often associated with Pynchon's writing is less evident here: the intertexts make contextual sense in that they fit neatly into the world of late-1960s hippie culture rather than reaching out to gesture beyond the limits of the focalising characters' expected sense-making capacities.

The comparative simplicity of *Inherent Vice*'s narrative, in its contrast with practically all of Pynchon's other work, draws attention to the often extreme complexity of his writing that has been a key object of attention throughout our discussion. The effect of this change is to make *Inherent Vice* appear a much more narratologically straightforward text than Pynchon's earlier works, a 'lite' reworking of his experimental aesthetic perhaps, but, despite this, a text that is still able to share some key continuities of theme, image and political engagement, which we shall examine in the following sections.

'American life was something to be escaped from': Pynchon's California

Inherent Vice is, as we have said, set in California at the end of the 1960s; or, more precisely, in the spring of 1970, with Richard Nixon in the White House, Ronald Reagan as California's Governor, and Charles Manson and the 'Manson Family' about to stand trial for a notorious series of murders. Geographically, it shares a space with *The Crying of Lot 49* and *Vineland* as one of Pynchon's California novels, and chronologically it stands at the mid-point in a series that runs from the 1960s of *Lot 49* to the 1980s of *Vineland*. This

spatial and temporal locale is important to note, both in terms of
getting to grips with the novel's relation to Pynchon's other work,
and also as a means of understanding its explorations of history and
politics.

In terms of the geography, Bill Millard in his essay 'Pynchon's
Coast: *Inherent Vice* and the Twilight of the Spatially Specific' argues
that all three of the California novels mark a tightening of focus
on Pynchon's part as each follows a 'large-scale work of historical
fiction with alarming interdisciplinary breadth and deeply entangled
metaphysical implications' (*V.*, *Gravity's Rainbow* and *Against the
Day* respectively) and that, in contrast to these, Pynchon's 'California
novels are shorter and more focused, though in certain respects no
less ambitious, than the mammoth books that precede them. They
are temporally closer, more inclined to generate their atmosphere
through American pop-culture references than through ... equations,
benzene rings, and controversies in Cyrillic transliteration of Kazakh
consonants'.[5] Millard is correct about the comparative immediacy
of these novels and also to an extent about their tightening of focus,
though he perhaps underplays their capacity for sudden excursions into more diverse locations and periods (such as, to cite just
one example from *Lot 49*, the medieval and renaissance contexts
of the Thurn and Taxis postal systems and the mock-Jacobean *The
Courier's Tragedy*) but, more importantly perhaps, his identification
of Pynchon's use of specific popular-cultural reference and precise
geographical knowledge as a means of generating his fictional
worlds identifies astutely the effect of making the 'rendering of
southern California exceptionally credible and nuanced'.[6]

In terms of US history, as we argued in Chapter Five, Pynchon's
work is explicitly concerned with exploring American identity and
politics, and, especially in the California texts, the transition from the
left-wing political radicalism of the 1960s to the repressions of the
Reaganite 1980s, and the exploration of the going-sour of the hippie
/ surf-culture alternative to mainstream US politics in the early
1970s that is so central to *Inherent Vice* extends and deepens this
thematic interest. The 1960s are presented in the novel as a 'little
parenthesis of light' about to be extinguished:

> and here was Doc, on the natch, caught in a low-level bummer he
> couldn't find a way out of, about how the Psychedelic Sixties, this little
> parenthesis of light, might close after all, and all be lost, taken back
> into darkness ... how a certain hand might reach terribly out of the

darkness and reclaim the time, easy as taking a joint from a doper and stubbing it out for good. (*IV* 224–5)

This identification with the 1960s as a site of potential emancipation from the repressive mainstream of American culture that is under threat from commercial and political forces is shared with Pynchon's earlier works: from the alternative mail systems that form the modes of interaction and exchange for a seemingly endless array of preterite groups in *Lot 49* to the ghostly presences of not-quite-eclipsed resistances that have managed to survive into the otherwise bleakly right-wing context of 1980s California in *Vineland*, these countercultural possibilities present other worldviews, alternative opportunities for community, or, in the language of *Gravity's Rainbow*, the possibility of a 'fork in the road America never took' (*GR* 556). In the Californian context, these stem from the psychedelic counterculture of the 1960s, explored either as a potentiality that never quite comes to be realised by the end of *Lot 49* or as a moment of possibility quickly receding in *Vineland* and *Inherent Vice*.

In these three texts, Pynchon's California thus becomes a site of potentiality and resistance to the increasingly right-wing repressive commodification of experience in American mainstream culture. As Rob Wilson argues, in *Inherent Vice* California is presented as a 'worlding edge-space, as a temporal promise of social transformation and popular-cultural redemption not quite over'.[7] In other words, and this is shared with the California of all three texts, it becomes a locale in which alternatives to the hegemony of present-day technological rationality and capitalist economics can be suggested.

We argued in Chapter Five that, despite claims to the contrary by some critics, *Vineland*'s retrospective views of 1960s Californian culture are not simply nostalgic reminiscences about an earlier, more authentic time, but can be read as a search for possible alternative means of engagement with contemporary American politics, and the contrast between the 1960s and 1980s is both a critique of the economic and cultural values of the latter as well as an attempt to prevent the former from being 'taken back into darkness ... and stubb[ed] out for good'. The same appears to be the case with *Inherent Vice*. This searching-out of alternatives to established political and social orders, the attempt at finding a means to give voice to groups, worldviews and possibilities that have been side-lined or silenced by the 'elect' in power, is a constant in Pynchon's writing

from the very earliest short stories collected in *Slow Learner* to his
latest novel. In order to explore how this invocation of possibility
functions in that and his other work, the next section will discuss the
often tentative presentation of alternative and utopian possibilities
by reading *Inherent Vice* in relation to *Mason & Dixon* and *Against
the Day*.

'This dream of prerevolution was in fact doomed to end': Pynchon's precarious utopias

Our readings of *Mason & Dixon* and *Against the Day* developed
ideas introduced in earlier chapters to explore the ways in which
Pynchon's writing generates political questions and arguments by
presenting possible spaces that exist outside of or alongside the
rationalising imperatives of Enlightenment philosophy, modern
technology and capitalist economics. As we argued in the last
chapter, Pynchon's writing sets out to produce an anarchic postmodern challenge to such instrumental modes of thought, not simply
by presenting a straightforwardly oppositional political vision, but
by developing in a more complex and nuanced manner a narrative of tensions between aspiration and disappointment in which
such alternative spaces are generated both as images of hope and
parodies of simplistic revolutionary dreaming as their emancipatory
potential is simultaneously posited and undermined. In other words,
Pynchon's novels imagine resistances to the totalitarian, imperialist or corporate capitalist exploitation of the world's preterite as
both a utopian aspiration and an inevitably futile form of protest.
Mason & Dixon seeks out such sites of resistance in the history of
the mapping and colonisation of America, and *Against the Day* does
so in relation to anarchist resistances to global capitalist expansion
during the opening decades of the twentieth century. Although its
scale is considerably smaller and its focus tighter than either of these
novels, a very similar set of questions and possibilities are explored
in *Inherent Vice*.

Perhaps the clearest presentation of the sort of utopian projection
to be found in Pynchon's work is the one evoked in *Against the Day*
that we discussed in the last chapter:

> there might exist a place of refuge, up in the fresh air, out over the sea,
> someplace all the Anarchists could escape to, now with the danger so

> overwhelming, a place readily found even on cheap maps of the World
> ... a place promised them, not by God, which'd be asking too much of
> the average Anarchist, but by certain hidden geometries of History,
> which must include, somewhere, at least at a single point, a safe conju-
> gate to all the spill of accursed meridians, passing daily, desolate, one
> upon the next. (*ATD* 372–3)

We noted that this anarchist utopia is evoked only by means of
what is for Pynchon a typically tentative mode of phrasing, in which
the hope for the 'single point' of the 'safe conjugate' can only be a
projection of a possibility, a 'someplace' 'promised' that 'might exist'
'somewhere'. In opposition to this, however, the novel presents the
might of capital: 'Money speaks, the land listens ... money will beget
money, grow like bluebells in the meadow, spread and brighten and
gather force, and bring low all about it' (*ATD* 1001), asserts Scarsdale
Vibe triumphantly; and, although he is assassinated almost immediately afterwards, capitalism's eventual triumph over the anarchist
alternative is presented as increasingly inevitable as the First World
War approaches and 'every small victory Anarchism has struggled to
win' seems about to 'turn to dust' (*ATD* 938). In this manner, as we
argued in the last chapter, Pynchon evokes utopian alternatives, but
carefully hedges them around with assertions of the potential inevitability of their extinction in the face of modernity's growing systems
of power, control and exploitation, the 'vortex of corroded history'
that, Doc muses, promises a future that 'seemed dark whichever way
he turned' (*IV* 110).

This conflict between projected emancipatory potential and the
destruction of resistance and difference by mainstream capitalist
culture lies at the heart of *Inherent Vice*. In contrast to the focus
on time that we noted in *Against the Day*, and more like *Mason &
Dixon*'s investigations of mapping and measurement, *Inherent Vice*
explores the emancipation/constraint conflict in relation to space,
and, more specifically, to the transformation of California by real-
estate development. At the outset of the novel, Doc is hired to find
Mickey Wolfmann, the 'real-estate big shot' (*IV* 4) who has disappeared leaving his development Chanel View Estates, an 'assault
on the environment – some chipboard horror' (*IV* 8), unfinished.
From the outset, Wolfmann appears to be emblematic of the sort of
corporate 'They' familiar from Pynchon's other work, having gained
his reputation as 'Westside Hochdeutsch mafia, biggest of the big,
construction, savings and loans, untaxed billions stashed under an

Alp someplace, technically Jewish but wants to be a Nazi' (*IV* 7). However, as Doc's investigation progresses, a more complex figure emerges along with another real-estate project in the Las Vegas desert called Arrepentimiento ('Spanish for "sorry about that"'), Mickey's 'dream project' in which, in direct contradiction of the rules of capital, 'anybody could go live there for free, didn't matter who you were, show up and if there's a unit open it's yours, overnight, forever' (*IV* 248). This space for an alternative, non-commercial community is given as a potential reason for Mickey's disappearance, as Doc is told by Special Agents Borderline and Flatweed of the FBI, who are also on his trail:

> It's you hippies. You are making everyone crazy. We'd always assumed that Michael's conscience would never be a problem. After all his years of never appearing to have one. Suddenly he decides to *change his life* and give away millions to an assortment of degenerates – Negroes, longhairs, drifters. Do you know what he said? We have it on tape. 'I feel as if I've awakened from a dream of a crime for which I can never atone, an act I can never go back and choose not to commit. I can't believe I spent my whole life making people pay for shelter, when it ought to've been free. It's just so obvious.' (*IV* 244)

This moment of hippie revelation, an alternative vision to the commercial speculation driving his previous land development, brings down on Mickey's head the forces of the state (the FBI) as well as other shady groups (the mysterious Golden Fang). This alternative community remains finally unrealised as, with Mickey's disappearance, the project is abandoned part-way through leaving just a ghost town in the desert inhabited only by the paranoid Riggs Warbling, who is driven to distraction by the 'deliberate, authorized buzzing' of military jet-fighters that will one day be permitted to launch a 'rocket strike, and Arrepentimiento will be history – except it won't even be that, because they'll destroy all the records, too' (*IV* 251). As in Pynchon's earlier work, the posited utopian alternative is immediately qualified and withdrawn as a realisable possibility: the countercultural anti-capitalist free community remains unrealised and is imminently to be extinguished entirely at the moment that 'they' choose to wipe it out with a rocket strike and expunge it entirely from the historical record.

Arrepentimiento is, though, just one of the novel's visions of an alternative order – the closest to being realised, perhaps, but by no means the only utopian possibility that is evoked. Numerous potential utopias are suggested, often as the briefest moments of hope, and not all are closed off as resolutely as the unfinished desert town. Towards the end of the novel, the nautical lawyer Sauncho Smilax ties together the different threads of utopian and reactionary potential in an elegiac speech about a ship, both a particular vessel that has reappeared menacingly throughout the text and also the 'ship of state' itself:

> yet there is no avoiding time, the sea of time, the sea of memory and forgetfulness, the years of promise, gone and unrecoverable, of the land almost allowed to claim its better destiny, only to have the claim jumped by evildoers known all too well, and taken instead and held hostage to the future we must live in now forever. May we trust that this blessed ship is bound for some better shore, some undrowned Lemuria, risen and redeemed, where the American fate, mercifully, failed to transpire. (*IV* 341)

The ship, the United States, although continually threatened with having its 'claim jumped by evildoers known all too well' remains a subject of hope, retaining the subjunctive potential, within the parameters of Pynchon's fictional California, to arrive redemptively at 'some better shore'.

Despite its considerably simpler narrative form and less encyclopaedic range of references, then, *Inherent Vice* maintains the critical-political stance that we have detected in a good deal of Pynchon's writing: it challenges the reader to question common-sense assumptions about the rational structures of domination prevalent in technological thinking and capitalist economics that reduce identity and community to functions of calculation, and presents aesthetically the potential for alternatives to the status quo. Although describing a 1960s culture coming to a traumatic end, the publication of *Inherent Vice* in 2009 also asks us to reflect on the moment of its appearance, in which an increasingly polarised and reactionary American political culture accentuates the kinds of divisions that Pynchon's entire writing career has so forensically examined. As David Cowart has noted, *Inherent Vice* 'addresses the antipathy of left and right in terms somewhat more conducive to prospect than to retrospect',[8] for its depiction of the forces of conservatism corralling a populace into complacent conformity speak to our present and near future. Driving into Los Angeles, Doc reflects on the torpor of its inhabitants: 'People in this town saw only what they'd all agreed to see, they believed what was on the tube or in the morning papers half of them read while they were driving to work on the freeway, and it was all their dream about being wised up, about the truth setting them free' (*IV* 315). Unlike the easy mantras of west-coast popular culture, the 'truth' in Pynchon's work does not emancipate. Instead, the term itself is placed alongside other, contesting claims for our attention in such a way that the ideology of authorised narratives is unpeeled. Even if not overturned by a utopian reflex, the stories that we tell about ourselves, and especially those that get told on our behalf, are exposed to careful interrogation. Narratologically *Inherent Vice* might perhaps be 'Pynchon Lite', and it is certainly one of his most immediately accessible and funny texts, but it continues to offer serious commentary about an 'American life [that] was something to be escaped from' (*IV* 192).

Notes

1 Michiko Kakutani, 'Another Doorway to the Paranoid Pynchon Dimension', *The New York Times*, 4 August 2009. Online: www.nytimes. com/2009/08/04/books/04kaku.html?pagewanted=all.

2 Christopher Taylor, '*Inherent Vice* by Thomas Pynchon', *The Guardian*, 1 August 2009. Online: www.guardian.co.uk/books/2009/aug/01/ thomas-pynchon-inherent-vice-review.

3 This case is made even more strongly by Thomas Leveritt in his review for *The Independent*, which begins by tendentiously claiming that, in contrast to his reception in the United States as 'one of America's most important writers ever', the British have 'some problem' with Pynchon: 'Of those who've heard of him, few have read him, and of those who have read him, even fewer seem able to metabolise him' (Leveritt, '*Inherent Vice*, by Thomas Pynchon', *The Independent*, Sunday, 9 August 2009. Online: www.independent.co.uk/arts-entertainment/books/reviews/ inherent-vice-by-thomas-pynchon-1767732.html).

4 See Chapter Four; the quotations are from McHale, *Constructing Postmodernism*, 113, 63, 80.

5 Bill Millard, 'Pynchon's Coast: *Inherent Vice* and the Twilight of the Spatially Specific', *College Hill Review*, 4 (Fall, 2009). Online: www.collegehillreview.com/004/0040501.html.

6 Millard, 'Pynchon's Coast'. Millard also notes that so many of the references, especially in *Inherent Vice*, are to 'the actual landscape of greater Los Angeles in that given period that *Wired* magazine has posted an online interactive map' of Pynchon's California. See Mark Horowitz,

'The Unofficial Thomas Pynchon Guide to Los Angeles (and vice versa)', *Wired*, 17.08 (August 2009). Online: www.wired.com/special_multimedia/2009/pl_print_1708.

7 Rob Wilson, 'On the Pacific Edge of Catastrophe, or Redemption: California Dreaming in Thomas Pynchon's *Inherent Vice*', *boundary 2* 37.2 (2010): 217–25 (218).

8 Cowart, *Thomas Pynchon & the Dark Passages of History*, 128.

Works cited

Abrams, M. H. *The Mirror and the Lamp: Romantic Theory and the Critical Tradition*. Oxford: Oxford University Press, 1953

Adams, Henry. *The Degradation of the Democratic Dogma*. London: Macmillan, 1919

Adams, Henry. *The Education of Henry Adams*. London: Penguin Books, 1995

Adorno, Theodor W. and Max Horkheimer. *Dialectic of Enlightenment*. London: Verso, 1997

Anderson, Perry. 'From Progress to Catastophe', *London Review of Books* 33.15 (28 July 2011): 24–8

Anon. 'A Myth of Alligators', *Time*, 15 March 1963. Online: www.time.com/time/magazine/article/0,9171,870237,00.html

Apter, Emily. 'On Oneworldedness: Or Paranoia as a World System', *American Literary History* 18.2 (2006): 365–89

Attridge, Derek. *The Singularity of Literature*. London: Routledge, 2004

Badiou, Alain. *Saint Paul: The Foundation of Universalism*, trans. Ray Brassier. Stanford: Stanford University Press, 2003

Baker, Jeffrey S. 'Amerikka Über Alles: German Nationalism, American Imperialism, and the 1960s Antiwar Movement in *Gravity's Rainbow*', *Critique* 40.4 (Summer, 1999): 323–41

Baker, Nicholson. *The Fermata*. London: Vintage Books, 1994

Barnett, Stuart. 'Refused Readings: Narrative and History in "The Secret Integration"', *Pynchon Notes* 22–3 (1988): 79–85

Baudrillard, Jean. *The Spirit of Terrorism*. London: Verso, 2002

Benjamin, Walter, *Selected Writings*: Volume 4, *1938–1940*, ed. Howard Eiland and Michael W. Jennings. Cambridge, MA: Harvard University Press, 2003

Bercovitch, Sacvan. 'The Problem of Ideology in American Literary History', *Critical Inquiry* 12 (1986): 631–53

Berressem, Hanjo. *Pynchon's Poetics: Interfacing Theory and Text*. Urbana: University of Illinois Press, 1993

Berressem, Hanjo. 'Pynchon Reads Serres', *Postmodern Culture* 11.3

(2001). Online: http://muse.jhu.edu/journals/postmodern_culture/
v011/11.3berressemprs1.html

Bersani, Leo. 'Pynchon, Paranoia and Literature', *Representations* 25
(Winter, 1989): 99–118

Bérubé, Michael. *Marginal Forces / Cultural Centers: Tolson, Pynchon, and the
Politics of the Canon*. Ithaca: Cornell University Press, 1992

Best, Steven and Douglas Kellner. *The Postmodern Adventure: Science,
Technology and Cultural Studies at the Third Millennium*. New York and
London: Guilford Press, 2001

Brett, R. L. and A.R. Jones, eds. *Wordsworth and Coleridge: Lyrical Ballads*.
2nd edition. London: Routledge, 1961

Caesar, Terry and Takashi Aso, 'Japan, Creative Masochism, and
Transnationality in *Vineland*', *Critique* 44.4 (2003): 371–87

Call, Lewis. *Postmodern Anarchism*. Lanham: Lexington Books, 2002

Casey, Edward. 'The World of Nostalgia', *Man and World* 20 (1987):
361–84

Cavell, Stanley. *Conditions Handsome and Unhandsome: The Constitution of
Emersonian Perfectionism*. Chicago: University of Chicago Press, 1990

Cavell, Stanley. *Emerson's Transcendental Etudes*. Stanford: Stanford
University Press, 2003

Cavell, Stanley. *Philosophy the Day After Tomorrow*. Cambridge, MA: Harvard
University Press, 2005

Chambers, Judith. *Thomas Pynchon*. New York: Twayne, 1992

Clerc, Charles, ed. *Approaches to 'Gravity's Rainbow'*. Columbus: Ohio State
University Press, 1983

Clerc, Charles. *Mason & Dixon & Pynchon*. Lanham: University Press of
America, 2000

Clymer, Jeffory A. *America's Culture of Terrorism: Violence, Capitalism, and
the Written Word*. Chapel Hill: The University of North Carolina Press,
2003

Collignon, Fabienne. 'A Glimpse of Light', *Textual Practice* 22.3 (2008):
547–62

Cooper, Peter L., *Signs and Symptoms: Thomas Pynchon and the Contemporary
World*. Berkeley: University of California Press, 1983

Cowart, David. *Thomas Pynchon: The Art of Allusion*. Carbondale: Southern
Illinois University Press, 1980

Cowart, David. 'Pynchon and the Sixties', *Critique* 41.1 (Fall, 1999): 3–12

Cowart, David. 'The Luddite Vision: Mason & Dixon', *American Literature*
71.2 (1999): 341–63

Cowart, David. *Thomas Pynchon & the Dark Passages of History*. Athens:
University of Georgia Press, 2011

Crosthwaite, Paul. *Trauma, Postmodernism and the Aftermath of World War
II*. Basingstoke: Palgrave, 2009

Curtin, Maureen F. *Out of Touch: Skin Tropes and Identities in Woolf, Ellison, Pynchon and Acker*. New York: Routledge, 2003

Dalsgaard, Inger H., Luc Herman and Brian McHale, eds, *The Cambridge Companion to Thomas Pynchon*. Cambridge: Cambridge University Press, 2011

Danson, Edwin. *Drawing the Line: How Mason and Dixon Surveyed the Most Famous Border in America*. New York: Wiley, 2001

Davidson, Cathy N. 'Oedipa as Androgyne in Thomas Pynchon's *The Crying of Lot 49*', Contemporary Literature 13 (1977): 38–50

Davis, Mike. 'Fortress Los Angeles: The Militarization of Urban Space', in Michael Sorkin, ed., *Variations on a Theme Park: The New American City and the End of Public Space*. New York: Hill & Wang, 1992, 154–80

Davis, Robert M. 'Parody, Paranoia, and the Dead End of Language in *The Crying of Lot 49*', Genre 5 (1977): 367–77

Deleuze, Gilles and Félix Guattari. *A Thousand Plateaus: Capitalism and Schizophrenia*, trans. Brian Massumi. London: Continuum, 2004

Do Carmo, Stephen. 'History, Refusal, and the Strategic-Essentialist Politics of Pynchon's *Vineland*', Pynchon Notes 44–5 (1999): 173–94

Doane, Janice and Devon Hodge. *Nostalgia and Sexual Difference: The Resistance to Contemporary Feminism*. New York: Methuen, 1987

Doyle, Laura. 'Towards a Philosophy of Transnationalism', Journal of Transnational American Studies 1.1 (2009): 1–29

Dugdale, John. *Thomas Pynchon: Allusive Parables of Power*. London: Macmillan, 1990

Dussere, Erik. 'Flirters, Deserters, Wimps, and Pimps: Thomas Pynchon's Two Americas', Contemporary Literature 51.3 (2010): 565–95

Eagleton, Terry. *Against the Grain: Essays 1975–1985*. New York: Verso, 1986

Emerson, Ralph Waldo. *The Complete Works of Ralph Waldo Emerson*, Centenary Edition, 12 vols. Boston: Houghton Mifflin, 1903–04

Evans, David H. 'Taking Out the Trash: Don DeLillo's *Underworld*, Liquid Modernity, and the End of Garbage', Cambridge Quarterly 35.2 (2006): 103–32

Fisher, Philip. *Still the New World: American Literature in a Culture of Creative Destruction*. Cambridge, MA: Harvard University Press, 1999

Fluck, Winfried. 'A New Beginning? Transnationalisms', New Literary History 42 (2011): 365–84

Foreman, Joel, ed. *The Other Fifties: Interrogating Midcentury American Icons*. Champaign: University of Illinois Press, 1997

Franklin, Benjamin. *Writings*. New York: Library of America, 1987

Friedman, Ellen G. 'Where are the Missing Contents? (Post)Modernism, Gender, and the Canon', PMLA 108 (1993): 240–52

Giles, Paul. *Virtual Americas: Transnational Fictions and the Transatlantic Imaginary.* Durham: Duke University Press, 2002

Giles, Paul. *The Global Remapping of American Literature.* Princeton: Princeton University Press, 2011

Grant, J. Kerry. *A Companion to V.* Athens and London: The University of Georgia Press, 2001

Gray, Richard. *After the Fall: American Literature Since 9/11.* Oxford: John Wiley & Sons, 2011

Green, Geoffrey, Donald J. Greiner and Larry McCaffery, eds. *The Vineland Papers: Critical Takes on Pynchon's Novel.* Normal, IL: Dalkey Archive Press, 1994

Habermas, Jürgen. 'Philosophy and Stand-in and Interpreter', in K. Baynes, J. Bonham and T. McCarthy, eds, *After Philosophy: End or Transformation?* Cambridge, MA: The MIT Press, 1987, 296–315

Hardt, Michael and Antonio Negri. *Empire.* Cambridge, MA: Harvard University Press, 2000

Hawthorne, Mark D. 'Homoerotic Bonding as Escape from Heterosexual Responsibility in Pynchon's *Slow Learner*', *Style* 344.3 (2000): 512–29

Hayles, N. Katherine. '"Who Was Saved?" Families, Snitches, and Recuperation in Pynchon's *Vineland*', *Critique* 32.2 (1990): 77–91

Herman, Luc and John M. Krafft. 'From the Ground Up: The Evolution of the South-West Africa Chapter in Pynchon's *V.*', *Contemporary Literature* 47.2 (Summer, 2006): 261–88

Hinds, Elizabeth Jane Wall. 'Sari, Sorry, and the Vortex of History: Calendar Reform, Anachronism, and Language Change in *Mason & Dixon*', *American Literary History* 12.1/2 (2000): 187–215

Hinds, Elizabeth Jane Wall, ed. *The Multiple Worlds of Pynchon's Mason & Dixon: Eighteenth-Century Contexts, Postmodern Observations.* Rochester: Camden House, 2005

Hoborek, Andrew. *The Twilight of the Middle Class: Post-World War II American Fiction and White-Collar Work.* Princeton: Princeton University Press, 2005

Hofstadter, Richard. *The Paranoid Style in American Politics and Other Essays.* New York: Knopf, 1965

Horowitz, Mark. 'The Unofficial Thomas Pynchon Guide to Los Angeles (and vice versa)', *Wired*, 17.08 (August 2009). Online: www.wired.com/special_multimedia/2009/pl_print_1708

Huehls, Mitchum. *Qualified Hope: A Postmodern Politics of Time.* Columbus: Ohio State University Press, 2009

Hume, Kathryn. *Pynchon's Mythography: An Approach to 'Gravity's Rainbow'.* Carbondale: Southern Illinois University Press, 1987

Hume, Kathryn. 'The Religious and Political Vision of Pynchon's *Against the Day*', *Philological Quarterly* 86.1/2 (2007): 163–87

Hutcheon, Linda. *A Poetics of Postmodernism*. 2nd edition, London: Routledge, 2002

Hutcheon, Linda. *The Politics of Postmodernism*. 2nd edition. London: Routledge, 2002

Huyssen, Andreas. *After the Great Divide: Modernism, Mass Culture, Postmodernism*. Basingstoke: Macmillan, 1986

James, Henry. *The Critical Muse: Selected Literary Criticism*, ed. Roger Gard. London: Penguin Books, 1987

James, Henry. *The American Scene*. New York: Penguin Books, 1994

Jameson, Fredric. 'Periodizing the 60s', *Social Text* 9–10 (1984): 178–209

Jameson, Fredric. *Postmodernism, or, the Cultural Logic of Late Capitalism*. London: Verso, 1991

Jardine, Alice. *Gynesis: Configurations of Woman and Modernity*. Ithaca: Cornell University Press, 1985

Jarvis, Brian. *Postmodern Cartographies: The Geographical Imagination in Contemporary American Culture*. London: Pluto Press, 1998

Johnston, John. *Information Multiplicity: American Fiction in the Age of Media Saturation*. Baltimore: The Johns Hopkins University Press, 1998

Kakutani, Michiko. 'Another Doorway to the Paranoid Pynchon Dimension', *The New York Times* (4 August 2009). Online: www.nytimes.com/2009/08/04/books/04kaku.html?pagewanted=all

Kant, Immanuel. *Anthropology from a Pragmatic Point of View*, trans. Victor Lyle Dowdell. Carbondale: Southern Illinois University Press, 1978

Kaplan, Amy and Donald Pease, eds. *Cultures of United States Imperialism*. Durham: Duke University Press, 1993

Keesey, Douglas. '*Vineland* in the Mainstream Press: A Reception Study', *Pynchon Notes* 26–7 (1990): 107–13

Kellman, Steven G. and Irving Malin, eds. *Leslie Fiedler and American Culture*. Newark: University of Delaware Press, 1999

Keniston, Ann and Jeanne Follansbee Quinn, eds. *Literature After 9/11*. London: Routledge, 2010

Kermode, Frank. 'That Was Another Planet', *The London Review of Books*, 8 February 1990: 3–4

Kern, Stephen. *The Culture of Time and Space, 1880–1918*. Cambridge, MA: Harvard University Press, 1983

Kerouac, Jack. *The Dharma Bums*. London: André Deutsch, 1959

Knight, Peter. *Conspiracy Culture: From Kennedy to the X-Files*. London: Routledge, 2000

Kohn, Robert E. 'Pynchon's Transition from Ethos-Based Postmodernism to Late-Postmodern Stylistics', *Style* 43.2 (2009): 194–214

Kupsch, Kenneth. 'Finding *V.*', *Twentieth Century Literature* 44.4 (Winter, 1998): 428–46

LaCapra, Dominick. *History, Politics, and the Novel*. Ithaca: Cornell University Press, 1987

Latrobe, John H. B. *The History of Mason and Dixon's Line; Contained in an Address*. Philadelphia: The Historical Society of Pennsylvania, 1855

Leary, Timothy. 'Cyberpunks', *Spin* (April 1987): 88–93

Lefebvre, Henri. 'Reflections on the Politics of Space', trans. M. Enders, *Antipode* 8 (1976): 30–7

Lefebvre, Henri. *The Production of Space*, trans. Donald Nicholson-Smith. Oxford: Wiley-Blackwell, 1991

Leveritt, Thomas. '*Inherent Vice*, by Thomas Pynchon', *The Independent*, Sunday, 9 August 2009. Online: www.independent.co.uk/arts-entertain ment/books/reviews/inherent-vice-by-thomas-pynchon-1767732.html

Levin, Jonathan. *The Poetics of Transition: Emerson, Pragmatism & American Literary Modernism*. Durham: Duke University Press, 1999

Lifshey, Adam. *Specters of Conquest: Indigenous Absence in Transatlantic Literatures*. New York: Fordham University Press, 2010

Link, Arthur S. et al., eds. *The Papers of Woodrow Wilson*, vol. 35 (1 October 1915–27 January 1916). Princeton: Princeton University Press, 1980

Lowenthal, David. 'Nostalgia Tells it Like it Wasn't', *The Imagined Past: History and Nostalgia*, ed. Malcolm Chase and Christopher Shaw. Manchester: Manchester University Press, 1989

Lyotard, Jean-François. *The Postmodern Condition: A Report on Knowledge*, trans. Georges Van Den Abeele. Manchester: Manchester University Press, 1984

Lyotard, Jean-François. *The Lyotard Reader*, ed. Andrew Benjamin. Oxford: Blackwell, 1989

MacKey, Louis. 'Paranoia, Pynchon, and Preterition', *SubStance* 1.1, Issue 30 (1981): 16–30

McHale, Brian. *Postmodernist Fiction*. London: Methuen, 1987

McHale, Brian. *Constructing Postmodernism*. New York: Routledge, 1992

McHoul, Alec. 'TEENAGE MUTANT NINJA FICTION (Or, St. Ruggles' Struggles, Chapter 4)', *Pynchon Notes* 26–7 (1990): 97–106

McHoul, Alec and David Wills. *Writing Pynchon: Strategies in Fictional Analysis*, Urbana and Chicago: University of Illinois Press, 1990

Madsen, Deborah L. *The Postmodernist Allegories of Thomas Pynchon*. New York: St Martin's Press, 1991

Mailer, Norman. 'An Author's Identity: An Interview with Michael Lennon', in Mailer. *Pieces and Pontifications*. Boston: Little, Brown and Company, 1982, 151–7

Manning, Susan. *The Puritan-Provincial Vision: Scottish and American Writing in the Nineteenth Century*. Cambridge: Cambridge University Press, 1990

Marcuse, Peter and Ronald van Kempen, eds. *Globalizing Cities: A New Spatial Order?* Oxford: Blackwell, 2000

Mason, Hugh, ed. *The Journal of Charles Mason and Jeremiah Dixon.* Philadelphia: American Philosophical Society, 1969

Mattessich, Stefan. *Lines of Flight: Discursive Time and Countercultural Desire in the Work of Thomas Pynchon.* Durham: Duke University Press, 2002

Meiksins Wood, Ellen. *Empire of Capital,* London: Verso, 2005

Melley, Timothy. *Empire of Conspiracy: The Culture of Paranoia in Postwar America.* Ithaca: Cornell University Press, 2000

Mendelson, Edward. 'Encyclopedic Narrative: From Dante to Pynchon,' *MLN* 91 (1976): 1267–75

Mendelson, Edward, ed. *Pynchon: A Collection of Critical Essays.* New Jersey: Prentice Hall, 1978

Meyer, Eric. 'Oppositional Discourses, Unnatural Practices: Gravity's History and the 60's', *Pynchon Notes* 24–5 (1989): 81–104

Millard, Bill. 'Pynchon's Coast: *Inherent Vice* and the Twilight of the Spatially Specific', *College Hill Review,* 4 (Fall, 2009). Online: www.collegehill review.com/004/0040501.html

Miller, Mark Crispin. *Boxed In: The Culture of TV.* Evanston: Northwestern University Press, 1988

Milton, John. *Paradise Lost,* ed. Alastair Fowler. 2nd edition. London: Longman, 2007

Molloy, Seán. 'Escaping the Politics of the Irredeemable Earth: Anarchy and Transcendence in the Novels of Thomas Pynchon', *Theory & Event* 13.3 (2010). Online: http://muse.jhu.edu/journals/ theory_and_event/ v013/13.3.molloy.html

Moretti, Franco. *Signs Taken for Wonders: The Sociology of Literary Forms.* London: Verso, 1983

Nicholson, Colin and Randall Stevenson. '"Words You Never Wanted to Hear": Fiction, History and Narratology in *The Crying of Lot 49*', *Pynchon Notes* 16 (1985): 89–109

O'Donnell, Patrick, ed. *New Essays on 'The Crying of Lot 49'.* Cambridge: Cambridge University Press, 1991

O'Donnell, Patrick. *Latent Destinies: Cultural Paranoia and Contemporary U.S. Narrative.* Durham: Duke University Press, 2000

Olster, Stacey. 'A "Patch of England, at a Three-Thousand-Mile Off-Set"? Representing America in *Mason & Dixon*', *Modern Fiction Studies* 50.2 (2004): 283–302

Patell, Cyrus K. *Negative Liberties: Morrison, Pynchon, and the Problem of Liberal Ideology.* Durham: Duke University Press, 2001

Patteson, Richard. 'Architecture and Junk in Pynchon's Short Fiction', *Illinois Quarterly* 42.2 (1979): 38–47

Plater, William. *The Grim Phoenix: Reconstructing Thomas Pynchon.* Bloomington: Indiana University Press, 1978

Plimpton, George. 'The Whole Sick Crew: *V.* by Thomas Pynchon', *The New York Times*, 21 April 1963. Online: www.nytimes.com/books/97/05/18/ reviews/pynchon-v.html?_r=5

Pöhlmann, Sascha, ed. *Against the Grain: Reading Pynchon's Counternarratives.* Amsterdam: Rodopi, 2010

Poirier, Richard. 'Humans', review of *Slow Learner*, *London Review of Books*, 24 January 1985: 18–20

Poole, Robert. '"Give Us Our Eleven Days!"': Calendar Reform in Eighteenth-Century England', *Past and Present: A Journal of Historical Studies* 149 (1995): 95–139

Pratt, Ray. *Projecting Paranoia: Conspiratorial Visions in American Film.* Lawrence: University of Kansas Press, 2001

Punday, Daniel. 'Pynchon's Ghosts', *Contemporary Literature* 44.2 (2003): 250–74

Punday, Daniel. *Writing at the Limit: The Novel in the New Media Ecology.* Lincoln: University of Nebraska Press, 2012

Pynchon, Thomas. 'A Journey Into the Mind of Watts', *New York Times Magazine*, 12 June 1966: 34–5, 78, 80–2, 84

Pynchon, Thomas. 'To Richard Wilbur', in 'Presentation to Thomas Pynchon of the Howells Medal for Fiction of the Academy', in *Proceedings of the American Academy of Arts and Letters and the National Institute of Arts and Letters* 26 (1976): 43–6

Pynchon, Thomas. 'Is It O.K. to be a Luddite?', *New York Times Book Review*, 28 October 1984: 40–1

Pynchon, Thomas. *Vineland.* London: Vintage, 1990.

Pynchon, Thomas. 'Nearer, My Couch, to Thee', *New York Times Book Review*, 6 June 1993. Online: www.nytimes.com/books/97/05/18/reviews/pynchon-sloth.html

Pynchon, Thomas. *Gravity's Rainbow.* London: Vintage, 1995.

Pynchon, Thomas. *The Crying of Lot 49.* London: Vintage, 1996

Pynchon, Thomas. *Mason & Dixon.* London: Jonathan Cape, 1997.

Pynchon, Thomas. *Slow Learner.* London: Vintage, 2000

Pynchon, Thomas. *V.* London: Vintage, 2000

Pynchon, Thomas. Foreword to George Orwell, *Nineteen Eighty-Four* (London: Penguin Books, 2003), v–xxv

Pynchon, Thomas. *Against the Day.* London: Jonathan Cape, 2006.

Pynchon, Thomas. *Inherent Vice.* London: Jonathan Cape, 2009.

Raban, Jonathan. 'Try, Try and Try Again', review of *Slow Learner. Sunday Times* (London), 20 January 1985: 44G

Randall, Martin. *9/11 and the Literature of Terror.* Edinburgh: Edinburgh University Press, 2011

Reilly, Terry. 'A Couple-Three Bonzos: "Introduction"', *Slow Learner* and *1984*', *Pynchon Notes* 44–5 (Spring–Fall, 1999): 5–13

Ricoeur, Paul. *Time and Narrative*, vol. 1. Chicago: University of Chicago Press, 1990

Riesman, David. *The Lonely Crowd: A Study of the Changing American Character*. New Haven: Yale University Press, 1960

Rogin, Michael. *Ronald Reagan, the Movie and Other Episodes in Political Demonology*. Berkeley: University of California Press, 1987

Ronell, Avital. *Stupidity*. Champaign: University of Illinois Press, 2002

Roszak, Theodore. *The Making of a Counterculture: Reflections on a Technocratic Society and Its Youthful Opposition*. Berkeley: University of California Press, 1995

Rushdie, Salman. *Imaginary Homelands: Essays and Criticism 1981–1991*. London: Granta, 1991

Sanders, Scott. 'Pynchon's Paranoid History', *Twentieth-Century Literature* 21.1 (1975): 177–92

Sante, Luc. 'Inside the Time Machine', *The New York Review of Books* 54.1 (11 January 2007): 8–10, 12

Sates, Toon. '"Quaternionist Talk": Luddite Yearning and the Colonization of Time in Thomas Pynchon's *Against the Day*', *English Studies* 91.5 (2010): 531–47

Savvlas, Theophilus. 'Pynchon Plays Dice: *Mason & Dixon* and Quantum History', *Literature & History* 20.2 (2011): 51–67

Schaub, Thomas H. *Pynchon: The Voice of Ambiguity*. Urbana: University of Illinois Press, 1981

Schaub, Thomas H., ed. *Approaches to Teaching Pynchon's 'The Crying of Lot 49' and Other Works*. New York: Modern Language Association, 2008

Schroeder, Ralph. 'Weber, Pynchon and the American Prospect', *Max Weber Studies* 1.2 (2001): 161–77

Schuber, Stephen P. 'Rereading Pynchon: Negative Entropy and "Entropy"', *Pynchon Notes* 13 (1983): 47–60

Schwartz Cowan, Ruth. *A Social History of American Technology*. Oxford: Oxford University Press, 1997

Seed, David. *The Fictional Labyrinths of Thomas Pynchon*. Basingstoke: Macmillan, 1988

Severs, Jeffrey and Christopher Leise, eds. *Pynchon's 'Against the Day': A Corrupted Pilgrim's Guide*. Newark: University of Delaware Press, 2011

Slade, Joseph W., *Thomas Pynchon*. New York: Warner Paperback Library, 1974

Smith, Shawn. *Pynchon and History: Metahistorical Rhetoric and Postmodern Narrative Form in the Novels of Thomas Pynchon*. London: Routledge, 2005

Solomon, William. 'Secret Integrations: Black Humor and the Critique of Whiteness', *MFS Modern Fiction Studies* 49.3 (2003): 469–95

Staiger, Jeffrey. 'James Wood's Case Against "Hysterical Realism" and Thomas Pynchon', *Antioch Review* 66.4 (Fall, 2008): 634–54

Stewart, Susan. *On Longing: Narratives of the Miniature, the Gigantic, the Souvenir, the Collection*. Durham: Duke University Press, 1993

Stimpson, Catherine R. 'Pre-Apocalyptic Atavism: Thomas Pynchon's Early Fiction', in George Levine and David Leverenz, eds, *Mindful Pleasures: Essays on Thomas Pynchon*. Boston: Little, Brown, 1976, 31–47.

Tambling, Jeremy. *On Anachronism*. Manchester: Manchester University Press, 2010

Tani, Stefano. 'The Dismemberment of the Detective', *Diogenes* 120 (1982): 22–41

Tanner, Tony. *Cities of Words: American Fiction 1950–1970*. London: Jonathan Cape, 1971

Tanner, Tony. *Thomas Pynchon*. London: Methuen, 1982

Tanner, Tony. *The American Mystery: American Literature from Emerson to DeLillo*. Cambridge: Cambridge University Press, 2000

Taylor, Christopher. 'Inherent Vice by Thomas Pynchon', *The Guardian*, 1 August 2009. Online: www.guardian.co.uk/books/2009/aug/01/thomas-pynchon-inherent-vice-review

Taylor, Matthew A. 'The "Phantasmodesty" of Henry Adams', *Common Knowledge* 15.3 (2009): 373–94

Thomas, Samuel. *Pynchon and the Political*. New York: Routledge, 2007

Thomas, Samuel. 'Metković to Mostar: Pynchon and the Balkans', *Textual Practice* 24.2 (2010): 353–77

Thoreen, David. 'The President's Emergency War Powers and the Erosion of Civil Liberties in Pynchon's *Vineland*', *Oklahoma City University Law Review* 24.3 (1999): 761–98

Van Delden, Maarten. 'Modernism, the New Criticism and Thomas Pynchon's *V*.' *NOVEL: A Forum for Fiction* 23.2 (Winter, 1990): 117–36

Veggian, Henry. 'Thomas Pynchon Against the Day', *boundary 2* 35.1 (2008): 197–215

Versluys, Kristiaan. *Out of the Blue: September 11 and the Novel*. New York: Columbia University Press, 2009

Vidal, Gore. 'The Thinking Man's Novel', *New York Review of Books* 27.19 (4 December 1980): 10

Vidal, Gore. 'American Plastic: The Matter of Fiction', in Gore Vidal, *United States: Essays 1952–1992*. London: Abacus, 1997

Weber, Max. *The Protestant Ethic and the Spirit of Capitalism*. London: Routledge, 1992

Weisenburger, Steven. *A 'Gravity's Rainbow' Companion: Sources and Contexts for Pynchon's Novel*. Athens and London: University of Georgia Press, 2006

Whitman, Walt. *Leaves of Grass*. Boston: Thayer and Eldridge, 1860

Whyte, William H. *The Organization Man* (1956). Philadelphia: University of Pennsylvania Press, 2002

Wiener, Norbert. *The Human Use of Human Beings: Cybernetics and Society*. New York: Doubleday Anchor Books, 1954

Wilson, Rob. 'On the Pacific Edge of Catastrophe, or Redemption: California Dreaming in Thomas Pynchon's *Inherent Vice*', *boundary 2* 37.2 (2010): 217-25

Winship, Michael P. 'Contesting Control of Orthodoxy among the Godly: William Pynchon Reexamined', *William and Mary Quarterly* 54.4 (1997): 795-822

Winston, Mathew. 'The Quest for Pynchon', *Twentieth-Century Literature* 21.3 (1975): 278-87

Wood, James. *The Irresponsible Self: On Laughter and the Novel*. London: Jonathan Cape, 2004

Wood, Michael. 'Rocketing to the Apocalypse', *The New York Review of Books* 20.4 (22 March 1973)

Wood, Michael. 'Pynchon's *Mason & Dixon*', *Raritan* 17.4 (1998): 120-30

Wright Mills, C. *White Collar: The American Middle Classes*. New York: Oxford University Press, 2002

Žižek, Slavoj. *In Defense of Lost Causes*. London: Verso, 2008

Index

Lightning Source UK Ltd.
Milton Keynes UK
UKOW06f1439180615

253735UK00001B/1/P